T0330003

Knowledge Borders

NEW HORIZONS IN REGIONAL SCIENCE

Series Editor: Philip McCann, *Professor of Urban and Regional Economics, University of Sheffield Management School, UK*

Regional science analyses important issues surrounding the growth and development of urban and regional systems and is emerging as a major social science discipline. This series provides an invaluable forum for the publication of high quality scholarly work on urban and regional studies, industrial location economics, transport systems, economic geography and networks.

New Horizons in Regional Science aims to publish the best work by economists, geographers, urban and regional planners and other researchers from throughout the world. It is intended to serve a wide readership including academics, students and policymakers.

Titles in the series include:

Knowledge Borders

Temporary Labor Mobility and the Canada–US Border Region

Kathrine E. Richardson

Associate Professor, San José State University, USA

NEW HORIZONS IN REGIONAL SCIENCE

Cheltenham, UK • Northampton, MA, USA

Published by
Edward Elgar Publishing Limited
The Lypiatts
15 Lansdown Road
Cheltenham
Glos GL50 2JA
UK

Edward Elgar Publishing, Inc.
William Pratt House
9 Dewey Court
Northampton
Massachusetts 01060
USA

A catalogue record for this book
is available from the British Library

Library of Congress Control Number: 2016959916

This book is available electronically in the **Elgar**online
Economics subject collection
DOI 10.4337/9781785369032

ISBN 978 1 78536 902 5 (cased)
ISBN 978 1 78536 903 2 (eBook)

Typeset by Servis Filmsetting Ltd, Stockport, Cheshire
Printed and bound in Great Britain by TJ International Ltd, Padstow

Contents

Figures

Tables

Abbreviations

ACLU	American Civil Liberties Union
AILA	American Immigration Lawyers Association
APEC	Asia Pacific Economic Cooperation
ASEAN	Association of South East Asian Nations
BC	British Columbia
CBSA	Canada Border Services Agency
C-A4	Canadian Attorney '4', for example
C-IO 2	Canadian Immigration Officer '2', for example
CEO	Chief Executive Officer
CIC	Citizenship and Immigration Canada
CBR	Cross-border regions
DHS	Department of Homeland Security
ESDC	Employment and Social Development Canada
EE	Express Entry (Canada)
EU	European Union
EEA	European Economic Area
EFTA	European Free Trade Association
GATT	General Agreement on Tariffs and Trade
GATS	General Agreement on Trade in Services
HR	Human resource
HRDC	Human Resources and Development Canada
HRSDC	Human Resources and Skills Development Canada
IIRIRA	Illegal Immigration Reform and Immigration Responsibility Act 1996
IT	Information technology
JIT	Just-in-Time
LMIA	Labour Market Impact Assessment (Canadian)
MNC	Multinational Corporation
CNDH	National Human Rights Commission (Mexico) (Spanish: Comisión Nacional de los Derechos Humanos)
NAFTA	North American Free Trade Agreement
OECD	Organisation for Economic Co-operation and Development
PNWER	Pacific Northwest Economic Region
PRI	Policy Research Initiative (Canadian)

POE	Port of entry
POEs	Ports of entry
PNP	Provincial Nominee Program
R&D	Research and development
Firm-S1	Seattle Firm '1', for example
SIJORI	Singapore-Johore-Riau Growth Triangle
TPP	Trans-Pacific Partnership
TN	Treaty NAFTA
UK	United Kingdom
US	United States
US-A6	US Attorney '6', for example
US DHS	US Department of Homeland Security
US DOL	US Department of Labor
IIRIRA	US Illegal Immigration Reform & Immigration Responsibility Act
US INA	US Immigration and Nationality Act
US INS	US Immigration and Naturalization Service
US-IO 4	US Immigration Officer '4', for example
Firm-V8	Vancouver Firm '8', for example
WTO	World Trade Organization

Acknowledgements

This book could not have been produced without the support, work, and sincere efforts of so many people, many of whom I will probably inadvertently omit from this brief note of thanks.

A grand, thank you, goes to David Edgington, my former PhD supervisor of the Department of Geography at the University of British Columbia (UBC). Thank you, Dave.

I would also like to thank Pitman Potter of the Institute of Asian Research and Faculty of Law at UBC. I am deeply grateful for Pitman's leadership while I was at UBC.

I would also like to thank Richard Florida of the Martin Prosperity Institute, Rotman School of Management, University of Toronto and Kevin Stolarick of The Center for Political Leadership for the opportunity to research a very important issue that intrigued all three of us. I would also like to thank Karen King for being such a wonderful colleague and friend during my time at the Martin Prosperity Institute, and my dear cousin, Eve Richardson, who hosted me often while I was living in Toronto.

I would also like to recognize my Departmental and College of Social Sciences colleagues and staff at San José State University, who encouraged me to take a sabbatical so that I may write this book. Thank you all for filling in for me while I was away. I would also like to recognize the many undergraduate students that I have taught over the years. I have learned so much from them. I would also like to thank my graduate students, Flo Pucci, April Schneider, Jessica White, and Angela Ivanov. All four have been a wonderful source of inspiration for me over the past six years. I would also like to thank Angela, especially, for generating some of the graphs and figures that are used in this book. I would also like to recognize the professional editorial team at Edward Elgar Publishing. It was a pleasure to have the opportunity to work with all of you. Finally, I cannot forget the great people at Office Max in the Pearl District of Portland, Oregon, who expertly and patiently helped me assemble the many figures and graphs found in this book.

Although I cannot name research participants, I would like to sincerely thank the many immigration lawyers, immigration officials, and Vancouver, Seattle, and Silicon Valley high-tech and biotech firms who gave generously of their time and expertise to participate in my work. Without dedication towards my research project, this book would not have been possible. I hope that the findings from my work will help these professionals in a small way.

I must also recognize key people around the world who have been true supporters and friends through my time as a PhD student and now as a mid-career academic. These people include Pascale Soumoy, Natalia Santamaria Laorden, and Johanna Waters. I offer my kindest and sincerest thanks to these three people.

I want to thank Dave Rayat, my partner, who has spent many an evening listening to me talk about my research. I am very fortunate to have such an amazing person in my life.

A special thank you to my mom, Patricia Richardson, who offered encouragement, focus, and inspiration through the writing of the manuscript. I also want to thank my dear sister, Shasha Richardson O'Dea, my brother-in-law, Julian O'Dea, and their wonderful son, Evan, for hosting me at their home on Sunday afternoons as a form of a break from my writing and academic work.

Finally, I dedicate this book to my father, Henry Richardson, and my sister and brother, Frances and Jeb Richardson. The origins of this book and its completion would not have been possible if it were not for my sister and brother supporting me in the beginning and my father encouraging me at the end. Thank you all for your confidence in me, and more importantly, your love.

Kathrine Richardson
Vancouver, BC; Portland, Oregon; San José, California

PART I

General introduction and overview

1. Introduction

1.1 INTRODUCTION

The idea of borders as sieves or shields has come to the forefront of topics in the past few years. The opportunities presented by free trade and the emergence of cross-border regions have been compromised, beginning with the constraints imposed after the attacks on the World Trade Center in New York City in September 2001 (hereafter 9/11) and a growing number of terrorist attacks throughout the world over the past 15 years. In response, 'fortressing up' with drastic security measures taken not only along the United States (US) borders, but also along international borders throughout the world (Andreas, 2003, 2009) have now become the norm. The overall trend since the ending of the Cold War has been one of free access across international borders, especially for international trade and multinational business interests (Ohmae, 1995). In fact, the trend of globalization, in general, has been seen as a catalyst to making international borders more and more irrelevant, fostering the idea of borders operating as a 'sieve'. However, in a post 9/11 environment, 'borders are back', and a new set of security issues have arisen, which contribute to the idea of borders functioning again as 'shields', as they did during the Cold War, but now with an emphasis on shielding citizens from terrorists as opposed to rogue nation states (Andreas, 2003). In other words, borders represent a fascinating case study of a more general intersection between geography and contemporary public policy (Cox, 1997; Brunet-Jailly, 2004, 2007, 2008; Konrad and Nicol, 2008).

Borders have always been important to geographers and scholars of similar research interests since the signing of the Treaty of Westphalia in 1648. This treaty helped to end the Thirty Years' War in Europe and legitimately recognized the demarcations of a state's territory by physical boundaries or borders. In fact, the Treaty of Westphalia in 1648 helped to establish the creation of the borders and boundaries of many contemporary nation states, which evolved out of the kingdoms and territories of European royalty and nobles, starting in the eighteenth century. Moving forward to the early twenty-first century, new regional groups are beginning to form, which cut across the borders of nation states. This includes

the triad economy of North America under the North American Free
Trade Agreement (NAFTA) (which includes Canada, the United States,
and Mexico), the European Union (EU), the Association of South East
Asian Nations (ASEAN), and most recently the Trans-Pacific Partnership
(TPP). Within these larger regional trading blocs are sub national cross-
border regions; these include SIJORI (Singapore-Johore-Riau Growth
Triangle) (Yuan, 1997; Macleod and McGee, 1996) and Cascadia (the
Pacific Northwest and Northern California region of North America)
(McCloskey, 1989; Artibise, 2005; Richardson, 2006a), for example. In
fact, Cascadia may be considered a local example where issues of cross-
border flows are critical to the growth of a post-industrial high-tech
and biotechnology service oriented region that benefits from Seattle and
Vancouver's interaction and dynamism. Ideally, Chapter 16 of NAFTA
(the North American Free Trade Agreement), which is dedicated, in
part, to facilitating the movements of North American business persons,
traders, investors, and professionals, should help to foster movements of
these qualified people between Vancouver and Seattle and beyond. Thus,
this book analyses the intersection of the Canada–US border, the high-
tech and biotechnology economy in the Seattle–Vancouver corridor and
its connection to the Greater San Francisco/Silicon Valley area, namely
Cascadia, and how well NAFTA has contributed to the movement of
North American professionals between these cities of the North American
west coast.

The NAFTA, since its inception in 1994, was designed to allow for the
greater ease and cross-border mobility of goods, services, investment,
government procurement, intellectual property, competition policy, and
finally the mobility of business persons.[1] For the most part, NAFTA may
be considered a success in terms of the majority of factors in that it allows
facilitated cross-border entries. Within continental North America there
is a general perception that access into the US from Canada is almost
guaranteed for North American business people and vice versa. However,
as will be shown, the legitimate NAFTA information technology (IT) and
related professionals have perceived difficulties moving back and forth
across the Canada–US border for a variety of reasons. Unlike the EU's
Schengen Agreement developed through the 1990s (Anderson, 2000),
which allows for almost complete labor mobility between all signatory
countries, there has been no attempt to harmonize the regimes of NAFTA
entry for Canada, the US, and Mexico. Essentially, each NAFTA country
has set its own standards for the entry of skilled workers. Hence, there
are three country systems operating under NAFTA, which look alike
but are quite different from each other. These differences, coupled with
the growing post 9/11 restrictive nature at US ports of entry, have led to

considerable variability in border controls, not only between the US and Canada, but also between US ports of entry. In addition, there is a widening gap between the Canadian and American interpretations of NAFTA at the actual ports of entry as it applies to the North American business person. The following interview excerpt provides a rather vivid example of these complexities and of the difficulties encountered by one Canadian high-technology firm trying to seek entry of its workers into the US after 9/11 in order to perform a job for the US Navy.

I remember, a while back when I first spoke with you on the phone, you and your crew had a very interesting time in trying to get across the Canada–US border. Could you tell me about it? (Author)

Oh yes, that was our US Navy fiasco. We were contracted to do a job for the US Navy in San Diego. We expected some problems. So we got a letter from the US Admiral in charge. *He was an Admiral.* We were each issued letters from the US Navy and the State Department letterhead stating who we were and the fact that we had to provide work on US Navy equipment. We go to the POE [port of entry, *but it is actually the 'US preflight inspection area'*] at YVR (Vancouver International Airport). . . .I got through. The next guy goes through, the immigration officer talks to him and pulls him aside. He then pulled all the other guys aside, and refused entry to all of them! One of them had an H-1 card [a designated US work visa], but it had expired and he did not return it. (The card is the property of the US government.) For the other three, they said that the letter was not specific enough. We had the US immigration talk with the Navy [on the phone]. They [the border officials] considered our work 'maintenance', and said anyone can do this! They sent us home and told us to come back the next day. We went back the next day with additional paperwork from the Navy. However, they gave us a one-time entry, and as soon as we reentered any port in Canada we would lose this status. So we went to San Diego and performed the job for a week or so. The Navy did not want to pay for us to stay there, so they sent us home.

However, four days later the US Navy called us back saying they needed us right away. This was the worst time for this to happen, there was another terrorist threat or something like that . . . Essentially, the US border went on Orange alert in early October [of 2002]. I called the US immigration people at the Peace Arch/Douglas border crossing, and they said it would be highly unlikely that they would let us through. The Navy said we have to go, and told us to get there any way we can. So, we put all of our gear (work hats, equipment, everything) in a big box, shipped it to San Diego. We then rented a car, filled it with Doritos chips and pop and said we are going to Seattle [for the week] to do some shopping and maybe some fishing. We drove to Seattle, ditched the rental car in a hotel parking lot, took the shuttle bus to SeaTac [airport]. We went to San Diego for the week, got the job done. Came back home, drove through the [Canadian] border . . . The US Navy does not work that fast [with paper pushing]. I don't believe we did this, and I don't believe we didn't get nailed! In the end it all worked out well. I cannot believe we had a contract with the US Navy, and we had to sneak people into the US to get the job done. (Firm-V6)

Although not frequent, many of the smaller Canadian firms that were interviewed for this study stressed that they would take extreme measures in order to get into the US to perform a job, land a contract, or provide services to US firms or the US Military. The previous excerpt provides a very determined and creative example of what Canadian firms will do in order to continue their working linkages and networks not only with US firms, but also with powerful US governmental bodies, such as the US Navy. Even more interesting is the paradox or tension, which apparently exists between the US Department of Homeland Security (DHS), directed to guard the US's domestic borders, and the US Navy, mandated, among other things, to protect the US from enemy invasions by water and 'to hold the oceans'. Based on the above example, the US Navy found it in the best interest of the US to allow passage into the US for these five Canadian extreme equipment specialists. However, the US DHS port of entry (POE) officers were not convinced of their professional significance, and exercised their right as immigration officials first in the line of defense of the US's border to refuse entry to four of the five Canadian professionals.

The above example demonstrates that the examination of the role of the international border in the high-tech and biotechnology Cascadia region leads to a focus on the firms that need to send highly qualified employees across the border. In addition, the study analysed the role that the port of entry officials and other governmental officials played, especially with regard to their interpretation of NAFTA status provisions. Thus, this examination of border management also led to understanding the important role carried out by immigration lawyers who specialize in preparing complex visa applications for cross-border business travelers in both the US and Canada.

Overall, this study explores the plans, dreams, and goals of Cascadian firms, both US and Canadian, in relation to how they see themselves within a North American context, and how the Canada–US border affects their day-to-day operations and their long-term aspirations. An examination of the other players and actors, such as immigration officers and immigration attorneys, will also be analysed in hopes of gaining a better understanding of the similarities and differences between the Canadian and American experiences of moving across the Canada–US border under NAFTA and beyond.

1.2   GENERAL BACKGROUND

NAFTA intended to give freer mobility to high-tech professional workers across the international borders between Canada, the US, and Mexico. In fact, even prior to 9/11, there was a growing 'push' from key decision makers on both sides of the Canada–US border to create blanket North American visa policies and procedures, develop common terminology, streamline entrance and exit databases, and the possibility of greater harmonization of Canada–US immigration policies.[2] Despite these long-term coordinating efforts between Canada and the US, this study found that there is still considerable variability between the US and Canada when it comes to the actual inspection, facilitation, and admittance of North American business people across the Canada–US border, as discussed in the preceding section. This growing variability had tremendous impacts on the predictability of mobility for professionals, which arguably, in turn, may have severe impacts on the continued development and success of the integrated North American high-tech and biotechnology economy. For example, Vazquez-Azpiri (2000) argued that this fluid stream of legitimate professionals under NAFTA is crucial in moving both the US and Canada into a stable and growing information economy.

The need for greater ease and mobility of professionals or 'knowledge workers'[3] is especially relevant for the emerging new economy high-tech corridor in the more northern portion of Cascadia which transcends the international border between Vancouver, British Columbia and Seattle, Washington. These two urban settlements have developed successfully over the past 100 years into modern cities, both lauded internationally for their quality of life (MacDonald, 1987). Seattle is home to major high-technology companies such as the software giant Microsoft Corporation, and the commercial headquarters of the aircraft manufacturer Boeing, both world leaders in their respective industries. British Columbia (BC) is quickly developing its own critical mass of new economy industries. In fact, Vancouver is often stated as a city of choice for young high-tech specialists looking for quality of life as they embark on their fast paced careers in software development (Littlemore, 2015; Mackie, 2000). Additionally, over the past 15 years, Vancouver has developed strong human and economic networks with three of the four East Asian tigers (Singapore, Hong Kong, and Taiwan) and South Asia. The city continues to maintain a robust trade relationship with Japan (Edgington, 1995) and, more recently, mainland China. As this study will demonstrate, there were also strong ties between Vancouver firms and the Greater San Francisco and Silicon Valley region.

1.3 RESEARCH QUESTIONS

Based on the chapter's introduction and background, this book examines how the particular provisions of Chapter 16 of the North American Free Trade Agreement (NAFTA) actually deal with temporary labor mobility of North American high-tech and biotechnology professionals across the Canada–US border, with particular emphasis in the Pacific Northwest region of Canada and the United States. The empirical research included the Vancouver, BC–Seattle, Washington corridor and to a lesser extent the Greater San Francisco and Silicon Valley area, namely the more western portion of much of the Cascadia region (see Figure 1.1 for an illustration of Cascadia's high-tech corridor). In principle, the NAFTA status (visa) provisions should have made the temporary movement of professionals easier across the border of all NAFTA countries (Canada, the United States, and Mexico), and facilitate cross-border trade and enterprise. However, in the case of software engineers and related professions, which are a very important category for the expanding high-tech and biotechnology service industries of Vancouver and Seattle, this study argues that it is not so. Drawing from four primary literatures, which include material on high-tech/industrial clusters; borders and borderlands in a post 9/11 era; transnationalism and labor mobility; and transborder institutions, the research aims to comprehend the dynamics of transitory immigration of 'knowledge-workers' between Vancouver, Seattle, and the Greater San Francisco/ Silicon Valley area. A greater understanding of these dynamics also helps to shed light on whether or not the Canada–US border is an impediment to the development of a cross-border high-tech cluster in the Cascadia region. In essence, is the border a sieve or shield to successful regional development in this part of North America?

1.3.1   The Primary Research Question

More concretely, the primary research question for the study is as follows: Is the Canada–US border an impediment to the development of a high-tech industrial cluster in the Cascadia region? This is of critical importance because much of the new economy[4] in the Cascadia region (as in other similar regions) is dependent on the free movement of highly skilled peoples over international boundaries who can respond quickly to the ever changing needs and developments of firms that develop and work with new technologies (Richardson, 2006a). Historically, over the past 300 years since the development of nation state borders, one primary purpose of the border was to keep people residing in one nation state from moving and residing in another nation state. Now, networks of firms involved in information technology, and the new economy in general, span international borders. Thus, the information technology sector needs to draw from a talented pool of well-educated professionals residing throughout the globe as these firms compete in a 'high stakes game' of product development where timing and cleverness are keys to success or failure (Saxenian, 2002,

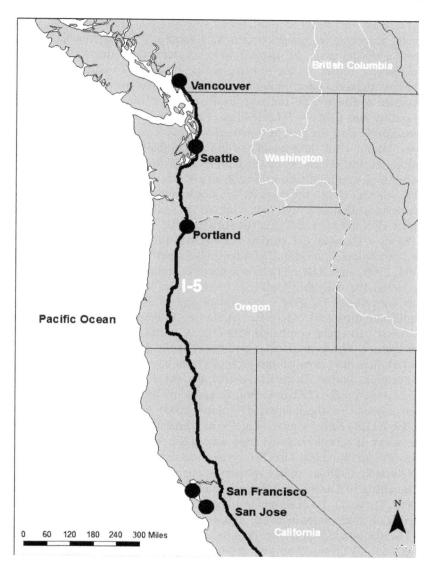

Figure 1.1   Cascadia's high-tech corridor

2006). And so, the immediate needs of the new economy require more cross-border integration and more predictable transparent border regulations when it comes to the movement of professionals across international boundaries.

The need for greater ease and mobility of professionals is especially true for the emerging high-tech corridor of Cascadia. For Vancouver, BC and Seattle, Washington, the two city-regions share the natural drainage of the Georgia Basin, but are bisected politically by the Canada–US border. These settlements have similar histories as two new northwest coast cities designed to function as outposts in the export of natural resources, such as timber and fisheries (MacDonald, 1987). In fact, both have developed successfully over the past 100 years into modern settlements, both lauded internationally for their quality of life and globally competitive high-tech industries. In the context of the high levels of growth and success of bio-technology and high-tech in Seattle and Vancouver, the question emerges as to whether or not the Canada–US border impedes their integration and the development of a high-tech complex, as has been the case with Silicon Valley in Northern California (Lee et al., 2000).

From a Canada–US studies perspective, the impact of the NAFTA and its implementation in Cascadia is also a pertinent issue (Brunet-Jailly, 2004, 2006, and 2008). There is a need to understand how NAFTA has impacted the emerging high-tech cross-border complex. While NAFTA was introduced in 1993 to facilitate cross-border trade, its detailed implementation and outcomes remains a relatively understudied area of research. Moreover, compared with other Canada–US border regions (e.g. the Detroit–Windsor corridor and the Atlantic Maritime and Northeast States) very little detailed research has been carried out on the industrial connections within Cascadia. Historically, there has been more scholarly work done on the Canadian branch economy located within the Golden Horseshoe of southern Ontario (Holmes, 2003). Here a sophisticated Just-in-Time (JIT) delivery process of the big three auto manufacturers created networks of production that span across the Ambassador Bridge linking Detroit and Windsor. This JIT system has carefully integrated Canadian production facilities into a powerful chain of auto production plants originating in Detroit and extending into Ohio and Tennessee (Holmes, 2000). However, no research to date has attempted to 'map out' similar chains of interactions between high-tech firms in the Vancouver, BC and the Seattle corridor and their possible extensions to Greater San Francisco and Silicon Valley, and beyond. Additionally, rather than moving car parts, as is frequently the case between Detroit and Ontario, the Cascadia area has a greater potential of moving knowledge workers across its regional borders due to the fact that the high-tech industry is much more dependent on flows of people as opposed to goods (Florida, 2005).

Based on the above, this research study places special emphasis on the movement of knowledge workers across the Canada–US border in Cascadia, and how Chapter 16 of NAFTA, which deals with labor mobility, has affected these movements. Indeed, it is intended that a primary outcome of this work will be a better understanding of how high-tech and biotechnology firms span across the Canada–US border within the Cascadia region, and whether the border impedes possible flows of peoples working in the high-tech and biotechnology industries.

1.3.2 Methodology and Other Primary Research Questions

The methodology for the study involved over 80 semi-structured interviews conducted between 2002–15 with the human resource (HR) managers, chief scientists, and executives of 25 biotechnology and high-technology firms based primarily in the greater Vancouver and Seattle areas and to a lesser extent the Greater San Francisco and Silicon Valley area at various stages of firm development; 5 executive officers of two regional biotech-nology and high-technology industrial associations; 23 professional immigration attorneys; 22 US Department of Homeland Security, Citizenship and Immigration Canada and Canada Border Services Agency port of entry (POE) officers; and 5 senior Canadian and US policy development advisors that specialized in Chapter 16 of NAFTA. Additional material came from the web pages of the surveyed firms, company reports, and published materials on the high-technology and biotechnology industries of Vancouver, BC, Seattle, and the Greater San Francisco area, which included 'Silicon Valley'.

The semi-structured in-depth interview format was chosen as the major approach to gathering information due to the lack of consistent quanti-tative data on knowledge workers crossing the Canada–US border. This assessment of NAFTA in the case of highly skilled labor immigration was used due to the fact that there was a lack of documentation regarding the varied experiences of North American professionals seeking entry across North American borders for the purpose of work. As well, the interview process was considered semi-structured due to the fact that many of the interviewees added other dimensions to the interview that could not be captured by the initial questions that were asked (Fontana and Frey, 2000).

Despite the flexibility in the research structure, there were four questions that were asked to all interviewees. These questions include the following: Is the Canada–US border an impediment to a high-tech industrial cluster developing along the Vancouver/Seattle corridor?; How has Chapter 16 of NAFTA influenced this region and/or your work/firm?; How did 9/11 influence the flows and experiences of high-tech professionals moving back and forth across the Canada–US border; and What was the relationship between all of the actors involved?

1.4   EMPIRICAL RESEARCH AND THE INTERVIEWS

Using the questions discussed in the preceding section, semi-structured interviews were conducted with CEOs, vice presidents, and human resource managers from a variety of firms that engage in high-tech and biotechnology work in Vancouver, BC, Seattle, Washington, and the San Francisco/ Silicon Valley area. These companies employed software engineers, scientists, and related professionals who had to cross the Canada–US border often for purposes of work (e.g. sales, research, and service activities). These firms also recruited specialists, such as software engineers, scientists, computer graphic design artists, and engineers in general from either side of the Canada–US border in order for the firm to remain competitive in its respective industry. Canadian and US immigration lawyers practicing law primarily within the Vancouver–Seattle–San Francisco corridor were also included in this study for their background and understanding of the Treaty NAFTA (TN) status and the US H-1B visas. Interviews with professional immigration attorneys were important in order to determine if intermediaries, or auxiliary professionals, were significant in the management of the US border within the Cascadia region. Specifically, the attorneys contributed tremendous insights into the culture and spirit of both the Canadian and US immigration services, in addition to providing leads to companies that move people back and forth across the Canada–US border under NAFTA. Canadian and US front-line immigration officials and POE directors were also interviewed for this research since their understandings, interpretations, and adjudications of NAFTA statuses (in addition to being the gatekeeper to the flows of people, in general) were pivotal to learning how the border acts as a shield and/or sieve when allowing for the legitimate movements of professionals. Finally, interviews with key officials within institutions, primarily governmental, which affect or have influence on the policy development and or adjudication of cross-border labor mobility policies were also included as part of this study due to the fact that many of the ideas and policy influence regarding the border originate with these actors in the major ministries and departments in Ottawa and Washington DC. The following section expands on the nature of these three types of actors involved in cross-border regulations.

1.4.1   The Firms

Currently there is a sparse amount of literature that explores the development and operations of clusters of high-tech firms and biotechnology firms that operate in a cross-border transnational setting. However, there appears to be a growing trend in the need for smaller, non-multinational firms to have a global reach upon firm inception, and the necessary requirement to move beyond the borders of nation states. For example, Saxenian (2000) demonstrated that Chinese and Indian engineers started 29 percent of Silicon Valley's technology companies between the years of 1995–98, and spend considerable time traveling between their operations in Silicon Valley and China and Taiwan, which contributed to a growing transnational economic network between North America and Asia. Saxenian expanded on this idea two years later in a study conducted for the Brookings Institution by stating the following,

> As recently as the 1970s, only giant corporations had the resources and capabilities to grow internationally, and they did so primarily by establishing marketing offices or manufacturing plants overseas. Today, new transportation and communications technologies allow even the smallest firms to build partnerships with foreign producers to tap overseas expertise, cost-savings, and markets. Start-ups in Silicon Valley are often global actors from the day they begin operations. (Saxenian, 2002)

The above quote helps to confirm Canada and the US's growing experience in transcending international boundaries as a part of daily operations for the emerging information and technology sector. This phenomenon will be explored later in the book in the hopes of contributing to this nascent body of literature.

Based on the notion of firms needing to transcend international borders, the sample for this study included firms based in the broader notion of Cascadia that had any sort of activities that included moving professional employees across the Canada–US border. All firms interviewed were associated with the high-tech or biotechnology sectors, or had a major component of the firm's purpose associated with high-technology or biotechnology. This included firms associated with the forestry industry, software development, printing technology and services, aerospace, marine industries, the film and gaming industry, and biotechnology and medical devices. The firms ranged in staff size from over 50,000 employees worldwide to fledgling start-ups with just two employees. Six of the firms could be considered Fortune 500 firms. Two of the firms were based in Seattle, 20 were based in Vancouver, and 3 were based in San Francisco/Silicon Valley. Both Seattle firms and two of the San Francisco/Silicon Valley firms had considerable research and development (R&D) operations in the greater Vancouver area, and the third Silicon Valley based firm was in the process of moving its headquarter operations to Vancouver during the time of the research interview.[5]

The interviews with the two Seattle based firms revealed four key themes: (1) for the most part, the firms sometimes did have difficulties bringing in software engineers and related professionals from Canada, especially after 9/11; (2) both firms noted that due to the fact that, since they used an in-house attorney and had experienced human resources professionals, they were usually capable of avoiding any serious problems; (3) for the most part, the US firms lauded the Canadian experience when sending employees across the border as intracompany transferees, new American hires, or for services contracts; and (4) finally, US firms found the Canadian immigration service to be professional, knowledgeable, and most importantly, predictable in their adjudications and issuing of working permits/visas, stressing that the US side could possibly learn from this management style. These findings will be explored in more detail in Chapter 4 of the study as well as in the Conclusion.

By comparison, the Vancouver firms were much more varied and significantly smaller than the Seattle firms. Firms interviewed ranged from relatively small-scale firms that developed world class marine products to large-scale companies in leading edge hydrogen fuel cell and professional printing technologies. Additionally, the largest firm based in Vancouver employed a total of about 1,200 people within the greater Vancouver area. Despite these employment size differentials between key firms in Seattle and Vancouver, Vancouver was beginning to 'come into its own' with key world class technologies and firms that aimed to prosper and flourish within the next decade. Interviews from these Vancouver firms revealed four key themes: (1) firm size was significantly smaller than the Seattle based firms, and led to less firm recognition and 'clout' when trying to cross into the US; (2) the mobility of employees was based on time zones and regions, not countries; (3) the Canada–US border has become much more unpredictable since 9/11; and (4) firms were turning more and more to attorneys for advice on NAFTA applications and general cross-border mobility strategies when moving employees or potential employees across the Canada–US border for work. These findings will be explored in detail in Chapter 4 of the study as well as the Conclusion.

Importantly, Vancouver was also an emerging site for the establishment of major research and development (R&D) facilities for Seattle and San Francisco/Silicon Valley based high-tech firms. For example, Microsoft Corporation established an initial development center in the greater Vancouver area in 2007, and unveiled an even larger site situated in the heart of downtown Vancouver in June of 2016. Amazon.com established a key development facility in downtown Vancouver in 2014, and now Tableau Software, Inc., a smaller high-tech firm[6] also based in Seattle, established a temporary office in downtown Vancouver in late 2015 with intentions of securing a permanent Vancouver facility for product development. Providing reasoning for locating major R&D facilities so close to headquarters, all three Seattle based firms cited the fact that there was a strong base of 'homegrown talent' of high-tech professionals in Vancouver and other uniquely Vancouver attributes that were positive pull factors for these Seattle based firms. However, evidence is growing that it was in fact Canada's open immigration policies that initially lured two of these Seattle based firms north to Vancouver (Stewart, 2016). (See Richardson, Florida, and Stolarick (2012) for an in-depth discussion on these uniquely Vancouver attributes and R&D site selection for a large Seattle based high-tech firm.) As well, Vancouver has served as a key R&D facility for California based firms for over the past 20 years. This includes EA (Electronic Arts), PMC Sierra, and most recently, Pixar Studios.[7] This concept and growth potential will be explored more deeply within Chapter 4 and the Conclusion.

1.4.2 Immigration Officials

Historically, the state has played the most important role in modern times when it comes to controlling movements of people (J. Scott, 1998). Despite the increasing inquisition of the state over time in the movements of people across international boundaries, the freest time for the movements of wealthy foreigners occurred in Europe, just prior to World War I (Torpey, 2000). During this time period, there was emphasis placed on the fact that these foreigners could bring considerable wealth into foreign cities and nation states. This welcoming attitude of the state towards foreigners ended abruptly during World War I. Emphasis is now placed on controlling the entry of foreigners into other nation states, and there has been a growth of discretionary power of immigration officers who represent and execute the will of the state towards foreigners. Since 9/11, there is a growing literature on this topic area, and so Chapters 2 and 3 comprise a more detailed review of this literature. For the purpose of this study, a greater understanding of the nature and culture of immigration officers is extremely important since much power rests in the hands of the reviewing officer at each POE for NAFTA applications. The next few paragraphs will provides a short review of the types of immigration officers involved in this study, and the key findings, which emerged from this component of the research.

Immigration officers include district directors, special agents, port directors, and front-line supervisors for both the BC/Yukon District of Citizenship and Immigration Canada and Canada Border Services Agency and the Seattle District of the US Department of Homeland Security (formerly the US Immigration and Naturalization Service). Immigration policy experts employed by Citizenship and Immigration Canada and the Department of Homeland Security who were based in Ottawa or Washington DC were also included in the study within the cohort of interviewees. The rationale for interviewing front-line Canadian and US immigration officials for this research project was that this cohort is a primary official gatekeeper/facilitator to labor mobility across the Canada–US border under NAFTA. In addition, the need to interview a number of key policy officials who wrote and annually amended Chapter 16 of NAFTA (either in Washington DC or in Ottawa) was essential to understand the ideas behind the origins of Chapter 16 of NAFTA (e.g. how changes are negotiated between all actors involved and the dissemination and implementation of these changes with front-line immigration officials at the POE.) To provide some background for the reader, NAFTA was written originally in the early 1990s in such a way that a person applying for a NAFTA status might go to a POE of the receiving country with completed application materials. Then, ideally, he/she would be issued a NAFTA status within ten minutes to a few hours of applying. This procedure has given powers of review and adjudication rights to front-line immigration officers at the POE, which was not the case prior to NAFTA, and understandably the change in border policy has had tremendous influence in the gatekeeping/facilitation mechanism of North American labor flows under NAFTA (Vazquez-Azpiri, 2000).

Regarding the actual interviews, each interviewee was asked a series of approximately 19 questions relating to the Canada–US border. From these questions, six themes began to emerge: (1) the impact of NAFTA on labor mobility between Canada and the US and the Cascadia region specifically; (2) the types of professions that were difficult to interpret under NAFTA; (3) how immigration officials are educated about Chapter 16 of NAFTA; (4) the issue of port shopping (i.e. choosing the 'easiest' port of entry); (5) how immigration officials saw the role of attorneys in the NAFTA application process; and (6) how 9/11 had influenced the flows of professionals across the Canada–US border. These themes and possible consequences towards the development of a high-tech corridor within Cascadia will be explored within Chapter 5 and the Conclusion of the study.

1.4.3   The Immigration Attorneys

Overall, the 'migration industry' (i.e. the lawyers who prepare immigration and visa applications and argue cases on behalf of their clients) may be considered a 'meso-structure' which acts in the space between micro (local) – and macro (international) – structures, by linking individual activities to the state and the economy (Castles et al., 2009). This meso-structure or layer is especially true for the role of business immigration attorneys. This group not only serves as an interface between individuals, firms, and front-line immigration officials at ports of entry, but the immigration attorneys also act as key spokespeople and lobbyists to the national government officials who create immigration policy and also to the public at large. In regards to this study, many of the attorneys interviewed had served since the early 1990s in a capacity as professional advocates and facilitators for NAFTA applicants. They also have a wide breadth of knowledge about the labor mobility process and immigration law, especially when it involved crossing the US–Canada–Mexico borders. Consequently, understanding their part in how the Canada–US border operated in the Cascadia region was critical, and a key pillar within the empirical work of this study. This component was also significant as there is very little literature, if at all, on the role of attorneys in the movements of professional foreign workers across international boundaries. Therefore, it is hoped that the outcomes and findings of this study will help to provide more academic insights into the role and capacities that business immigration attorneys fill in the movement of professionals across North American borders.

The majority of immigration attorneys interviewed had law offices primarily in the Vancouver or Seattle areas. Three attorneys were located outside of the Vancouver–Seattle corridor. One practiced law in Toronto at a medium sized firm; a second practiced law in San Francisco at a large and well-established firm; and a third practiced law at a large and well-established firm in Dallas, Texas. Many of the attorneys stressed that although much of their client base came from the North American west region, they also had clients throughout greater North America, Europe, and Asia. Similar to immigration officials, each lawyer was asked a series of approximately 15 questions relating to the Canada–US border. From these interviews, seven major themes became apparent: (1) how NAFTA influenced labor mobility between Canada and the US, and the Cascadia region specifically; (2) the power and 'clout' of large versus small firms; (3) the types of professions that were especially difficult to interpret under NAFTA provisions; (4) how immigration officials were educated about Chapter 16 of NAFTA; (5) the issue of port shopping (i.e. choosing the 'easiest' port of entry); (6) the seemingly indisputable power of the front-line immigration officials and the 'disconnect' between distant policy makers in national capitals and these front-line officials; and (7) how 9/11 has influenced the flows of professionals across the Canada–US border and the attorneys' line of work. These themes and possible consequences for the development of a high-tech corridor within Cascadia will be explored within Chapter 6 and in the Conclusion of the study.

1.5   CHAPTER SUMMARY

This chapter has provided a general introduction and reasoning for the purpose of writing this book. Part I will continue with Chapter 2, which will review the appropriate realms of literatures that provide a theoretical and conceptual structure to the text. Chapter 3 will explore the concept of the region of Cascadia and how it operates economically. Part II of the study focuses on the empirical work covered in the study, with Chapter 4 exploring the firms' experiences in moving people back and forth across the Canada–US border, and whether or not there was a difference in experience between the larger and smaller firms when navigating the Canada–US border. Chapter 5 explores the role of immigration officials, both front-line officials at the various ports of entry in addition to key immigration policy officials based in Ottawa and Washington DC. The relationship and interplay between these governmental policy makers and the officials who interpret and adjudicate NAFTA applications 'on the ground' will be examined in addition to how other actors see and interpret their experiences with these primary gatekeepers and policy makers. Chapter 6 examines the role of immigration attorneys in the movement of professionals across the Canada–US border. Particular emphasis is placed on how immigration attorneys are seen and portrayed by other actors in addition to their own reflections of themselves and their profession. Part III of the study will include Chapter 7, which provides a discussion of the research findings, policy implications and recommendations, and a conclusion of the study's research and possible next steps.

NOTES

1. Chapter 16 of NAFTA includes the preferential treatment of North American business visitors, traders, investors, intracompany transferees, and 65 professional job categories.
2. The Canada–US Smart Border Declaration, signed in December 2001 had been in development between senior Canada and US officials since the early 1990s.
3. A knowledge worker is a term originally developed by Peter Drucker in 1959 and generally refers to a person who works primarily with information or one who develops and uses knowledge in the workplace.
4. The new economy is a term that was developed in the 1990s to describe OECD countries' transitions from industrial/manufacturing based economies into a high technology based economy, arising largely from new developments in the technology sector.
5. For the most part, both California headquartered firms encouraged the autonomy of their acquired Vancouver R&D facilities by wanting to facilitate and capture a particular 'creative spirit' unique to Vancouver (Richardson, 2006a). Thus, the study will categorize all Vancouver based and San Francisco/Silicon Valley based firms as 'Vancouver Firms', and all Seattle based firms with R&D facilities and activities as 'Seattle Firms'.
6. Tableau Software, Inc.'s total firm size regarding employees is approximately 2,400 worldwide.
7. Pixar Studios closed its Vancouver location in October 2013, after only three years of operation.

2. Borders and the movement of the highly skilled

2.1 INTRODUCTION

In order to begin to answer the question as to whether the international border impedes the development of Cascadia as a high-technology and biotechnology region, a number of more general themes are relevant in framing this study. Clearly, scholars have long been interested in borders and borderlands, and this suggests a rich array of literature to review. Similarly, Cascadia has been identified as a high-tech region, albeit growing on either side of an international border. The growth of the knowledge intensive firm and the workforce in the past 20 years or so provides a hint that highly skilled labor is important to the success of Cascadia, and that mobility of labor is as equally important as the mobility of goods and services within the Cascadia region. Still, understanding the dynamics of the Cascadia economy is complex, and so requires a review of diverse literatures and frameworks that have hitherto rarely been juxtaposed, namely the geography of borders and borderlands; the spatial dynamics of high-technology regions; transnationalism and labor mobility of the highly skilled; and cross-border institutions that facilitate or impede labor mobility. These general literatures are discussed within the following chapter, which closes with a discussion of how they might be applied to research on highly skilled labor mobility within the Cascadia corridor.

2.2 BORDERS AND BORDERLANDS: THEIR HISTORY, CURRENT SITUATION, AND POSSIBLE FUTURES

Boundaries have been long associated with kingdoms, tribal territories, and tribal kingships. However, not until the Peace of Westphalia in 1648, when the Holy Roman Emperor conferred sovereign independence on princes who remained formally within the Empire,[1] ending the Thirty Years' War which involved much of Europe, did the inviolable nature of territory, and its respective boundaries, begin to be associated with the modern state (Muir, 1983: 20). Since this inception in the mid-1600s, national boundaries in Europe have been riddled with conflict between any two neighboring nation states (see for example, Prescott, 1965; Eyre, 1968; Hodder, 1968; and Rushworth, 1968). For instance, it was not until the latter part of the twentieth century that regions spanning international boundaries were seen as having economic promise and opportunity to literally transcend the nation state (Anderson and O'Dowd, 1999; Anderson, 2000). This section provides a brief introduction to how borders have been interpreted over the past century; how these current trends towards globalization have shifted the image of border regions; and, currently with a greater emphasis on meso-scale regional development, how various border regions might be perceived due to the globalization of neo-liberal regimes. It should also be stressed that due to a post 9/11 world, borders throughout the world have taken on a much more security focused position. This trend will also be explored in the remaining sections.

2.2.1   The Historical Importance of Borders and Borderlands

Borders may be seen as one of the important variables that allow any particular state to be part of an international system composed of sovereign nations. Specifically, a state's sovereignty terminates at its boundaries, as this represents the interface between two or more neighboring territories. It is here that the roles of boundaries and borders have been crucial for over the past 300 years. Historically, boundaries have always been problematic in a political or administrative sense, although the nature and degree of potential conflict has greatly varied from border to border (Sahlins, 1989; Martinez, 1986; Muir, 1983). Therefore, borders have typically been seen as buffer zones, and this perception has often diminished opportunities for both wide-scale international trade as well as international conflict. In fact, historically, there have been often few incentives to develop and populate borderlands especially since frequent warfare in continents such as Europe resulted in constant alterations of nation state boundaries. Nations that often lost part of their borderland territories in conflict had good reason not to develop or populate their remaining borderlands in order to keep the national heartland at a safe distance from aggressive neighbors. For example, the Scottish–English border region created an extremely unstable environment with devastating consequences for the local border communities over the course of three centuries. George MacDonald Fraser, in his book *The Steel Bonnets: The Story of the Anglo-Scottish Border Reivers*, captures this situation well:

> Whoever gained in the end, the Border Country suffered fearfully in the process. It was the ring in which the champions met; armies marched and

counter-marched and fought and fled across it; it was wasted and burned and despoiled, its people harried and robbed and slaughtered, on both sides, by both sides. Whatever the rights and wrongs, the Borderers were the people who bore the brunt; for almost 300 years, from the late thirteenth century to the middle of the sixteenth, they lived on a battlefield. (Fraser, 1989 [1994: 13])

As well, the experiences of *tejanos* (Texas Mexicans) in the nineteenth century were similar to those living along the Scottish and English borders, although the period of instability was much shorter (Martinez, 1994). Oscar Martinez, in his book *Border People: Life and Society in the US–Mexico Borderlands*, describes this war-torn borderland:

During the Texas rebellion of the 1830s and the US–Mexico War in the fol-lowing decade, the Texas–Mexico border became a ravaged wasteland, forcing many borderlanders to choose between remaining in their war-torn land and abandoning it for safer ground. Scores of tejanos sought asylum in Mexican territory, returning to their homes years later after the issue of a permanent boundary had been settled. (Martinez, 1994: 13)

The decline of territorial conflicts after World War II and advancements in technology allowed countries to both modernize their transportation and communication systems as well as steadily increase international trade. In fact, interdependence between once warring countries has quickly become a way of life, as can be seen with the strong economic relationship between two former enemies, namely Germany and France, and the experience of the larger European Community following 1945. Since the 1970s with the onset of globalization, border regions found in North America, Europe, and Asia (with some important exceptions being North and South Korea, for example) have begun to have a more prominent role in labor exchanges, commercial transactions, and binational industrialization due to growing international trade (Perkmann, 2003; Held and McGrew, 2000; Edgington et al., 2003; Anderson and O'Dowd 1999; Scott, 1999). These concepts and others will be explored more thoroughly in the following sections. Figures 2.1 and 2.2 provide visual depictions of two of the better known border regions throughout the world.

2.2.2 The Contemporary Importance of Borders and Borderlands

In an era of globalization, transborder trade and movements of people across international borders is key. Ohmae has explored these concepts in a popular fashion in his 1990 book, *The Borderless World* and empirically the issue has been treated in *Regions and the World Economy* (1998) by Alan Scott. In the post cold war period, border regions have been perceived as

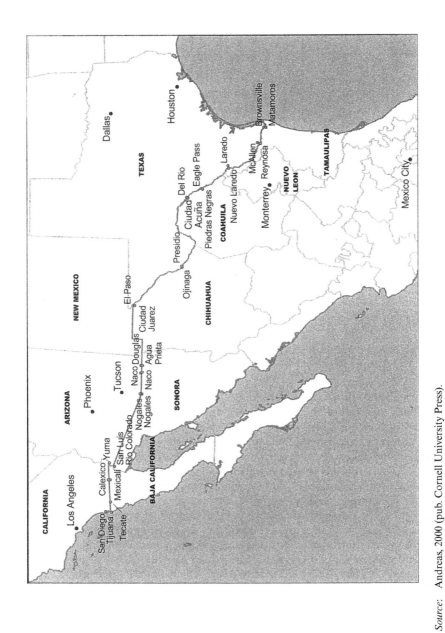

Source: Andreas, 2000 (pub. Cornell University Press).

Figure 2.1   The US–Mexico borderlands

22

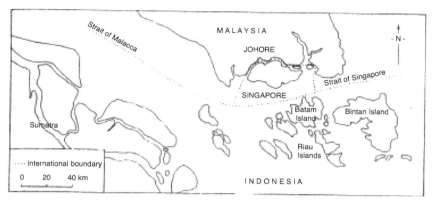

Source: Macleod and McGee, 1996 (pub. United Nations University Press).

Figure 2.2 Singapore–Johore–Riau Growth Triangle

having many positive prospects rather than being characterized by the more traditional problems such as illegal migration, smuggling, air pollution, water contamination, and trade protection, although these latter issues remain important. In fact, border regions once seen as national hinterlands are now cooperating with cross-border partner regions to form cross-border regional alliances, such as the Regio Basiliensis, formed in 1963, which includes Alsace (France), South Baden (Germany), and the border cantons of Switzerland (Briner, 1986). This trinational body, which has received endorsement from each nation's respective government, assesses the needs of the common border area, collects data, and engages in transportation and environmental planning for the region as a whole. The Regio Basiliensis provides a positive model for not only the European Commission, in its long, yet deliberate, process of integrating Europe's borderlands with capital for transnational economic development, but also for other regions throughout the world which are separated by international boundaries, but are drawn to one another in an age of global economic integration.

Although the above paragraph may appear optimistic about the overall future progress of cross-border cooperation and integration, it should be noted that the three major global triads, Europe, Asia, and North America, are at very different stages of meso-regional integration. While there has been an acceleration in the number of regional trading block agreements in recent years (e.g. the European Union, the North American Free Trade Agreement (NAFTA), and the Association of South East Asian Nations) most outside of the European Union are very limited in the depth and extent of their integration and these differences have commensurate implications for particular cross-border (or meso-level) regions (Wu, 2001). Only Europe has advanced to the stage of a formal economic union, with the harmonization of certain economic and social policies under supranational control. North America, which includes Canada, Mexico, and the United States, has not integrated beyond a simple free trade agreement, namely the NAFTA – although labor and environmental side agreements were an important part of NAFTA. Even slower in formal integration is Asia, which has not progressed beyond the stage of international free trade commitments, such as the ten nations involved in the Association of South East Asian Nations (ASEAN), or the Asia Pacific Economic Cooperation (APEC) forum, which has scheduled a reduction of trade barriers by 2020 in the Bogor Agreement (APEC, 2006). The Trans-Pacific Partnership, if ratified by the congresses of the 12 different signatory Pacific Rim countries, which includes the United States and Canada, will allow even freer trade, services, and labor mobility between all signatory countries. Ultimately, at whatever level of economic and political integration that these regional entities finally achieve, it is the borders and borderlands of component nations that will likely receive a tremendous amount of influence and change from their roles as peripheries of the nation state to the gateways of international regional economies.

2.2.3   The Potential Futures of Borders and Borderlands

The future focus of borders lies within the cross-border or transborder regions in which they transect. For example, the means by which binational communities in Europe such as France and Germany have made dramatic efforts to make their national borders more porous to facilitate trade and economic growth also provides a solid and inspiring model for other cross-border regions to follow. However, even the success of Europe's border region integration is not uniform. By way of illustration, the economic integration of the Dutch–German border is much more complete than that of Spain and Portugal (Perkmann, 2007; Capellin, 1993). Additionally, the Nijmegen Centre for Border Research at the Radboud University Nijmegen, established in 1998, has an extensive listing of recent publications dedicated to the European challenge of debordering, rebordering, and reordering its boundaries, both inside and outside the EU. Wong-Gonzalez (2001) captured well the opportunities, but also the struggles that many of these emerging transnational regions face in an era of globalization,

The relationship between territory and globalization can be said to have a double face ... On one side, it supposes the creation of a single world space of interdependencies that constitutes the scope of the new global economy and culture; on the other, it entails the restructuring of existing territories, a new division of international labor, and a new geography of development with winning and losing regions, becoming a factor of both opportunity and danger. In this sense, the possible regional impacts of globalization will depend strongly on the specific territorial response; that is, the modality of integration – the exogenous condition – and on the region's endogenous ability to enhance such a process ... The emergence of transborder regions is noteworthy as a part of this change in economic geography and territorial division of labor on a global scale, resulting from the processes of globalization and international integration; these are entities with qualifications superior to those called simply border regions. (Wong Gonzalez, 2001: 59)

Overall, even in an era of free trade the successful development of transborder regions depends on specific circumstances, agencies, and willingness to cooperate. It is the painstaking details of transborder development and the institutions, structures, and agencies that make this happen, which will help to determine if these new meso-scale regions will succeed in increasing trade and economic growth in addition to the development of the transborder region's own culture. Alain Vanneph in Wong-Gonzalez (2001) explained this idea, as a 'region of the third kind'. He states,

When market forces transcend the obstacles conventionally established by people and generate a migratory and economic dynamics, inducing such evolutions, [such as] solidarities and convergences on both sides of the border, that a single transitional space is created between them or, better said, about them; a 'region of the third kind' – with all the interest that covers this hybrid, this 'cross fertilization,' creator not only of change and wealth but also of a new culture or a new space of cultural identity from the neighborhood to the region. (Vanneph, 2001 [2001: 59])

The above implies that there is much potential not only economically and geographically with the development of transborder regions, but also the opportunity to develop a hybrid culture between and within the transborder region. Examples of this include Cascadia (McCloskey, 1994), the many communities along the US–Mexico border (Martinez, 1994), and the domestic settlements that have straddled international borders throughout Europe for centuries (Ratti, 1993). What is most interesting about these referent examples of cross-border regions is that there is a strong transborder culture, which has existed long before the emergence of globalization and its subsequent transborder regional development. Thus, the communities situated along these international borders might be in a stronger position to develop a 'region of the third kind' as compared to newer transborder regions, driven primarily by globalization and economics. However, a new factor that has been added to the mix of transborder regions is the concept of 'security', especially following 9/11. In fact, security is now the number one priority for all border regions that deal with the US when it comes to shipping, or staging, goods and services, and/or moving people either into or out of the US (Rudd and Furneaux, 2002). In the foreseeable future, it is likely that the successful facilitation of NAFTA at all North American borders, as well as the smooth implementation of trade policies around the world, must succumb to the ever changing concept of security and its increasing influence (Rudd and Furneaux, 2002).

The next section moves from a general history of the role of borders and border regions to the more specific notion of developing cross-border regions. It briefly explores the idea of cross-border regional development in theory and practice. The chapter will then move to some of the primary concepts regarding post 9/11 security within North America. It will place particular emphasis on continental perimeter security as well as the Mexican experience along the US–Mexico border, and how these new security policies may influence the movements of legitimate travelers that influence cross-border development.

2.3   CROSS-BORDER REGIONAL DEVELOPMENT IN THEORY AND PRACTICE

Besides a historical perspective, discussion of theories relevant to cross-border regions (hereafter CBRs) and their development in an era of globalization is also pertinent to this study. Thus, a literature has emerged that examines many different perspectives of these changing borders. From a more tangible approach, CBRs have specific characteristics that distinguish them from other types of regions located within a nation state (e.g. their intersections with boundaries between provinces and states). Consequently, theorizing and policy formation regarding their long-term development has been relatively complex and difficult. In concrete terms, the major theoretical foundations of regional theory and analysis centering around traditional models – such as regional growth theory (Perloff and Dodd, 1963), location theory (Losch, 1954), the original regional development formulations of John Friedmann, and the growth pole theory of Peroux (Friedmann, 1965; Darwent, 1969) do not apply easily to those regions containing cross-border areas. For example, much of the literature using these theoretical models was dedicated to British post-World War II new towns, in an effort to decentralize growth away from the central city of London. Hence, the following section will begin to discuss why particular regional growth theories, which are based on regional linkages within nation states, do not adequately represent the needs and unique characteristics of regional cross-border development.

2.3.1 Similarities in the Development of Cross-border Regions

Although there are differences between cross-border regional development and conventional regional development, as noted in the preceding section, there are also similarities. Indeed, a number of studies have been carried out on cross-border regions. However, these studies have been primarily focused on describing particular cross-border flows. (See for example, *Regional Studies*, *Geojournal*, and the *Journal of Borderland Studies*). There has been relatively little literature that has attempted to analyse the importance of border management to the overall growth of these regions. Thus, one objective of this book will be to provide a solid analysis of how, as a whole, Cascadia's international border separating Vancouver and Seattle is administered, and whether this serves the growing needs of the region. This section reviews studies that focus on the particular needs of cross-border regions, which points out the similarities between cross-border regions and more conventional regional development theories. According to Wu (1998: 5) there are four aspects that are more or less similar in importance to their successful development: the role of infrastructure, the significance of transportation costs, the importance of factor supplies, such as labor and comparatively inexpensive land, and the crucial role of government in promoting development. Thus, appropriate infrastructure is considered crucial in promoting economic development as the 'backwardness' of formerly remote locations close to borders can affect cross-border transportation costs as well as business investment location decisions. Wu argues that the strongest attribute with remote border locations is often the availability of inexpensive land and labor. The fourth factor seen as important to development of cross-border regions is government intervention in the form of seed capital and effort has been seen as essential for a region to succeed in attracting investment and engaging in sustained regional economic development.

Of course all of these factors identified by Wu can also be considered key elements in the success of conventional regional development as well as cross-border development. However, according to Wu (1998), there are a number of aspects of economic growth in cross-border regions that are unique from other types of regional development, and which are not considered in the conventional regional development literature.

The first of these differences includes complementary factors of production. A key point is that cross-border development hinges on the complementarities of factors across borders, such as high levels of capital in California alongside low wage labor and relatively inexpensive land in Mexico.

A second example of the above concept includes cross-border regions that profit from providing expertise, adding value, or storing a good until it is purchased as it moves from one country to the other (e.g. the Hong Kong–Shenzhen corridor). Essentially, these border regions often specialize in the disjuncture and different trade policies within a natural geographical region divided by an international border. Compared with the reality of cross-border zones, conventional regional development theory often assumes the mobility of factors of production, including labor across borders. Finally, unlike regions lying completely within any nation state, one of the greatest challenges with a cross-border region involves the transaction costs and delays that are an inherent attribute of all but the most intricately integrated borders, such as the Benelux region of Europe (Bertram, 1998).

Third, yet another challenge of developing a cross-border region is integrating two or more areas with incompatible economic systems. For example, Hong Kong–Shenzhen, Germany and Poland, and the border areas of Thailand–Laos have proved to be very complicated in blending various transitional economies with market based ones. An even greater challenge in this mix is where transitional economies are also going through political reforms. Bertram (1998) calls these cases 'double transformations'. Wu (1998) noted that developing cross-border regions with incompatible economic systems may pose other challenges. These include the fact that there is the issue of additional institutional learning that must occur as the economy moves from one system to another, as well as the challenges of being a latecomer to industrialization.

Fourth, the role and stability of national institutions are pivotal to the success of any cross-border development. For example, much of the delay in achieving results in the Hong Kong–Shenzhen region has been due to institutional problems. Specifically, the Chinese government had to progressively liberalize many restrictions such as wages and lease of land to non-Chinese citizens (Wu, 1998).

Fifth, economic complementarities must be present in order for cross-border development to work. This is the most important attribute to successful cross-border development. Essentially, cross-border development fixes differences in space, and attracts movement of investment across the border to the region, which has the less expensive labor force and land (Wu, 1998: 7). (Conventional theory by comparison expects movement of labor towards the center or urban core of a region.) The US–Mexico border is probably the best example of this dynamic. Within Cascadia, there is some activity that fits into this type of cross-border complement-arity. (See Merrit, 1996 and Richardson, 1998.) However, since the greater Vancouver area can be described as a post-manufacturing economy, and with land and labor costs in the neighboring US county not being that dramatically different compared to the greater Vancouver area, there is not the same ferocity of economic activity that can be found in key urban corridors along the US–Mexico border where *macquiladora* zones attract US direct foreign investment that takes advantage of low wages in Mexico (Andreas, 2000).

Finally, much of conventional regional development theory has revolved around the importance of large-scale industrialization and the formal economy (Wu, 1998). However, by comparison, many cross-border developments focus on trade within small-scale industries (e.g. clothing, house-hold goods, electronics, and so forth), and also within the service sector, and cross-border regions have taken advantage of exchanges between the small-scale informal economies. For example, cross-border areas strad-dling between the transitional market economies of Russia and China and China and Vietnam have engaged in cross-border trade since it provides an opportunity for residents on either side of the border to buy affordable consumer goods or hard currency, in exchange for agricultural products or raw materials. Over time, this small-scale trading potentially allows entrepreneurs to invest in larger trading operations or diversify into other activities (ibid.).

As mentioned previously, the development of cross-border regions to facilitate international trade and economic development is a relatively new and changing phenomenon. Therefore, in the literature, other than the recent conceptual work of Lundquist and Trippl (2013), which shall be discussed in an upcoming section, there has been little theoretical work dealing rigorously with the underlying cycles and dynamics of cross-border regions broadly, even though there are a considerable number of specific case studies to describe these recent and unfamiliar activities. This section's discussion has attempted to demonstrate that border regions have many unique attributes, which are not dealt with by conventional theories of development. Hence, due to this dearth of literature, which critically examines cross-border theorization, there is a need for more articulate research on this topic area. The following section will examine various types of cross-border development drawing from European, Asian, and North American experiences in an attempt to gain a greater understanding of possible theories, which might be derived from these new activities.

2.3.2   Types of Cross-border Regions and their Development

Although the various meso regions within the 'global triad' have had different histories, and most likely will experience different futures, many cross-border regions, whether in Europe or South East Asia, appear to be going through significant transitions. This section reviews a series of representative case studies from the various meso-scale cross-border regions of Europe, Asia, and North America, stressing their unique features but also drawing attention to their commonalties.

Wu (1998), in a review of the European and Asia Pacific situations, emphasizes that cross-border regions have a number of different characteristics, but fall primarily into three different types (see Table 2.1). Wu calls his first category 'border regions', which are primarily the least developed regions of the three types and have the least potential for trade and other forms of cross-border interaction. The Russia–China–North Korea border area is an example of this type of border region (see Figure 2.3). The second type he calls 'cross-border regions'. These are

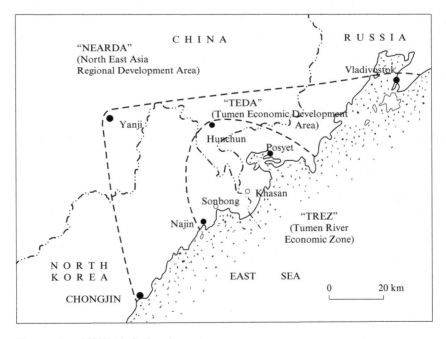

Source: Lee, 1998 (pub. Springer).

Figure 2.3   Tumen River area development zone

Table 2.1 *Typology of border region development*

Type of Border Region	Economic Relations	Institutional/Governmental Frameworks	Types of Enterprises	State of Infrastructure Networks	Migration	Differences in Labor Cost	Examples
Border Regions	Few and strictly controlled	Few	Individuals or small enterprises	Bottlenecks due to strict and cumbersome border controls	Strictly controlled (frontier)	Extremely high	Russia–China (Tumen) China–Vietnam
		Emerging, but one-sided	Spontaneous development	(as above)	(as above)	High	Thailand–China–Burma–Laos
Cross-Border Regions	Dependent relations	Emerging consultative mechanisms	Enterprises large and small acting on their own – largely contractual relationships-joint ventures	Consultative planning-border controls still important	Controlled migration (shoppers who commute university students also commute	High	Poland–Germany
							Hong Kong–Shenzhen
						Diminishing	*CASCADIA*
Trans-border Region	Symbiotic	Cooperative institutions	Enterprise networks; technology transfer or sharing networks	Joint planning of infrastructure networks	Simplified procedures and relatively free movement	Little or none	European Union (planned)

Source: Adapted from Wu, 1998: 198 (pub. Springer).

Source: Dorrenbacher and Schulz, 1999 (pub. Dorrenbacher and Silesian Institute in Opole).

Figure 2.4   *Direction of transboundary commuter relations (Bassin
              Houiller Lorraine–Saarland), within the larger Saar–Lor–Lux
              border region*

characterized by interdependent economic relations and substantial trade,
but some types of flows (e.g. immigration) are still tightly controlled. The
Hong Kong–Guangdong Province in Asia and the Cascadia Corridor
in North America are examples of this type of border region development. He notes that these types of regions have the greatest potential in
achieving a 'trans-border region', which is the most open of the three
border types that he recognizes (Table 2.1). This third type of region
is characterized by true symbiotic economic development, a joint management regime, and almost free movement of regional citizens across

international borders. The Benelux region of Belgium, the Netherlands, and Luxembourg is an example of this type of border region development, as well as the 'Saar–Lor–Lux' region of Luxembourg, Germany, Belgium, and France (see Figure 2.4).

The most difficult objective to attain regarding the above three factors is the free mobility of people across international boundaries. Much of the existing literature on cross-border regions has tended to focus on core and periphery regions such as Singapore–Johore, Hong-Kong–Guangzhou, and Los Angeles–Tijuana.

In this case, interactions across the border, which bisect CBRs, are defined by traditional core-periphery relations, for example direct foreign investment from the core flowing to a cheap wage periphery. However, little has been written on core–core regions such as the Vancouver–Seattle–San Francisco/ Silicon Valley corridor, where wages and levels of development are roughly similar. Perhaps the European Union may provide examples of core to core cross-border economic connectivity due to its efforts to unite the continent economically for the past 40 years (Trippl, 2012; Anderson, 2000). In fact, the EU is the only meso-scale region that has allowed for almost complete employment mobility for its citizens through EU labor mobility policies as part of the European Economic Area (EEA) and facilitated by the Schengen border system.[2] As will be discussed in Chapter 6, the Canada–US relationship has not evolved to this level of trust between nations when it comes to its citizens. For example, even before 9/11, under Section 110 of the Illegal Immigration Reform and Immigration Responsibility Act (IIRIRA) of 1996, US Congress was seriously considering that all Canadians attain visas upon entering the United States, even for a simple shopping trip.[3] This portion of the bill was finally defeated in 2000. However, the spirit of restrictiveness when it comes to allowing familiar foreigners, such as Canadians, to traverse easily into the US was mounting long before 9/11.

2.4 POST 9/11 SECURITY MEASURES AND THEIR INFLUENCE ON BORDERS AND THE MOVEMENTS OF PEOPLES

Finally, in considering the theoretical literature on borders and CBRs, the impact of events following the terrorist attack of 9/11 in the US must be considered. The horrific events of 9/11 placed a spotlight on America's borders, and how porous they are to terrorists. While gazing at America's own borders, attention was also drawn specifically to the Canada–US border, and US Congress raised strong concerns about the perceived openness and little security, which might be found on the Canadian side of the border. Thus, Senator Hilary Clinton, remarked erroneously that four of the terrorists involved with the 9/11 hijacking had slipped into the US from Canada (Biersteker, 2003). Senator Clinton later retracted these comments when it was determined that all 19 terrorists directly involved with 9/11 had directly entered the US legally. However, there was a time lag of a few weeks between Senator Clinton's comments and factual evidence that these comments were incorrect. Within this time period of only a few weeks, many alarmist articles in US papers were generated about the perceived laxness of Canadian security along its borders, and the fact that this irresponsible neighbor shares the longest demilitarized border with the US (Klein, 2003). This created a public relations nightmare for the Canadian government, since much of the openness of the Canada–US border rests on the American perception that Canada is a safe, non-threatening country. Still senior levels of the Canadian government had anticipated a scenario of this sort occurring long before 11 September (Rudd and Furneaux, 2002). In fact, the Canadian federal government has been working with the US government on tighter and more harmonious border controls since the early 1990s. A product of these joint efforts was the signing of the Ridge-Manley Smart Border 30 Point Declaration on 12 December 2001 by Governor Tom Ridge[4] and Foreign Minister John Manley. These products are examples of long-term Canadian planning and advancement when it came to the Canada–US border that allow it to remain relatively open, with seemingly unofficial preferential treatment for Canadians entering into the US,[5] but also to establish more restrictive measures using sophisticated technology for all others entering the US through Canada.

The above paragraph draws attention to the fact that there was a scramble after 9/11 by US politicians from across the political spectrum to be seen as doing something about the perceived leaky and dangerous border between Canada and the US (Andreas, 2003). In fact, the more traditional topics of trade issues and immigration/labor mobility have been seen through a lens of security since 9/11. Andreas (2003) considers that the growing momentum developed through the 1990s regarding talks and efforts towards open borders in North America have been replaced by discussions regarding security perimeters and homeland defense. Moreover, he notes that it is now seen as politically incorrect to talk about open borders. He stresses,

> Any politician who does talk about open borders may be quite possibly muted, attacked, and ostracized by their political opponents. (Andreas, 2003: 2)

Based on the darkened mood emanating from the terrorist events on 9/11 towards borders and security, Andreas (2003) concluded that 'borders are back' with a vengeance. However, Biersteker (2003: 160), writing in the same collection of essays, reflects on the fact that borders are not fixed, but are 'socially constructed by the practices of state and nonstate actors'. In fact, during the latter part of the twentieth century, many states have lifted controls on goods, currency, and ideas, but have continued to control the cross-border movement of a majority of people. He notes that the range of activities controlled by the state at borders, and also the points and places of inspections, also varies. Biersteker goes on to point out the changing and elusive natures of borders in addition to the different actors, both state and nonstate, that have control within these zones of power and authority:

> Thus, when thinking about the nature of borders and boundaries, the important point to remember is that the border changes in two dimensions: both over what it attempts to control, and where it attempts to assert its controlling authority. Its salience and meaning vary according to the ease with which different types of goods and services are allowed across it (the porosity of the border), and it varies according to the actual physical location at which the state attempts to assert its authority . . . Perhaps the most significant aspect of the line to demarcate the border is not the actual physical location of the inspection of goods and people, but the jurisdiction under which the inspections take place . . . In the final analysis, state jurisdictional claims of authority define the operational meaning of the border, both how hard or how soft it is, and precisely where (in legal, not physical space) the authority is exercised. Not only are the issues over which states claim authority (and the need for control) variable, but the location of the assertion of that control also changes. (Biersteker, 2003: 160–61)

Indeed, controls over flows and networks across borders (Luke, 1991) are becoming as important as the actual 'traditional territorial imaginary of international political economy' (Biersteker, 2003: 161). Added to these new developments around transnational movements and imaginary boundaries are the development of transborder regions, as has been discussed in the previous section, which physically emerge along international borders, and serve as a site of facilitation and a catalyst towards moving and developing goods, services, and even people, from one nation state to another. Biersteker (2003) used the example of the dramatic fall of the Mexican peso in 1994 to demonstrate that it had major short-term impacts on the regional economies of the American Southwest, which was highly dependent on the economy of northern Mexico, but very little impact, if at all, on the economy of Boston, Massachusetts. Thus, the idea of a transborder region may be expanded to different scales, with perhaps the nexus being the strength of the social and economic networks that have emerged between these different regions.

Cascadia has been identified as a core–core CBR, one with the potential to emerge as a high-technology region in continental North America.

Accordingly, as part of the review of relevant literature framing this study, an upcoming section shall continue to explore the idea of innovative regions and their spatial implications as they apply to high-tech companies and their networks of operations. However, before the book moves to explore innovative regions, the concept of border management will be explored.

2.4.1   Border Management

The concept of border management has taken many different forms over the past century. This range and variety of management agencies and raisons d'être is reflected in the many different governmental agencies responsible for some part of managing the goods, people, and services that flow from one country to the next. It was not until the formation of the EU in the late 1980s and the aftermath of 9/11 that Europe and North America began to take a more integrative and 'upfront' approach to how borders were managed. From the perspective of the EU, this may be demonstrated in the development of the Schengen Acquis[6] in the early 1990s (Anderson, 2000). Although originally heralded as a progressive approach to regional international cross-border labor mobility, the Schengen system has become increasingly strained over the past few years. This is especially true after the Arab Spring of 2011 and the recent Syrian refugee crisis. Thus, due to challenges with EU external border management, many European counties have experienced considerable increased migration flows from the Middle East and Africa, two regions close to Europe, but still outside of the EU zone. This has led to the questioning of the long-term viability of free movement throughout the EU region (Collett, 2013).

The North American effort towards the joint modern management of borders begins in the early 1990s, and finally led to the ratification of the Ridge-Manley Smart Border Declaration and Action Plan in December of 2001 between then Canadian Minister of International Affairs, John Manley, and Tom Ridge, the first appointed Secretary of the US Department of Homeland Security. Despite these initial collaborative efforts between the US and Canada regarding shared understandings and possibly seamless management of the two countries' borders, the 2011 Smart Border Declaration was more of a broad based visioning statement and listing of all current collaborative work rather than a strategic foundation for joint Canada–US policy work. What followed in 2005 was the signing of the Security and Prosperity Partnership between US President George W. Bush, Canadian Prime Minister Paul Martin, and Mexican President Vincente Fox as part of the North American Leaders Summit. One of the more interesting features of this particular agreement was that it made provisions to include leaders within the North American private sector as part of the Partnership discussions. Moving forward to 2011, the 2011 Canada-US Beyond the Border (BTB) Action Plan, signed by Prime Minister Stephen Harper and US President Barak Obama, among other mandates, gave a directive of 'faster and more predictable crossings for business travelers' (Dawson, 2012). However, it has been argued that these more recent Canada–US border management and action plans have only half-heartedly facilitated more effective and predictable flows of people (Richardson, 2011; Cryne, 2013).

More importantly, perhaps, the events following 9/11 made policy experts in the US take a closer look at how exactly the US manages its border, especially from the perspective of the movements of people. Thus, the Migration Policy Institute (MPI), based in Washington DC, conducted some analysis on this topic area in 2005 in the form of two publications. They focused directly on the management of borders as it relates to people. The first relevant publication was entitled *Secure Borders, Open Doors: Visa Procedures in the Post-September 11 Era* (2005) authored by Stephen Yale-Loehr, Demetri Papademetriou, and Betsy Cooper (2005) and the second was Deborah Meyers' report, *One Face at the Border: Behind the Slogan* (2005). The first report, *Secure Borders, Open Doors*, provided detailed analysis as to how visa procedures were administered after 9/11, and the effectiveness of these procedures in relation to US security needs. The second report, *One Face at the Border*, examines the effectiveness of changes within the legacy US Immigration and Naturalization Service (US INS) as a result of the organization's amalgamation into the Department of Homeland Security in 2003. Overall, both reports provide a detailed analysis of the changes in the US government's management towards the facilitation of foreigners into the US since 9/11. However, both reports found many flaws in these new US governmental procedures and approaches and cautioned that, due to these flaws, the US government may continue to compromise, inadvertently, the security of the US and its people, despite the fact that the majority of these changes were instituted in an attempt to provide better security for the US regarding the admittance of foreigners.

A different perspective towards the approach of managing the finite details of borders in a post 9/11 climate is the one taken by Policy Horizons Canada, formerly the Canadian Policy Research Initiative (PRI), based in Ottawa, Canada. The initiative is sponsored by the Canadian government and examines key issues pertinent to Canada and its people. One main focus of the initiative is the study of Canada's relationship to the United States, or 'North American Linkages'. The effort began in the early 2000s with a major conference on the Canada–US border hosted in Vancouver, BC in October 2000. The former Canadian Policy Research Initiative subsequently followed up on this conference platform with key publications, such as *North American Linkages*, in June 2004; the November 2005 *Interim Report on Cross-Border Regions*; and *The Emergence of Cross-Border Regions* in February 2006. The initiative funded a series of studies as Policy Horizons Canada (Richardson, 2011; Bristow, 2010; Taylor, 2010; Vance, 2011) after the 2008 financial crisis to examine as to whether or not the Canada–US border remained an impediment to Canadian and US businesses. Rather than security, the main thrust of these reports focuses on trade and economic relationships between the different cross-border regions between Canada and the US, and Canada and the US in general. Beyond Richardson (2011), no other study mentioned high-tech clustering or connectivity between the different Canada–US cross-border regions, which further bolsters the importance for a study of this sort.

Overall, the above review of some of the current border management work conducted by the Migration Policy Institute, based in the US (and dedicated to US federal policy development), and the Policy Horizons Canada (dedicated to both federal policy and also geographically regional Canadian initiatives) helped to demonstrate the conflicting priorities and concerns regarding border management within North America. Specifically, the difference in the scale of perspective was very important here. The more federally based perspective, namely the Migration Policy Institute, placed considerable emphasis on the shield effects of the US border, while the more regionally focused efforts of Policy Horizons Canada emphasized more border management flexibility, or a sieve approach.

The Wilson Center based in Washington DC also began a series of symposia, or discussions, focused on major Canada–US issues over the past ten years. The series, entitled One Issue: Two Voices, is committed to covering and exploring key issues that are important to both Canadian and American societies. One of the symposia held in 2013 was, in fact, dedicated to cross-border labor mobility for professionals with an emphasis on Chapter 16 of NAFTA. This particular symposium did, indeed, try to grapple with the tension between the federal shield priority of security and the regional sieve needs of cross-border economy and more predictable cross-border management. The symposium's speakers concluded that many professions in the NAFTA list were outdated; there was increasingly inconsistent decision making at the ports of entry regarding NAFTA applications; and subsequently, Canada and the US should take more visionary risk-based professional labor mobility solutions that go beyond the 2011 Beyond the Border Action Plan (Shotwell and Yewdell, 2013) in an effort to better facilitate North American business interests and overall collective continental wellbeing.

Overall, the tension regarding Chapter 16 of NAFTA between federal policy priorities and cross-border regional economic needs has not been solved at this time. The following section shall begin to explore high-tech companies within innovative regions and their demand for internationally highly skilled labor.

2.5 CROSS-BORDER HIGH-TECH REGIONS AND EMERGING INNOVATION SYSTEMS, HIGH-TECH COMPANIES, INNOVATIVE REGIONS GENERALLY, AND THEIR DEMAND FOR LABOR

While growing scholarly attention has been paid to cross-border regions, Cascadia is a special type of emerging cross-border region, one to be shown later that is focused on high-technology and biotechnology. Thus, this type of region requires a special type of cross-border literature that is dedicated to understanding and supporting the dynamics of an advance core city to core city relationship that transcends an international border. The following literatures will begin to build a knowledge base around this regional dynamic and its demand for highly skilled labor.

2.5.1 Cross-border High-tech Regions and Their Emerging Innovation Systems

There is a nascent literature on cross-border high-tech regions. For example, Trippl (2010) argues that biotechnology cross-border clusters such as the biotechnology sector in the Öresund region (Coenen et al., 2004; Moodysson et al., 2005; Tödtling et al., 2006; OECD, 2013) can be acknowledged to constitute a key element of a cross-border regional innovation system since the region in question reflects high levels of economic integration and innovation-related intersections. The author stressed that cross-border areas differ enormously regarding their capacity to develop an advanced integrated innovation space. In a study that examined new innovation networks found in the metropolitan city of Vienna and its neighboring cross-border region of Centrope, which is made up of Eastern Austria and the adjacent regions of Hungary, the Czech Republic, and Slovakia, Trippl (2012: 297) found that a majority of firms had very few, if any, cross-border knowledge links, especially to these Centrope countries. The firms surveyed had much stronger and longer established links at other spatial levels, which included the local, national, and international. Trippl concluded that it remained unclear as to the relative importance of different kinds of proximities (e.g. cognitive, institutional, social and functional distance) when it came to shaping the prospects and challenges for enhanced transborder knowledge circulation. The author stressed that the influence of firm strategy and networking capacities of firms in relation to better understanding their cross-border knowledge-sharing activities required greater study.

Most recently, Lundquist and Trippl (2013: 455–58) developed a conceptual analysis of the three different stages of a cross-border regional innovation system, which can be summarized as follows:

> Stage I – Weakly integrated systems. Includes low levels of economic relations and an absence of knowledge interactions and innovative linkages. Region lacks a common culture, language, and leadership, as well as difficult physical accessibility from one side of border to the other. Thus, hard to brand region. German–Polish border as an example.

> Stage II – Semi-integrated systems. An emerging knowledge driven system. Opportunities for new and mutual beneficial connections and linkages on either side of border. Pockets of possible cross-border clusters, but not a coherent transfrontier innovation system along the entire border. Deemed 'islands of innovation' in an otherwise fragmented cross-border relationship. Increasing flows of students, researchers, professionals, university–industry partnerships, and enhanced institutional networking. Oresund region of Denmark and Sweden, and possibly Cascadia as examples.

> Stage III – Strongly integrated systems. Represents the most advanced stage of innovation-driven integration for a cross-border regional innovation system. Characterized by a considerable flow of knowledge, expertise, and skills across borders and demonstrated by intense mobility of students and professionals, as well as innovation related networking between firms, academic, and university–industry located within cross-border region. Cross-border innovation linkages are now comparable to other innovation linkages, rather than being subordinate. Seen as the utopia as cross-border region building. Difficult to achieve in practice.

Overall, Lundquist and Trippl (2013) developed an insightful conceptual model in order to begin to understand cross-border regions in a more complete and holistic manner, especially when examining several dimensions and their respective dynamics. Although the authors suggest that Cascadia may be an example of a Stage II cross-border innovation system when it comes to cognitive and functional proximity, as described by Brunet-Jailly (2008), there still remains the need to better understand Cascadia's possible connections and flows when it comes to knowledge workers, which is a critical factor in determining a cross-border region's ability to develop into a cross-border regional innovation system.

Based on the above, there has been substantial research on high-tech companies, their vocational preferences together with the notion of learning regions, and the geography of innovation, which has emphasized the importance of labor mobility. Thus, this section reviews the major pieces of literature within this topic area, and closes with how these themes may be applied to an analysis of the Cascadia region.

2.5.2 High-tech Companies and Their Regions

High-tech companies, and the regions that they are located in, emerged through the interactions of three major developments: the technological revolution, the formation of a global economy, and the emergence of an informational form of economic production and management (Castells and Hall, 1994). These advanced activities and the areas they occupy may be considered the mines and factories of the information age. However, despite the new economic wealth that these regions have generated over the past 30 years, albeit unevenly, they are still poorly understood in regards to their composition, and the fundamental dynamics contributing to their success. Many regional economic development agencies envision that clusters of successful firms will eventually cause a spill-over into the larger region with more and more firms growing and benefiting from success as has been the case in Silicon Valley. However, in recent times, high-technology regions have had a volatile cycle of development. For instance, the high-tech industry has experienced a massive 'bust' with the bursting of the dotcom bubble in 2000, followed by the slowing of the North American economy immediately after 9/11 and the 2008 global financial crisis. These negative events impacted the high-tech industry in the form of massive employee layoffs as well as firm closures during 2000–2003 and again from 2008–11. Regarding the dotcom bust of 2000, it was not until 2005 that high-tech firms began to hire in substantial numbers, led by Silicon Valley (Tam, 2006), only to go through another round of major layoffs beginning in late 2008. A more recent phenomenon has been the outsourcing of certain high-technology jobs, reflected, for example, in the hiring of high-tech software professionals found in India.

These dramatic and fast moving circumstances have caused regional development agencies to reassess what type of industries they wish to generate and foster within their region, and how they can attract, draw, and retain key talented employees who, ideally, will contribute to building a successful region. As well, in light of the two financial crashes of the early 2000s, there is also an academic trend to develop the perfect, yet elusive, circumstances that will facilitate a 'resilient region' (Donald et al., 2013; Cooke et al., 2012). Nonetheless, despite the volatility of information technology firms and associated high-tech sectors, many regional economic development agencies continue to strive for the next Silicon Valley, with a combination of research facilities, access to venture capital, a well-educated workforce, and a strong quality of life. Analysis of other successful high-tech regions can be found in Kenney (2000) (Silicon Valley); Gray et al. (1999a) (Seattle); Saxenian (1994) (Boston and Silicon Valley); and Bresnahan and Gambardella (2004) (Silicon Valley, Israel, Ireland, India, Cambridge UK, Scandinavia, and Taiwan). The evaluation of Silicon Valley[7] is of special interest to an analysis of Cascadia, as it hints at what the northern portion of Cascadia might become. As well, this book will demonstrate that a certain number of firms in both Vancouver and Seattle were highly dependent on firms and funding based in Silicon Valley for their continued growth and development.

2.5.2.1   Silicon Valley

Silicon Valley is a region or social system located originally in the southern portion of the San Francisco Bay area, which historically extended from San Carlos in the north to San José in the south, covering approximately a 35-mile corridor. As of the early 2000s, the term has extended itself to also include San Francisco and portions of the 'East Bay', which include Berkeley and Lawrence Livermore National Laboratories. It is not a formal geographical area, but encompasses much of San Mateo and Santa Clara counties and now San Francisco and Alameda counties – now a considerable portion of the Greater San Francisco Bay area. (Please see Figure 2.5.) Over the past five decades, Silicon Valley has commercialized some of the most important electronics and biomedical technologies developed in the second half of the twentieth century (Kenney, 2000: 1). The region is the product of a rich overlay of at least five distinct institutional groupings: an impressive cluster of innovative new media and electronics firms: Stanford University and its nonprofit research spin-offs; large domestic computing and instrumentation firms, many of them branch operations; research, marketing, and information-gathering operations of foreign firms; and a military-industrial component of both private corporations and government offices (Gray et al., 1999b: 307). Saxenian (1994), through her study of small and medium sized electronics firms, described a 'fuzzy' mutually beneficial social relationship within this network of firms. Primary characteristics of this relationship were based on egalitarianism, trust, and cooperation. These attributes enabled these smaller firms to quickly reposition themselves in response to industry change in the late 1980s and continue to succeed. These behaviors were contrary to electronics firms in the Boston area, which she characterized as larger, hierarchical, and more culturally conservative.

Gray et al. (1999b), along with others such as Storper (1999), is rather firm in the argument that the success of Silicon Valley is likely very

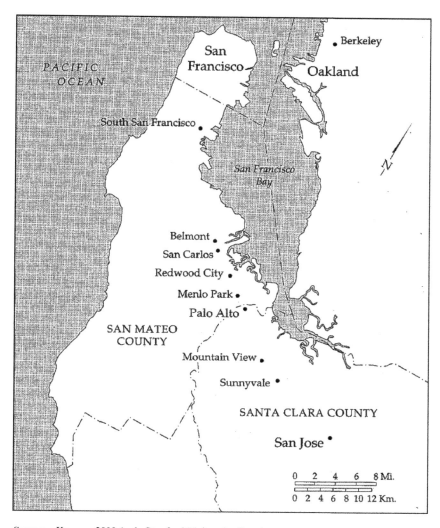

Source: Kenney, 2000 (pub. Stanford University Press).

Figure 2.5   Silicon Valley

difficult to replicate elsewhere for a variety of factors, based on its specific history, the influence of the military in Northern California, big firm leadership, and continual massive foreign direct investment within the region. Additionally, Silicon Valley is not without a number of social challenges. For instance, the region's income distribution is highly skewed and collective bargaining to protect the wages of the working class is almost nonexistent. Hence, Gray et al. (1999b) has stressed that perhaps the dynamics or 'milieu' behind the success of other high-tech clusters such as the 'Third Italy' (Piore and Sabel, 1984), North Carolina's Research Park (Luger and Goldstein, 1990) and Seattle (Gray et al., 1999a) may provide more appropriate case studies for many other regions wanting to achieve similar high-tech success due to their more manageable nature and greater income equity, as compared to Silicon Valley. These three geographic regions, in addition to other high-tech areas, are associated with various characteristics, such as innovation and learning institutions. They appear to have an ability to attract and retain highly skilled workers (whether foreign or domestic). Thus, these factors together may have the synergistic effects of contributing to a successful prosperous new economy region. Hence, the next two sections review these concepts, and how they might be applied to the Cascadia region.

2.5.3   Regional Innovation and its Institutions

Innovation, in a regional context, is often seen as the consequence of the critical institutional or organizational frameworks of production in an attempt to make, change, or create something new. Storper (1999) argues that there are two schools of American thought dedicated to what factors are important to regional development. These factors include innovation, high-technology, institutions, and regional development. The first stresses the university–production link and uses the experiences of Silicon Valley and Boston's Route 128 as their examples. (See Markusen et al., 1986.) The second approach focuses on a regional politics, and stresses the importance of the dynamics of regional coalitions that rally to attract certain high-technology, allowing for the transfer of high-technology resources into the region's economy. For example, much of the 'gunbelt' economy of New England and Southern California developed because of influential federal politicians representing New England and Southern California who lured substantial amounts of federal monies to their regions for the purpose of defense research. Storper adds that both approaches to successful regional development have flaws to their arguments. For instance, the first approach emphasizes university–industrial linkages and it only works well with a significant formal science base, such as advanced science based universities and the semiconductor industry. However, there were no strong research universities in the Los Angeles area in the 1920s and 1930s when the development of the airplane industry began in this region (Scott, 1993; Storper, 1982). The second argument is also flawed. Again, the importance of an external influence such as military investment (using the Southern California aerospace industry example) was in place long before the development of a military-industrial complex. In sum, for Storper, the American school on what factors make for a successful high-tech region has still not developed a coherent and convincing theory linking high-technology development to regional development (Storper, 1999).

Another, perhaps more convincing, approach has been developed by the GREMI group (Group de Recherche Europeen sur les Milieux Innovateurs) which is made up principally of Franco-Italian-Swiss regional economists. Their ideas on innovation and regional development revolve around the notion of a *milieu*. Storper (1999:35) essentially summarizes the work of various academics who specialize in this topic area (Aydalot, 1986; Aydalot and Keeble, 1988; Camagni, 1991; Maillat and Perrin, 1992; Maillat et al., 1993; Maillat et. al., 1990; Camagni, 1995) by stating that the milieu is a context for development, which motivates and guides 'innovative agents' to be able to innovate and coordinate with other innovative agents. The notion of milieu might be described as a *system* of regional institutions, rules, and practices, which lead to innovation. It is essentially a territorial version of the embeddedness of social and economic processes described initially by the sociologist, Mark Granovetter (1985). The milieu revolves around the concept of a network of actors, such as producers, researchers, and politicians, for example. Such a network is embedded in a milieu, which helps to provide these actors with what they need in order to succeed with innovation. In closing, though, the GREMI group cannot explain the logic or the essence of the intangible that they seek. In sum, the essential factors behind successful innovative regions are largely unclear (Storper, 1999).

2.5.4 Institutions, Learning, and Labor in High-technology Regions

The growth of any high-tech region generates a commensurate demand for skilled labor. In changing economic times, great emphasis is placed on the ability of regional based institutions to acquire, absorb, and diffuse relevant knowledge and information throughout the region that affect the process of economic development and change (Gertler and Wolfe, 2002), leading to what Florida (1995) deemed a 'learning region'.[8] Additionally, Gertler (2004: 10) stressed the need for institutions and related industrial practices to rethink their existing policies and approaches to innovations and industrial development within a region. He stressed that a matrix regulating investment decisions and time horizons, labor market decisions, and labor–management relations in the workplace have the most impact from a perspective of innovation and learning within an industrial region.

Thus, this section briefly examines the role of institutions and the process of learning, both within and between institutions situated within a given geographical space in addition to the essential ability to draw and retain labor to a region. Based on the foundational works of Weber, Veblen, Schumpeter, and Karl Polanyi, economic processes are embedded in a variety of institutions such as local customs, government, firms, associations of firms, religion, culture, and the legal framework within a society. This being the case, the ability of these institutions to respond to and flourish within changing economic times is critical to a region's success. The other critical attribute of these local institutions is their ability to retain and transmit learning and knowledge to their members (Gertler and Wolfe, 2002). Hence, the continued success of a region may be attributed to the abilities of its institutions, down to the firm level, to capitalize on social learning and increased networking between firms and other organizations within a geographical space.

By way of example, Cooke et al. (2012) present the idea that local and regional territories are no longer self-contained poles of growth and development, but that they transcend international borders to attract talent, resources, and opportunities beyond the local and regional. This is a considerable change to what Cooke (2002) discussed when examining to what degree European regions were able to support innovation at the firm level. Drawing from research conducted in the 1990s, his findings were interesting in the sense that they revealed that most of the firms he interviewed operated in regional and national markets rather than international ones. Gertler (2002) substantiated Cooke's (2002) findings by examining the relationship between German manufacturers and North American clients. His research found that the importance of institutional forces beyond the level of the nation state was rarely taken into consideration. Although firms tried to collaborate at the international level, much of their knowledge and experiences had not been shaped by a similar set of national institutions. This often led to confusion and misunderstandings between actors, and lessened considerably the likelihood of achieving interfirm learning beyond regions located within a nation state.

A decade later, Saxenian (2012) writing in the same collection of essays as Cooke et al. (2012) noted the importance of 'global search networks' that firms, or other actors, used to find a solution or solve a problem. She drew her example from highly skilled first generation immigrant professionals in US technology industries who collaborated with colleagues in their home country (namely, Taiwan) for entrepreneurial development. Her key argument was that these new Argonauts are ideally positioned to go beyond prevailing routines and identify opportunities for complementary 'peripheral' participation in the global economy (pp. 9–10).

The different findings of Gertler (2002) and Saxenian (2012) when it comes to learning, innovation, and global adaptation stratified within high-technology regions perhaps foreshadows the many varied outcomes of high-tech firms in an increasingly global era. Thus, there may be challenges for the concept of Cascadia when it comes to achieving high-tech aspirations, since it does straddle an international border. Even though there are many different types of institutions and understandings formulated and reassured by the two different nation states, namely Canada and the United States. However, management of the border and achieving harmonization of practices and procedures when interpreting 'rules of crossing' is of the upmost importance. Both Gertler's (2002) and Saxenian's (2012) findings provide an interesting departure point to the next paragraph, which shall briefly introduce the critical importance of the access and availability of skilled labor within a region.

The literature in the above paragraphs helps to draw attention to the factors of regional based institutions and learning within key firms and how these attributes ripple outward to the larger region. One additional factor that is essential to the growth and development of a high-tech region is the availability of local highly skilled labor and/or a region's ability to attract highly skilled labor, whether domestic or international in origin. Thus, it is not only important for a cluster to create networks within the local environment, but also to develop and maintain crucial alliances and networks both within the region and also externally beyond the region. Bresnahan and Gamberdella (2004) noted that the key ingredients that are needed to operate a regional cluster, in general, included entrepreneurship, linkages to a major and growing market, and the availability of skilled labor. Biotechnology firms, especially, have been seen as operating along these complex local to global networks in the development of strategic alliances regarding financing, research and development (R&D), and scientific innovation. These factors have been argued to be important if the firm stands a strong chance of success (Darby et al., 1999).

The reason for these vast and complicated networks is that the global biotechnology industry, for example, is an inherently risky and complicated one with many processes and potential pitfalls. Thus, any innovative firm requires extensive finances and seasoned experience, which is sometimes beyond the realm of the immediate firm. In addition to these needs, a biotechnology cluster, for example, specifically needs close physical proximity to key research centers that attract star scientists (Zucker and Darby, 1999), and a subsequent entourage of leading international researchers and graduate students with (or developing) highly sophisticated skills. Zucker and Darby (2007) stressed that the labor mobility of

these star scientists is very important when a new discovery has both a
commercial value and a combination of scarcity and tacitness that defines
natural excludability. In fact, Wolfe and Gertler (2004: 1087), based on
an extensive study of various types of industrial clusters throughout
Canada, bolstered this milieu of critical factors, stressing that the central-
ity of skilled labor was seen as the single most important local asset to
a successful high-tech cluster. They elaborated on this phenomenon as
follows:

> The local endowment of 'talent' in the labor force is emerging as a crucial deter-
> minant of regional-industrial success. This endowment is created and main-
> tained by the retention and attraction of highly-educated, potentially mobile
> workers who are drawn to thick, deep, opportunity-rich local labor markets.
> The emergence of a strong, concentrated talent pool in local and regional econ-
> omies also serves as a key factor in launching individual clusters along the path
> to sustained growth and development. Critical mass appears to be important
> here: Until this is achieved, local employers will fight a losing battle in attempt-
> ing to retain or attract the skilled talent they need, particularly in the context of
> a highly competitive North American labor market for highly educated workers.
> Once it is achieved, this set in motion a positive self-reinforcing circle through
> which regions with a critical mass of highly skilled workers in a particular sector
> are able to attract still more workers of this kind.

The next section of the literature review shifts from a focus upon critical
institutions to examining the concepts of labor mobility, immigration, and
transnationalism, which are also essential to a successful high-tech region,
as argued by Florida (2002). Despite the many challenges and confusions
that arise between actors originating from different regions and learning
experiences, there is still a great desire, opportunity, and need for highly
skilled people to move across international boundaries for the purposes of
work and immigration.

2.6 TRANSNATIONALISM, LABOR MOBILITY OF THE HIGHLY SKILLED, AND THEIR SHORTCOMINGS

2.6.1 Introduction

As noted in Chapter 1, a critical component to a high-tech firm's success
is its ability to draw from a talented pool of well-educated professionals
residing throughout the globe as these firms compete in a high stakes game
of product development where timing and cleverness are keys to success
or failure (Florida, 2005). Thus, the immediate needs of the new economy

require more cross-border integration and more predictable and transparent border regulations when it comes to the movement of professionals across international boundaries.

In fact, a report issued by management consultants McKinsey & Company, stressed that firms that could find, recruit, and retain the most talented executive leadership would win the global 'war for talent' (see Michaels et al., 2001 and Faulconbridge et al., 2009). The firms that were most successful in luring and retaining this global talent would benefit through increased innovation (and profits) in a globally knowledge driven era, and also bring benefits to the city that hosts this talent.

Regarding talent, Faulconbridge et al. (2009) define this notion of elite talent as workers fulfilling positions at the top of organizational structures (e.g. chief executives, chief financial officers) or specialist skilled roles (e.g. in the oil and gas industry; Chinese equity analysts; and research and development scientists in particular niches of the bio-tech sector). Beaverstock (1996), Beaverstock and Smith (1996), and Findlay et al. (1996) have substantiated this definition by expressing that there is a growing need for highly competitive firms associated with the fields of high-technology and biotechnology to have access to the globally highly skilled, especially when it comes to leading global cities (Sassen, 2012).

In reference to second-tier global cities, Richardson (2016) conducted a study on how Vancouver's biotechnology sector attracted and retained foreign talent during and after the economic crisis of 2008. As well, Richardson et al. (2012) conducted an informative study which examined why a large high-technology firm based in Seattle, Washington, would place a major development center outside of Vancouver, BC, just a two and a half-hour drive north of the firm's headquarters. Beyond these two studies, there is still very little research on Vancouver or Seattle regarding labor mobility of the knowledge worker across international boundaries, especially in the growing information technology (IT) industry and within the regional area of Cascadia.

It should be noted that the mobility of international workers to some degree has been continuous for over 300 years. Yet, historically, the majority of skilled migrations were regional rather than truly global in nature (Held et al., 1999). For example, from the seventeenth century onwards, mercantilist-oriented states drew on the flows of skilled labor such as the Dutch moving to Germany and England for land drainage projects and Peter the Great attracting artisans and gunsmiths to imperial Russia (Lucassen, 1987). Thus, current professional labor movements within North America may be described as part of a more historic and natural pattern of labor movements that occurred before technological and military capabilities allowed for more global labor movement (Held et al., 1999).

2.6.2   Transnationalism

From a broader perspective of transnationalism, Ong (1999) has captured theoretically the experiences of the mobile elite, for example, moving from Hong Kong to North America and returning yet again to Asia, in the form of a circular mobility. Among other things, Ong discusses the apparent ease and agility that these flexible elites experience as they move from one country to another. This global fluid mobility has been an experience of a select elite originating in the capital cities of great colonial powers over the past three centuries. In this regard, Carlos and Nicholas (1988) found that imperial trading companies used an extensive and elaborate network of salaried managers, usually expatriates, to oversee and monitor the hundreds of thousands of annual company transactions. Also, the Japanese *soga shosa* (general trading companies) have moved much of their managerial personnel around the world to support their global networks for the past century. Now, a considerable number of transnational elites originate in powerful cities in the Asian Pacific (e.g. Singapore, Hong Kong, and Bangalore, India) (Sassen, 2000 and Waters, 2004). Instead of moving from the capital city of London, to Burma on behalf of a British trading company, as in the nineteenth century, these new transnationals from Asia gain a professional education at leading education institutes throughout the world (Waters, 2004). Based on the caliber of their education (and class agility) many of these elites are then offered a job in a primary city or region, which focuses on leading edge activities such as banking in London or New York City or high-tech development in Silicon Valley (Florida, 2005; Saxenian, 2000).

The above scholarly work emphasizes the experiences of an elite, which has always found relative predictability and ease in moving across the boundaries of one nation state to another for either work or pleasure. Now, with the growth of knowledge workers throughout the western world in the face of global restructuring, there is a greater need to draw larger pools of global talent. Often this labor force comes from not only the developed world, but also increasingly the developing world (Florida, 2005). These knowledge workers might not have been born into a privileged background, but through the experience of a good education, they often have the opportunity and eligibility to work for a powerful or quickly growing high-tech firm in North America.

2.6.3   Labor Mobility and the Internationally Highly Skilled

Compared with the mainstream flows of overseas migration whose goal is typically full-time settlement, skilled transient migratory movements often go highly unnoticed both within the receiving country at large and within the academic literature. Possible reasons for this may be that this type of temporary migration poses no threat in terms of social and economic burdens to the host countries, as well as often being invisible ethnically and culturally (Findlay, 1995). A majority of these skilled migrants move from core country to core country (e.g. between Western Europe, United States, Canada, Australia, and Japan). However, there still is a brain drain of well-educated professionals immigrating from Asia, Eastern Europe, and Africa to the western world. Nonetheless, the majority of highly skilled migrant movements are between core economies, such as the US, Japan, and Western Europe, for short durations of time, namely anywhere from two to five years. The majority of these migrants move as intracompany transferees within these global firms. Historically, much of these movements have been reserved for executive and management personnel. However, now, with an economy based on information and highly sophisticated technologies, the cross-border movements of highly skilled professionals are becoming more commonplace (Findlay, 1995). This can be seen within a North American context, especially with the onset of NAFTA in the early 1990s. Since NAFTA's inception in early 1994, over 250,000 Canadians have entered the US on professional work statuses for temporary employment (US DHS statistics, various years; interview with Senior US Policy Analyst, January 2005).

The international hiring and movements of skilled professionals and star junior executives is a dynamic activity, historically dominated by large multinational corporations (PricewaterhouseCooper, 2002). However, a new type of mobile highly skilled professional is emerging. The ideal type of this new mobile professional may be captured by Boyle and Motherwell (2005) in their policy study, which examined how to lure highly skilled Scots away from the vibrant city of Dublin, Ireland, back to Scotland. The study worked to move beyond the traditional motivators of the highly skilled being better employment opportunities, more stable political environmental and social conditions, and tertiary job opportunities (Sassen, 2012; Abella and Kuptsch, 2006; Solimano, 2008) by using key cultural indices developed by Florida (2002).[9]

It should also be stressed that a majority of these highly skilled expatriate Scots worked for smaller less established firms in Dublin, which seemed to contribute to the 'Bohemianness' of Dublin (Boyle and Motherwell, 2005). From a more clinical perspective on this topic area, Saxenian (2000) demonstrated that Chinese and Indian engineers started 29 percent of Silicon Valley's technology companies between the years of 1995–98.

The above helps to demonstrate that in an era of globalization there are different types of firms, especially smaller start-up firms, needing to hire and retain international highly skilled talent. Additionally, the new type of the internationally highly skilled professional may not be of a traditional corporate culture, but one with many different diverse backgrounds, as described by Boyle and Motherwell (2005) and Florida (2002, 2005).

Overall, the phenomenon of the movements and intermittent and final destinations of the internationally highly skilled is a relatively under-studied one within the academic literature for a variety of reasons. This includes the fact that data and general information regarding international personnel are hard to extract at the firm level due to corporate confidentiality policies. Also, once a highly skilled migrant is within the host country, there is a likelihood that the person may move from one type of work visa to another, which makes tracking these types of immigrants through government immigration data a serious challenge.

Highly skilled professionals' origins, patterns, and durations of stay can be described as somewhat different compared to the more predictable and secure forms of migratory movements for corporate elites.[10] For example, professionals may originate from many different countries other than the country that hosts a multinational corporation's headquarters, whereas a majority of these corporate elites originate from the country that hosts the headquarters of multinational corporations. As well, international professionals are transferred to other international corporate sites for projects, training, and generally shorter term assignments as compared to corporate elites. Additionally, they are usually not given the privileged pay structure and moving allowances given to international corporate elites.

In an era of flexible accumulation, larger global firms have developed many sophisticated strategies to using and moving highly skilled professional people's expertise, without taking direct responsibility for these professionals as corporate employees. For example, many larger multi-national firms contract out work responsibilities to smaller and local high-tech firms. It then becomes the burden of the smaller firm to move their highly skilled professional employee across the border for meetings with, or to provide direct services for, the larger multinational. Findlay (1995) has stressed that these firms' patterns possibly indicate a new production regime involving sophisticated networks of high-technology contractors and suppliers, which transcend international boundaries (see also Sunley, 1992). Based on his research of electronics firms in Hong Kong, Findlay (1995) concludes that there are scarce technical skills residing in key individuals, which allow the relatively uninhibited movement of those with skills, and these movements do not necessarily need to be channeled through the international labor markets of large firms. Second, global cities with clusters of high-tech specialized firms may prove attractive to high-tech international professionals since they can locate within these clusters, and have the option of moving to another firm within a cluster. Ideally, the international migrant can position himself/herself for future international employment without being directly tied to a multinational company. Hence, the highly skilled professional migrant can operate as his or her own independent actor within the global economy. Richardson (2016) had similar findings when it came to attracting and retaining highly skilled staff in Vancouver's biotechnology sector. Despite this apparent free mobility of elite knowledge workers suggested by Findlay (1995) and Richardson (2016), the next section reviews some of the major constraints on the autonomy of the global professional worker.

2.7 CROSS-BORDER INSTITUTIONS IN THE FACILITATION/IMPEDING OF TRANSBORDER LABOR MOBILITY AND SOJOURNER RIGHTS

Historically, the state has played the most important role in modern times when it comes to controlling movements of people. Torpey (2001) emphasized that perhaps the freest time for the movements of wealthy foreigners occurred in Europe, just prior to World War I. He cites the work of Bertelsmann (1914), who stressed the fact that foreigners moving throughout Europe were no longer viewed with suspicion, but welcomed by a host state since it was recognized that these foreigners bring 'tremendous economic value in goods and exchange'. This spirit of open borders did not last for long, and immediately after the commencement of World War I, states recommenced monitoring and controlling the movements of its own citizens, as well as the entry and movements of foreigners, which lasted well into the latter part of the twentieth century. However, beginning in the early 1980s, states began to respond to a resurgence of international trade and commerce, and started to rethink and consider the facilitation of foreigners involved in these activities (Sassen, 1996). This was especially true in Europe, since the Berlin Wall fell in late 1989 and allowed many undocumented migrants from Eastern Europe to enter Western Europe free from historical barriers placed between East and West Germany. It was also at this time that supranational organizations, such as the European Union (EU) and the World Trade Organization (WTO), began to reconfigure the responsibilities and rights normally attributed to the state, such as mobility of persons within the EU and international human rights codes (Sassen, 1996). Additionally, the emergence of supranational legal trade regimes, such as the General Agreement on Tariffs and Trade (GATT), NAFTA, and EU policies towards labor equalization and the EU's Schengen Agreement, intervened in many aspects of international

trade, services, finance, and, most notably, cross-border labor mobility –
within the EU region and in other global regions such as continental North
America and East Asia. Finally, since 9/11, transnational legal regimes,
such as NAFTA, have undergone a heavy veil of security measures and
surveillances, which were not originally anticipated when initially written.
The roles of these supranational legal agreements on cross-border labor
mobility will be reviewed in the following sections. Special emphasis will be
placed on NAFTA, and the various actors involved in its original development, its daily implementation/facilitation, and what type of actors makes
use of this trade agreement.

However, before turning to these supranational institutions, it should
be underlined here that the general culture and management of US
borders over the past 20 years has deteriorated regarding port of entry
officer professionalism and general respect for basic human rights for all
persons seeking entry into a nation state. As will be noted in the empirical chapters of the study, this is a critical issue in the flow of knowledge
intensive workers across the border in Cascadia. In fact, a reoccurring
theme for many people seeking entry into the US, whether legally or illegally, has been a rather hostile one when encountering any US immigration
officer responsible for inspecting the person seeking entry (Nevins, 2002).
Although cross-border mobility was often perceived as on the rise during
the latter part of the 1980s and early 1990s (Ohmae, 1995), as part of
globalization, for many seeking entry into foreign countries the experience
is frequently not a humane or welcoming one. This is a far too common
experience for many seeking entry into the US, either legally or illegally. In
fact, there has been a growing number of books over the past five years
on this topic. For example, the second edition of *Operation Gatekeeper
and Beyond* by Joseph Nevins (2010) explores the remaking of the US–
Mexico border in an era of globalization primarily under the Clinton
Administration. The book places particular emphasis on the project's
failure to hold back the tide of undocumented immigrants while at the
same time the legacy Immigration and Naturalization Service's treatment
of undocumented aliens worsened. In fact, the drastic measures placed
along the US–Mexico border contributed to a dramatic rise in death rates
as Mexican and other Central and South Americans seek more difficult
and dangerous entry points along the border. The following is a quote
from the executive director of the American Civil Liberties Union (ACLU)
of San Diego and Imperial Counties regarding a recently released report,
Humanitarian Crisis: Migrant Deaths at the U.S.–Mexico Border (Jimenez,
2009), commissioned by the American Civil Liberties Union of San Diego
and Imperial Counties and Mexico's National Commission on Human
Rights (CNDH) on the 15-year anniversary of Operation Gatekeeper,

The current policies in place on both sides of the US–Mexico border have created a humanitarian crisis that has led to the deaths of more than 5,000 people . . . Because of deadly practices and policies like Operation Gatekeeper, the death toll continues to rise unabated despite the decrease in unauthorized crossings due to economic factors.

Kevin Keenan, Executive Director of the ACLU of San Diego and Imperial Counties, September 2009

Overall, the driving thesis of Nevins' work is that the state has actually created the crisis of illegality, and now increasing deaths, along the US–Mexico border that it is now responding to. In *Detained: Immigration Laws and the Expanding I.N.S. Jail Complex*, Michael Welch (2002) reveals the unrelenting power given to the legacy INS as a result of the Illegal Immigration Reform and Immigrant Responsibility Act (IIRIRA) passed by the US Congress in 1996. Among other unchecked powers, the legacy INS was given the right to 'expedited removal', which is discussed at length in this study, and 'indefinite detention', which may be applied to asylum seekers waiting for a hearing, which may never occur. Overall, this has led to growing levels of incarceration rates and a rise in detention centers, which are usually run for profit – all of this is spurred by the US's moral panic towards perceived outsiders. These draconian measures against immigrants were in place before the events of 9/11 and before the passing of the US Patriot Act in 2001, which shall be explored later in the book.

Both of the above studies discuss in elegant detail how immigration law passed by US Congress over the past 20 years has allowed and even encouraged drastic and inhumane approaches to dealing with foreigners at the US's boundaries, especially the southern border in an era of globalization and pre 9/11 'open borders'.

2.7.1 The Role of Supranational Agreements or Institutions that Affect International Labor Mobility

On a global basis, the most important formal arrangements regulating international labor mobility include the World Trade Organization's General Agreement on Trade in Services (GATS), the North American Free Trade Agreement (NAFTA), and the European Union's (EU) policies on labor mobility which allow for the transnational movements of each signatory country's citizens for purposes of work within the territories of all signatory countries. Although each of these agreements were designed to facilitate easier mobility of foreigners for purposes of work, they are quite different in their make-up and intricacies. These differences are briefly explored in the following paragraphs.

2.7.1.1 General Agreement on Trade in Services (GATS)

Mode 4 of the GATS recognizes the need for the temporary movement of natural persons for purposes of service deliveries. It has usually been applied to higher-level personnel, especially to intracorporate transferees, whose mobility is basically an adjunct of foreign direct investment (Winters, 2002: V). The GATS is usually used by citizens of developing countries when seeking access to developed countries, since there are other supranational agreements, such as the NAFTA, allowing for the movement of North American executives, service providers, traders and various professionals, and EU policies, designed to create a pan-Europe dynamic knowledge based economy, and the Schengen Agreement which specifically allows for open borders and free movement of all EU citizens. One drawback to the GATS is that it has not allowed for easy movements of medium skilled service providers (such as professional assistants, trades people, and technical support personnel, which would include systems analysts and programmers) due to its complicated nature regarding interpretation. For example, among other structural problems, there is a lack of uniformity in the definition and coverage of the various categories of service personnel, allowing too liberal interpretations by immigration officials and consular offices (Chanda, 2001). These problems also contribute to the difficulties of entry under the GATS for medium skilled personnel, where developing countries have more of a comparative advantage over developed countries, which more frequently export highly skilled and executive level personnel. Additionally, similar to NAFTA and the EU's European Economic Area and Schengen Agreement, the GATS is subject to immigration legislation and labor market policy rather than international trade policy (Winters, 2002).

2.7.1.2 The European Union's policies on labor mobility and the Schengen border system

The European Union has developed aggressive policies designed to encourage spatial job mobility across state borders. In fact, through the European Economic Area Agreement, the EU has made tremendous efforts to create an EU-wide acceptance of educational and skills certificates and in gearing social security systems towards a balancing of all EU countries, so that the EU labor market may become more transparent. These open labor market policies are coupled with the Schengen border system,[11] which allows for the creation of a free movement area without border controls between EU member states (Anderson, 2000). Despite these well-thought-out efforts and transparent preferential policies, the vast majority of Europeans are still rather immobile. In fact, van Houtum and van der Velde (2004) identified a study conducted by Fischer et al. (2000) where only 4 percent of people in their study had actually moved from one EU country to another EU country since the late 1980s. Additionally, Fischer et al. (2000) found that only 1.5 percent of the people living within EU border regions commute across the border for purposes of work. Thus, van Houtum and van der Velde (2004) concluded that spatial job immobility, not mobility, is usually the dominant spatial practice of people living within the EU. Hence, national borders still play an important influence on the socially constructed frameworks of familiar locales. Additionally, these new EU citizens have not been able to conceptualize, nor operationalize, the possibility of including other countries into their ideas of feasible work opportunities.

2.7.1.3 The Trans-Pacific Partnership

The Trans-Pacific Partnership (TPP), a large-scale trade agreement, awaits ratification by 12 signatory countries found in the Pacific Rim, which includes Canada, the US, and Mexico. In addition to providing freer movement of finances, goods, services, and labor between all signatory countries, many claim that the TPP would expand Canada's preferential access to the US, as mandated under the current NAFTA. There is also great anticipation that the TPP would update NAFTA's listing of 65 professions, which are increasingly out of date with professions found in new economy enterprises such as high-technology, biotechnology, and the creative design industries (Richardson, 2011; Cryne, 2013).

In the process of ratifying the TPP, there is growing concern that the TPP may not advance North American mobility needs when it comes to Canadian highly skilled labor. Even though Canada has updated its listing of permissible professions that would be considered under the TPP, the US has not updated its listing of permissible professionals that would be considered under the TPP, and, at this time, has no intention of doing so (Richardson, 2017). There is even greater concern that the TPP would, in fact, diminish Canadian professionals' current preferential access to the US, as allowed under the current NAFTA. Thus, it is unclear at this time as to whether or not the TPP is in the best interest of Canadian professionals seeking employment in the US. In sum, the question remains as to whether or not the TPP is the best next step beyond the NAFTA for Canada and the US.

2.7.1.4 The North American Free Trade Agreement (NAFTA)

The NAFTA is yet another supranational legal regime which allows for the preferential status/visa treatment for four different types of North American business persons. This includes business visitors, traders, investors, intracompany transferees, and certain professionals established under NAFTA (Folsom, 1999). A primary idea behind the development of the NAFTA visa status was that it was to allow preferential entry for these business persons so that the other provisions of NAFTA, which deal with services, investments, and goods could be carried out with ease. However, these business persons can enter into all signatory countries on their own right. Provided that a NAFTA applicant has the correct and required documentation, they are only subject to public safety and national security reviews at international borders. NAFTA professionals and intracompany transferees do not have to undergo labor certification screens, which the US Department of Labor and the Employment and Social Development Canada (ESDC) usually require before a foreigner is issued a professional work status/visa. Private interests saw this particular requirement as a big drawback to NAFTA's predecessor, the US's H-1B visa. Hence, the NAFTA status, or 'TN Status', especially for professionals, was heralded in the early 1990s as a vast improvement over the H-1B visa, famous for its slow cumbersome nature, and its application cost, which could run into the thousands of dollars. Another salient point of the NAFTA status was its port of entry adjudication. The H-1B visa required that all paperwork be mailed to a US Department of Homeland Security case processing center, and an average H-1B application took anywhere between 4 to 6 months to process. Thus, the NAFTA TN status was framed to US Congress as a much more efficient and immediate way to allow for North American professionals to access Canada, the US, and Mexico in an era of globalization and fast moving capital. Ideally, port of entry adjudication would take anywhere from ten minutes to an hour for the majority of NAFTA applicants. These factors have contributed to NAFTA's rising success as a supranational legal document that has allowed for over 250,000 Canadians to enter into the US as NAFTA professionals with annual rising increments of approximately 7,000–9,000 Canadians annually during periods of economic growth (US DHS/INS statistics, various years; interview with US Policy Advisor, 2006), see Figure 2.6.

2.7.1.4.1 NAFTA and its actors From the rising number of NAFTA statuses issued since 1994, one may conclude that Chapter 16 of NAFTA, which covers labor mobility, has, in general, been a positive factor for the North American business community and the mobile North American professional. However, certain professions listed under NAFTA, which include software engineers, computer systems analysts, management consultants, and scientific technicians, have had a more difficult time crossing borders with NAFTA visa statuses than the other 65 professions listed under NAFTA for a variety of reasons, see Tables 2.2 and 2.3 for

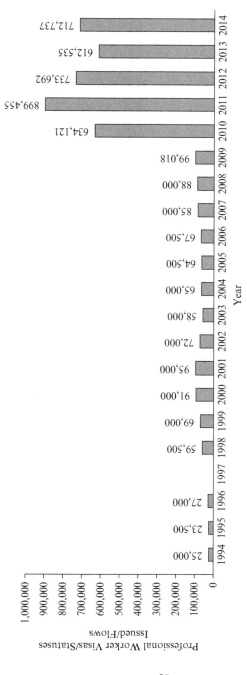

Notes: No data exists for 1997.
Beginning in 2010, the US DHS began to officially record number of TN 'entries' rather than 'persons'. Thus, the reason for the dramatic increase in values between 2009 and 2010 (Monger and Mathews, 2011).

Source: US Immigration and Naturalization Service, 1994–2014.

Figure 2.6   Professional worker visas/statuses issued/flows under the NAFTA to Canadians from 1994 to 2014

Table 2.2   List of NAFTA professionals, general

Profession	Minimum Educational Requirement/ Alternative Credentials
General Accountant	Baccalaureate/Licenciatura Degree; or C.P.A., C.A., C.G.A. or C.M.A.
Architect	Baccalaureate/Licenciatura Degree, or state/provincial license
Computer Systems Analyst	Baccalaureate/Licenciatura Degree
Disaster Relief Insurance Claims Adjuster (claims adjuster employed by an insurance company located in the territory of a party, or an independent claims adjuster)	Baccalaureate/Licenciatura Degree, and successful completion of training in the appropriate areas of insurance adjustment pertaining to disaster relief claims; or three years' experience in claims adjustment and successful completion of training in the appropriate area of insurance adjustment pertaining to disaster relief claims
Economist	Baccalaureate/Licenciatura Degree
Engineer	Baccalaureate/Licenciatura Degree, or state/provincial license
Forester	Baccalaureate/Licenciatura Degree, or state/provincial license
Graphic Designer	Baccalaureate/Licenciatura Degree, or Post-Secondary Diploma or Post-Secondary Certificate, and three years' experience
Hotel Manager	Baccalaureate/Licenciatura Degree in hotel/restaurant management; or Post-Secondary Diploma or Post-Secondary Certificate in hotel/restaurant management
Industrial Designer	Baccalaureate/Licenciatura Degree, or Post-Secondary Diploma or Post-Secondary Certificate, and three years' experience
Land Surveyor	Baccalaureate/Licenciatura Degree, or state/provincial/federal license
Landscape Architect	Baccalaureate or Licenciatura Degree
Lawyer (including Notary in the Province of Quebec)	LL.B., J.D., LL.L., B.C.L., or Licenciatura Degree (five years); or membership in a state/provincial bar
Librarian	M.L.S. or B.L.S. (for which another Baccalaureate or Licenciatura Degree was a prerequisite)

Table 2.2 (continued)

Profession	Minimum Educational Requirement/Alternative Credentials
Management Consultant	Baccalaureate/Licenciatura Degree; or equivalent professional experience as established by statement or professional credentials attesting to five years' experience as a management consultant, or five years' experience in a field of specialty related to the consulting agreement
Mathematician (including Statistician and Actuary)	Baccalaureate/Licenciatura Degree; an actuary must satisfy the necessary requirements to be recognized as an actuary by a professional actuarial association or society operating in the territory of at least one of the Parties.
Range Manager/Range Conservationalist	Baccalaureate/Licenciatura Degree
Research Assistant (working in a post-secondary educational institute)	Baccalaureate/Licenciatura Degree
Social Worker	Baccalaureate/Licenciatura Degree
Sylviculturist (including Forestry Specialist)	Baccalaureate/Licenciatura Degree
Technical Publications Writer	Baccalaureate/Licenciatura Degree; or Post-Secondary Diploma or Post-Secondary Certificate, and three years' experience
Urban Planner (including Geographer)	Baccalaureate/Licenciatura Degree
Vocational Counsellor	Baccalaureate/Licenciatura Degree

Source: NAFTA Appendix 1603.D.1 in Cheetham et al., 2006 (pub. American Immigration Lawyers Association).

a listing of these professions. Specifically, the way NAFTA was crafted, the rather esoteric job descriptions and nature of the above mentioned professions (exclusive of management consultants) and the variety of ways that front-line immigration officials understand and interpret NAFTA at each Canada–US port of entry can lead to a host of problems for firms trying to hire these professionals under NAFTA (Vazquez-Azpiri 2000; Richardson, 2010).

Richardson (2010) has provided analysis and discussion regarding the

Table 2.3   List of NAFTA professionals – medical/allied professional,
scientist, and teacher

Profession	Minimum Educational Requirement/ Alternative Credentials
Medical/Allied Professional	
Dentist	D.D.S., D.M.D., Doctor en Odontologia or Doctor en Cirugia Dental; or state/provincial license
Dietitian	Baccalaureate/Licenciatura Degree, or state/provincial license
Medical Laboratory Technologist (Canada)/Medical Technologist (Mexico/US)	Baccalaureate/Licenciatura Degree, or Post-Secondary Diploma or Post-Secondary Certificate, and three years' experience
Nutritionist	Baccalaureate/Licenciatura Degree
Occupational Therapist	Baccalaureate/Licenciatura Degree, or state/provincial license
Pharmacist	Baccalaureate/Licenciatura Degree, or state/provincial license
Physician (teaching or research only)	M.D. or Doctor en Medicina; or state/provincial license
Physiotherapist/Physical Therapist	Baccalaureate/Licenciatura Degree, or state/provincial license
Psychologist	State/provincial license or Licenciatura Degree
Recreational Therapist	Baccalaureate/Licenciatura Degree
Registered Nurse	State/provincial license or Licenciatura Degree
Veterinarian	D.V.M., D.M.V. or Doctor en Veterinaria; or state/provincial license
Scientist	
Agriculturist (including Agronomist)	Baccalaureate/Licenciatura Degree
Animal Breeder	Baccalaureate/Licenciatura Degree
Animal Scientist	Baccalaureate/Licenciatura Degree
Apiculturist	Baccalaureate/Licenciatura Degree
Astronomer	Baccalaureate/Licenciatura Degree
Biochemist	Baccalaureate/Licenciatura Degree
Biologist (includes Plant Pathologist)	Baccalaureate/Licenciatura Degree
Chemist	Baccalaureate/Licenciatura Degree
Dairy Scientist	Baccalaureate/Licenciatura Degree
Entomologist	Baccalaureate/Licenciatura Degree
Epidemiologist	Baccalaureate/Licenciatura Degree
Geneticist	Baccalaureate/Licenciatura Degree
Geologist	Baccalaureate/Licenciatura Degree

Table 2.3   (continued)

Profession	Minimum Educational Requirement/ Alternative Credentials
Geochemist	Baccalaureate/Licenciatura Degree
Geophysicist (including Oceanographer in Mexico and the US)	Baccalaureate/Licenciatura Degree
Horticulturist	Baccalaureate/Licenciatura Degree
Meteorologist	Baccalaureate/Licenciatura Degree
Pharmacologist	Baccalaureate/Licenciatura Degree
Physicist (including Oceanographer in Canada)	Baccalaureate/Licenciatura Degree
Plant Breeder	Baccalaureate/Licenciatura Degree
Poultry Scientist	Baccalaureate/Licenciatura Degree
Scientific Technician/Technologist	Possession of (a) theoretical knowledge of the following disciplines: agricultural sciences, astronomy, biology, chemistry, engineering, forestry, geology, geophysics, meteorology, or physics; and (b) the ability to solve practical problems in any of those disciplines, or the ability to apply principles of any of those disciplines to basic or applied research
Soil Scientist	Baccalaureate/Licenciatura Degree
Zoologist	Baccalaureate/Licenciatura Degree
Teacher	
College	Baccalaureate/Licenciatura Degree
Seminary	Baccalaureate/Licenciatura Degree
University	Baccalaureate/Licenciatura Degree

Source: NAFTA Appendix 1603.D.1 in Cheetham et al., 2006 (pub. American Immigration Lawyers Association

varied norms and rules that NAFTA adjudications operate within, both between each signatory country and also between each nation state's ports of entry. In fact, Richardson (2010) draws from the work of Finnemore and Sikkink (1998) who generally discuss the relationship between rules and norms in the context of how certain norms at the bureaucratic level influence international politics. Finnemore and Sikkink's 1998 study spends considerable time defining exactly what norms are, the relationships between domestic and international norms, and whether norms are agents of stability or change. Although their research is aimed at examining dynamic international issues, such as women's suffrage and the banning of land mines, Richardson (2010) argued that the study's topic area and concepts may be applied to the detailed implementation of a regional trade agreement, such as NAFTA. Specifically, Finnemore and Sikkink (1998: 891) stress that norms involve a prescriptive (or evaluative) quality of 'oughtness' that set norms apart from other kinds of rules. The authors go on to stress that there are no 'bad norms' from the vantage point of those promoting the norms. For example, slaveholders and non-slaveholders believed that slavery was an appropriate behavior, for without this belief, the institution of slavery would not have been possible (ibid.). Although norms may be difficult to document empirically prima facie, norms promote shared moral assessment among participating actors and leave extensive trails of communication and evidence of their influence. Additionally, norms are usually found naturally within the community or regional level (i.e. in this case, the respective Canadian and US immigration authorities), but usually not at the international level, and vary between countries in their strength and influence.

The above intellectual context of the definition of what a norm is and where it might be found provides a framework for explaining why variability exists in interpreting NAFTA between Canadian and US border officials and the many US ports of entry (POEs). To begin, although the actual rules of NAFTA have been constructed and approved by each signatory country, there is considerable leeway between each particular country in the inter-pretation and implementation of NAFTA. Thus, it is up to each country (Canada, the US, and Mexico) as to how its front-line officials understand and interpret NAFTA applications. These domestic norms then set the tone as to the actual interpretation of NAFTA applications. As will be explained in detail in the empirical section of the text (Chapters 4, 5, and 6) this leeway of interpretation has proven to be a significant impediment to the easy mobility of high-tech firms' employees and new hires between Vancouver and Seattle.

Overall, the challenges found within the use and implementation of NAFTA and the three primary actors involved, namely government officials, immigration attorneys, and the firms and individuals who use NAFTA statuses, serve as the departure point for Chapter 3, which examines the Cascadia region specifically.

2.8   CHAPTER CONCLUSION

This chapter has reviewed the existing literature on cross-border regions and analysed its strengths and weaknesses in framing a study of the role of the border in the Cascadia region. It has revealed that existing studies of CBRs have focused on some of the factors behind their success, but have rarely focused on how the management of international borders, per se, has influenced patterns of development. Similarly, scholarship of innovation and high-technology regions have pointed to the important role of skilled labor and also the institutions in social learning and the transmission of knowledge in regional networks, but has generally underplayed the significance of institutions that facilitate labor mobility. Studies of international labor mobility have suggested an increasing importance of footloose knowledge intensive workers, but have rarely focused on the very real constraints imposed by regulatory mechanisms embedded in the WTO, the EU, and NAFTA. Building on this narrative, the study will indicate the importance of the international border for Cascadia and spotlight the role of a number of significant actors. Overall, one outcome of the review reveals the transition of border regions in the popular imagination – from the concept of being a shield to a sieve in the late 1980s and 1990s, and now back to a rather ambiguous shield rather than a sieve in light of 9/11. However, despite this new trend, the US is still committed to business interests and globalization in general in the form of open borders.

At a broad scale, this rapid transition of the concept of borders in the imagination, as well as the actual practices of regulating movement across North American borders, warrants the need for a more concrete study; one that examines in detail this rapid transition, and how it has influenced flows of professionals back and forth across the Canada–US border. As stressed earlier, Cascadia is a particular type of border region, which for the most part contains a critical mass of high-technology companies, and one that suggests a strong demand for highly skilled labor. As stressed earlier in this chapter, high-tech regions grow best when supported with suitable institutions, and in the Cascadia case those that facilitate the mobility of labor are equally, if not more important, than those that support the mobility of goods. Chapter 3 will build on this argument by exploring the economic history and contemporary economy of the Cascadia corridor, and how NAFTA, with a focus on the research framework adopted here, may be central to its future success.

NOTES

1. Sovereignty involves the recognition by the sovereign of the exclusive rights of other sovereigns to govern within their respective states, and of the inviolable nature of the territory of other states (Muir, 1983: 20).
2. The European Economic Area (EEA) includes EU Member States and three of the European Free Trade Association (EFTA) States (Iceland, Liechtenstein and Norway) and was established by the EEA Agreement, signed in 1992. The EEA Agreement

enabled the EU Member States and the three EFTA States to participate fully in a single market and covers the four freedoms, i.e. the free movement of goods, capital, services and persons included within the territory of all signatory countries in addition to competition and state aid rules and horizontal areas related to the four freedoms (European Free Trade Association, 2017). The EU Schengen border system includes the creation of a free movement area without border controls and also covers measures to increase security at the EU's external frontier, to combat illegal immigration, to enhance police cooperation, and to improve judicial cooperation between all member states (Anderson, 2000).

3.   Theodore Cohn (1999) has provided a thorough analysis of the development and possible impact that Section 110 would have on Canada–US cross-border travel, and the ripple effect within border communities and beyond if this portion of the IIRIRA Act were to be enacted into US law.

4.   First Secretary of the US Department of Homeland Security

5.   Unlike many western European countries, Canadians, for the most part, are still visa exempt when it comes to seeking entry into the US.

6.   A combination of the Schengen Agreement (1985) and the 1990 Schengen Application Convention (Anderson, 2000).

7.   Silicon Valley is a similar 60 to 80 mile north–south corridor, albeit lying within one country rather than straddling an international border, as is the case with the northern portion of Cascadia.

8.   Richard Florida (1995) defines this term as collectors and repositories of knowledge and ideas that provide an underlying environment or structure which facilitates the flow of knowledge, ideas, and learning (p. 528). See Rutten and Boekema (2007) for an advanced analysis of this concept area.

9.   According to Florida, members of the creative class are essential to the success, dynamism, and ability to innovate for regional economies. Although Peck (2005) and Houston et al. (2008) have criticized Florida's (2002) place specific attributes, many cities and regions around the world have used creative class elements to lure the highly skilled, whether foreign or domestic.

10. This is reflected in many foreign work visas' length of time to remain in host countries. The US, for example, allows a professional, usually on an H-1B visa (which will be explained in more detail in Chapter 3), three years to remain in the US, whereas a foreign executive working for the same firm is usually allowed five years to remain in the US for purposes of work.

11. The Schengen border system includes a compilation of the 1985 Schengen Agreement and the 1990 Schengen Application Convention. The Schengen Agreement brought together the Benelux Common Travel Area with the proposed open frontier agreement between France and Germany to abolish all border controls on goods and persons between them. The Application Convention set up a series of arrangements, including a strengthening and standardization of controls at the external border, and of police and judicial cooperation between the EU member states (Anderson, 2000: 21–22). (See Endnote 2 in this chapter, as well.)

3. The Cascadia region in its wider context

3.1 GENERAL INTRODUCTION – PURPOSE OF CHAPTER

This chapter builds on the literature review carried out in Chapter 2 and argues that the Cascadia cross-border region is significantly different from the more traditional goods and trade oriented border zones between the US and Canada, such as the Detroit–Windsor and the San Diego–Tijuana, Mexico border regions.

In particular, cross-border flows of skilled labor are much more important in Cascadia than cross-border flows of parts or assembled final goods. Cascadia, from a development perspective, may be characterized as a natural resource intensive and post-industrial services based economy. It contains mature firms, such as the multinational timber giant, Weyerhaeuser, operating alongside new high-tech firms such as Microsoft Corporation, the e-commerce giant Amazon.com, and the North American headquarters of Nintendo, which are based in the Seattle area, and MacDonald, Dettwiler and Associates and Ballard Fuel Systems, based in the Vancouver, BC area. Besides being a cross-border region of intense transnational interaction, Cascadia has many links to the Asia Pacific region, and also southwards into California. Edgington (1995) revealed the importance of Cascadia's cross-border connection with Japanese *soga sosa* (or trading houses). Artibise (1996, 2005) has documented the social and potential economic connectivity within the more northern portion of Cascadia, which includes the greater Vancouver and Seattle areas. David McCloskey has done the initial work of exploring the historical and environmental connectivities within the region of Cascadia and also developed the regional ecological interpretation of Cascadia (1989, 1994). The second purpose of this chapter is to provide a framework of the many institutional apparatus that range from the international to the continental and finally to the domestic level that may affect cross-border labor mobility within the Cascadia region.

Overall, the frequency of cross-border mobility of professionals in Cascadia is likely to be more similar to the movement of EU cross-border regions, such as the 'Blue Banana', which includes portions of London, England through Germany, the Randstad of the Netherlands, and on to Northern Italy (Dunford and Kafkalas, 1992) and the Dutch–German border region (Perkmann, 2007). Essentially, Cascadia may be considered an area with an advanced service-based economy that has developed over the past 30 years. Additionally, this advanced service-based economy has created a need for professionals moving across borders, and this mobility is essential to the evolving success of the region (Richardson et al., 2012; Richardson, 2011). The next section explores the concept of Cascadia, and how the Cascadia region is different from other cross-border regions. It then speculates as to how the region may have an economic future as a symbiotic high-technology/biotechnology zone, and the implications on the need to hire North American and foreign skilled personnel. Both the Seattle and Vancouver economies, post the bursting of the dot-com bubble in 2000 and 9/11 as well as the 2008 financial crisis, are explored in some detail. The chapter also examines other immigration/labor mobility options. Finally, the role of Chapter 16 of NAFTA and how the Canada–US border works both as a sieve and a shield in light of this trade agreement is briefly examined. The chapter closes by introducing Part II of the book (Chapters 4, 5, and 6), which sets out the empirical work and focuses on the three major actors involved in the management of the international border and cross-border mobility.

3.2   CASCADIA AS A BORDER ZONE OF HUMAN CONTACT

3.2.1   Introduction

Since the late 1980s, there has been much rhetoric about the idea of a borderless world. As noted in Chapter 2, Kenichi Ohmae is one of the most recognized commentators in this regard, arguing in his 1990 book, *Borderless World*, that more borderless trade, or the continued elimination of tariffs and/or non-tariff barriers would lead to an even greater win/win situation for all involved. Holsti (2004) deals with borders and cites the works of Bernard Badie and Marie-Claude Smouts (1999: Ch. 1), and James N. Rosenau (1997), providing for more theoretical statements surrounding the idea of the diminishing relevance of borders. However, as explored in Chapter 2, the notion of borders, from a perspective of security, is back with 'with a vengeance' (Andreas, 2003). Biersteker (2003) tempered this statement by stressing that borders and boundaries are being used in many different ways that transcend physical demarcations, and powers of the state are now being vested to many different types of actors, both public and private. Several geographers have also contested this notion, however. For example, see Kevin Cox's (1997) discussion regarding the powers of the local in response to globalization. Additionally, as stated in Chapter 2, using Wu's 1998 border typology matrix, Cascadia may be considered somewhere between a transborder and cross-border region, since the movements of citizens within these regions are not completely liberalized, as is the case within the EU.

From a perspective of labor mobility and the growth networks between the new economy firms, the degree of globalization really depends on the actual partitioning of space between states and the continued impediments to cross-border travel, such as regulations prohibiting labor mobility between cross-border regions and cities. It is clear that the major impact of NAFTA and other recent free trade agreements has been in general to facilitate the cross-border flows of goods and investment capital. Thus, investments can now circulate more quickly between nations and/or sub-regions taking advantage of factors of production such as labor, land, ideas, and capital infrastructure that are unique to one particular area and guaranteed by the boundaries of a nation state. Indeed, it is often argued that this new world system of fast moving capital flows requires differences and inequities regarding factors of production, especially the New International Division of Labor (Frobel et al., 1980), in order to continue corporate profits and growth. However, one of the many downsides to the benefits of the globalization of capital is that it encourages many developing nation states and regions to continue comparative inequities with developed countries, such as low-cost labor, land, or lack of strong environmental laws, in order to continue to draw capital investments from beyond the boundaries of the local community.

Two classic examples of the New International Division of Labor, introduced above, are the US–Mexico border region and the Hong Kong–Shenzhen border region of Asia (Wu, 2001). Here, both urban centers in the American Southwest and Hong Kong supply capital and management while the Mexican *maquiladoras* zones and Shenzhen supply the sites of operations with an abundance of low paid and seemingly endless supply of workers. However, in bordering countries that have more equal development status (e.g. France–Germany and Canada–US), an opportunity exists to allow the more equitable exchange of professionals and workers in general. The European Union's policy on labor mobility and now NAFTA, in theory, are two good examples of this more equitable availability and accessibility of continental labor. Specifically, more progressive policies exist in the European Union where the EU parliament, working directly with concerned local governments, has taken deliberate policy steps to 'iron out' many of these differences and inequities with border regions based on so-called 'zones of contact' (Ratti, 1993) or 'trans-border regions' (Wu, 2001). In fact, many opportunities on the other side of international borders encourage the free movement of EU citizens seeking greater economic opportunities. Here, migration and labor mobility is defined by very simple procedures, and there are almost no differences in labor costs between adjoining regions (Wu, 1998: 198–99). Consequently, the European Union has developed policies and a culture that encourages the movement of professionals across borders with seemingly uneventful ease, which could at some point lead to a cross-border regional innovation system, as conceptualized by Trippl (2010) and Lundquist and Trippl (2013). Ideally, Chapter 16 of NAFTA, which focuses on the temporary movement of business people, should do something similar for continental North America, and the Cascadia region in particular, but does it? The following sections of this chapter examine the geographic area and the various economies of Cascadia in more detail, both as a notion of a region, and also the separate urban economies of Seattle and Vancouver.

3.2.2   The Cascadia Region

The idea of a Northeast Pacific Coast region has been in the imagination of novelists, journalists, and geographers for over the past 35 years. Ernest Callenbach in his 1981[1] novel, *Ecotopia Emerging*, was perhaps the first to capture this imaginary region. The book is a utopian futuristic look (based in 1999) at a politically autonomous Washington, Oregon, and North California. The society operates as an open equal one, and only small-scale environmentally friendly technologies are allowed within the region. San Francisco is seen as Ecotopia's capital, but the city is broken down into 'mini cities'. There is a strong emphasis on everyone within Ecotopia sharing the same ethos of an open and spiritually aware group of people dedicated to living in harmony with oneself, the community, and the environment at large. The vision is perhaps utopian in the sense that there are pockets of communities throughout the Northeast Pacific Coast that are still dedicated, for the most part, to this ethos (e.g. Bolinas, California; Bellingham, Washington; and Eugene, Oregon).

Realistically, the region, as a whole, has a much wider range of values and perspectives than what was originally developed by Callenbach. This is evident in Joel Garreau's 1981 book, *The Nine Nations of North America*. Garreau not only captured the 'spirit' of these environmentally based secessionists but also the tension between different perspectives found within this 'Ecotopia' region. For example, Garreau stressed that Washington State was also home to The Boeing Company, a leader in not only commercial aircraft, but also key missiles and other sophisticated defense artillery used by the US government in addition to housing a fleet of nuclear submarines in Bangor, Washington. Although Garreau had a much more encompassing perspective of the many realities found in this Ecotopia, he also expanded the boundaries of his imaginary of this region to include Southeast Alaska and Western British Columbia and south and eastward beyond Silicon Valley to Davis, California. He not only recognized the economic and political power of the Greater San Francisco Bay area, but also Seattle. Interestingly, Garreau's defining point of a boundary to his Ecotopia is not political, but is based on the abundance and immediate access to water and the fact that the mountains serve as a collector of these waters, which make this Ecotopia a distinctive region.

More recently, Douglas Todd, a spirituality writer for the *Vancouver Sun* newspaper, edited a collection of essays in the book, *Cascadia the Elusive Utopia: Exploring the Spirit of the Pacific Northwest*, in 2008. The book focused on just the British Columbia, Washington, Oregon region and explored the unique spirituality and culture found in Cascadia. Themes ranged from the notion of frontier utopian communities such as Indian yogi Bhagwan Shree Rajneesh's commune in Northern Oregon during the 1980s to Aboriginal spirituality. The book closed by stressing that it was a 'spirituality of place' that made Cascadia unique to other regions.

Finally, Donald Meinig, in his third volume of *The Shaping of America: A Geographical Perspective on 500 Years of History: Transcontinental America 1850–1915* (1986), provided a historical depiction of the regional connectivity of Washington and Oregon, specifically noting the strong historic economic and social connections between eastern Washington and western Oregon at the turn of the last century. Meinig discussed at length the political importance and wealth that Washington's Inland Empire[2] and Portland, Oregon amassed by shipping grain to various regions in Europe during repeated times of political turbulence in the late 1880s and early 1900s. Meinig also presented an elegant account of the overall regional Pacific Northwest and the politics between Eastern and Western Washington, the influence of Oregon and California in these matters, and the 'American Influence' in British Columbia during this time period. In sum, Meinig provided an excellent historical account of regional relations, roughly 100 years ago, that may still be found in this Ecotopia today.

This section's discussion of recent ideas, imaginaries, spiritualities, and histories surrounding the various regions located within the Northeast Pacific coastlands (and inland areas) helped to provide a foundation as to where the concept and term Cascadia may have originated. The original term Cascadia is historically credited to David Douglas, a nineteenth-century Scottish botanist, after whom the Douglas fir is named.

Douglas, while gathering plant specimens along the mouth of the mighty Columbia river, was in awe of the area's glorious 'cascading' rivers and waterfalls (Todd, 2008: 4). The original concept of the regional notion of Cascadia was also a natural, ecological one, developed by Professor David McCloskey at Seattle University in the late 1980s. McCloskey's northern boundary of 'Cascadia' was similar to Garreau's, being the pan-handle of Southeast Alaska and extending into British Columbia. The eastern boundary of Cascadia extends to the state of Montana with the continental Great Divide as a marker. However, McCloskey's southern boundary of Cascadia only extended to Mendocino, California. McCloskey argued that the commonality of this territory was the spine of its temperate rainforest ecology found in the BC Canadian Coastal/Washington-Oregon Cascade and California's Sierra Mountain Range[3] in the east and the Pacific Ocean to the west. Although McCloskey used physical features to determine Cascadia's boundaries, he argued that the word Cascadia represented the many waterfalls that may be found within this temperate mountainous area, similar to Douglas's original defining feature of the region. In fact, McCloskey's idea of Cascadia as 'a great green land on the Northeast Pacific Rim' may be defined as follows:

> Cascadia is a land rooted in the very bones of the earth, and animated by the turning of sea and sky, the mid-latitude wash of wind and waters. As a distinct region, Cascadia arises from both a natural integrity (landforms and earth-plates, weather patterns and ocean currents, flora, fauna, watersheds) and a socio-cultural unity (native cultures, a shared history and destiny). One of the newest and most diverse places on earth, Cascadia is flowing land poured from the north Pacific Rim . . . Cascadia is a land of falling waters. (McCloskey, 1989)

(Please see Figure 3.1 for a visual depiction of this original regional concept of Cascadia.) Since this time, the Cascadia concept has grown into a more political and economic term, and is currently used by a variety of academics and business organizations dedicated to a more pro-business environment within the Cascadia corridor. Specifically, Professor Alan Artibise, formerly at the University of British Columbia and now at Arizona State University, has developed ideas revolving around not only the cultural connectivity, but also the possible economic connectivity within the region of Cascadia. Aritibise's idea of Cascadia reaches more within the boundaries of British Columbia, Washington State, and Oregon with the Whistler, BC to Eugene, Oregon corridor deemed its 'Main Street' (Artibise, 1996; Piro, 1995). (Please see Figure 3.2 for a more economic depiction of Cascadia.)

Since the early 1990s, a substantial organizational infrastructure has grown up to discuss common goals and objectives in the development of

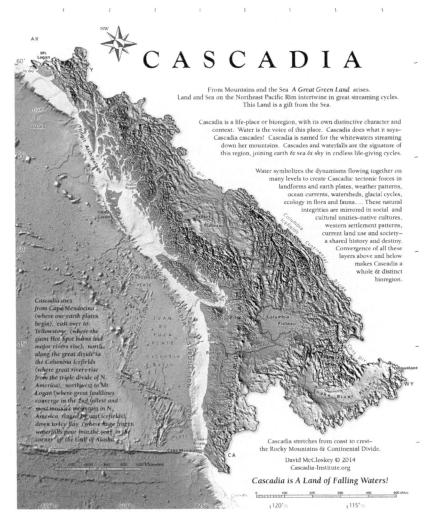

Source: McCloskey, 2014.

Figure 3.1   Cascadia

this CBR, as well as cross-border growth strategies and trends and patterns relative to the growth of the region. Specifically, the Pacific Northwest Economic Region (PNWER), based in Seattle, represents three Canadian provinces, namely, British Columbia, Alberta, and Saskatchewan; five US

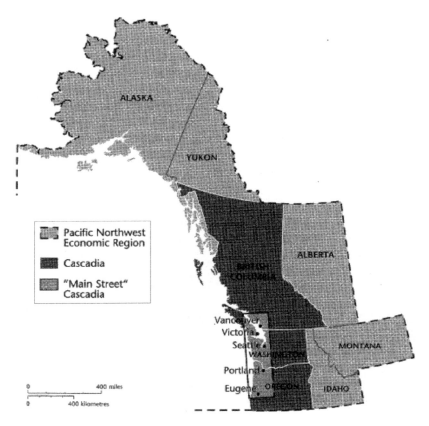

Source: Artibise, 2005 (pub. UBC Press).

Figure 3.2   Three views of Cascadia

states, namely, Washington, Oregon, Idaho, Montana, and Alaska; and
two Canadian territories, namely Yukon and the Northwest Territories.
PNWER has been in existence since 1991 and has not only worked to
lobby Washington DC and Ottawa on issues pertaining to its western
members, but also to develop and/or resolve issues between the region's
members, The Discovery Institute, also based in Seattle, may be considered
a conservative neo-liberal think tank and has been in existence since 1991.
Since the Discovery Institute's inception, it has worked on a number of
projects and issues related to the concept of Cascadia. However, through
the development of the Discovery Institute's identity over the past 15
years, it has finally settled on issues regarding transportation when it

comes to dealing with the Cascadia corridor. From a perspective of governance, there is an annual meeting of the two governors of Washington and Oregon with the Premier of British Columbia to discuss matters that affect all citizens within their areas of jurisdiction. As well, the Georgia Basin Initiative, developed by former BC Premier Mike Harcourt, is a joint initiative between BC and Washington State dedicated to the stewardship of the marine waterways and drainage basins that surround the lower portions of British Columbia and extend to the southern Puget Sound in Washington State.

Finally, the concept of Cascadia is not without its critics and observers. Matt Sparke (2000, 2003, and 2005), a professor of geography at the University of Washington, has offered a sustained neo-Marxist critique of the more business oriented approach to the idea of Cascadia. Although Sparke (2005) spends considerable time deconstructing the more business minded free market promoters found within the Cascadia region, there is very little effort in his work, if at all, towards a more acceptable vision of what his ideal construct of Cascadia would look like, and how it would actually function as a 'sustainable' region. Perhaps a more balanced critique of Cascadia may be found in the works of Professor Susan E. Clarke (2000, 2002 and 2004) at the University of Colorado. Over the past 15 years, Professor Clarke has observed the regional governmental, public, and private networks that have emerged within Cascadia. Based on her professional observations, she has offered varied critiques of these activities and actors, and how these activities and their actors may have long-term influences within the Cascadia region, as well as comparing the varied bottom-up activities within the Cascadia region to the more formal top-down activities emerging within Europe's border regions, as a result of direct EU governmental policy (op cit, 2002). Finally, Professor Emmanuel Brunet-Jailly of the University of Victoria has produced a series of publications over the past ten years dedicated to the notion of general cross-border management and border security within the region of Cascadia, especially in relation to the European Union (2004, 2006, 2007, and 2008).

The three preceding paragraphs touch on the many different ideas, institutions, activities, actors, and critics that surround the idea of Cascadia. However, there has been no research and policy development on professional labor mobility and common labor force issues per se. Thus, it is hoped that this book will contribute to providing a foundation of evidence towards the needs of cross-border labor mobility and common labor force needs within the Cascadia corridor. The following paragraph discusses in some detail historic relations between BC and Washington State, and then moves on to an introduction to the economies of Vancouver and Seattle.

From a more western regional perspective, despite its green calm 'Pacific' nature, Cascadia has been riddled with border conflicts, most recently due to the 1997 Fish Wars and continual softwood lumber disputes, which were settled between Prime Minister Stephen Harper and President George Bush in the Spring of 2006.[4] In part, many of these disputes are due to both sides of the border specializing in similar undifferentiated primary products (e.g. timber and seafood) exported either across the border or to the same third markets, such as Japan (Kresel, 1992:71). Unlike the more sophisticated cross-border production coordination of the Just-in-Time (JIT) auto manufacturing networks between Ontario/Michigan/New York, and the well-thought-out policies of the 1965 Auto Pact and now NAFTA (Hampson and Molat, 2000), there appears to be a 'winner take all' approach to competition and the sale of natural resources between British Columbia and Washington (Kresel, 1992). The mentality is that any sale in such an environment necessarily entails the diversion of a stream of revenue from one vendor to another (ibid.). Typically, the firm that loses 'the big contract' files a complaint with the relevant trade agency (such as the NAFTA or the WTO), as has been the case over the years.

However, it is important to note that although the firms and economies of the province of BC and Washington State appear to be severe competitors and may be regular petitioners in trade complaint procedures against each other, often over raw materials, this has little or nothing to do with relationships between the high-technology economies of Vancouver and Seattle (Kresel, 1992). Specifically, the Cascadia urban core region may be unique along the Canada–US border in that there is the possibility of a core city to core city relationship, namely between the advanced producer sectors of Vancouver and Seattle. Please see Figure 3.3 for a visual depiction of the numbers and types of Canadian entries at US ports of entry (hereafter POEs) into the US between the Seattle and Vancouver corridor. Figure 3.3 helps to demonstrate that business travel is still a relatively minor component (8 percent) compared to the other types of crossing from Canada into the US.

The following subsection explores the two separate economies of Seattle and Vancouver in more detail, and examines the two cities' future needs for foreign highly skilled workers. The next section of the chapter examines immigration visa/status regulators. It covers Cascadia's wider context and then assesses how NAFTA's Chapter 16, which was designed to facilitate cross-border labor mobility, provides an opportunity for closer integration as well as possibly imposing constraints on IT labor mobility within Cascadia.

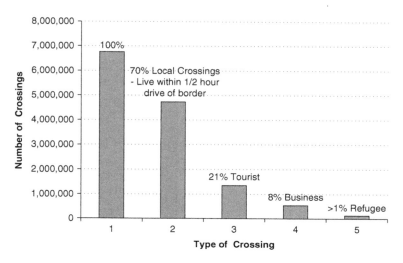

Source: Hacker (Thomas) and Associates, 1997; interviews with various DHS port of entry personnel, 2002–13.

Figure 3.3 Breakdown of border crossing types at four largest land border crossings between Vancouver, BC and Seattle, Washington (Canada entering US)

3.2.2.1 The Seattle economy
The city of Seattle and its surrounding region can be described, in general, as a great success story in its ability to grow from a mere trading post and logging village in the late 1800s to a city hosting the head offices of six fortune 500 companies, namely Boeing, Microsoft Corporation, Weyerhaeuser, Nordstrom, Amazon.com, and Starbucks Corp. Not only does Seattle support these major firms, but it also hosts over 1,000 high-tech firms, a robust and internationally competitive port and shipping industry, and an emerging biotech industry (Gray et al., 1999a). This section discusses some of Seattle's major strengths as an economy, and how the region is experiencing another boom after the 2008 financial crisis, and in light of the 'bursting' of the dot-com bubble in 2000 and the post 9/11 economic fallout.

3.2.2.1.1 Seattle's hub and spoke economy   Gray et al. (1999a) deemed Seattle as an outstanding American 'hub and spoke' city, which has been under-studied and unappreciated, both as a city and as a development concept. Essentially, a hub and spoke industrial district may be considered as a region that hosts one or more industries, each with one or a few dominant 'hub' firms surrounded by smaller firms which are tied, through origin and/or ongoing exchange relationships, to the larger firm (Gray et al., 1999a). However, the hubs are also usually engaged in various relationships, such as branch plants, suppliers, customers, and competitors. As well, there are also relationships outside of the region which can range anywhere from national to international in nature.

3.2.2.1.1.1 Aerospace and software sectors   The world's most successful aircraft manufacturer and military defense developer, namely Boeing Corporation, began south of Seattle in the early 1900s. Boeing's success over the years has made it the number one employer in the Seattle region, directly responsible for over 80,000 jobs as of 2015, in the state of Washington.[5] Boeing may be considered, therefore, as a 'hub' within the classic 'hub and spoke' model, since many smaller firms within the Seattle area are somewhat dependent on Boeing contracts. However, due to Boeing's international scope, especially with its commercial airplane sales, only about 15 percent of Boeing suppliers have been locally based (Beyers, 1993). Additionally, Boeing has a policy not to be supportive of the spin-off firms it generates, to the point that it refuses to purchase from companies owned by former employees for a period of five years (Gray et al., 1999a). Although some may consider this a strict and unbending policy, it has often forced local firms to not be entirely dependent on Boeing, and required that new supply firms also develop their own relationships with other firms and government. So, when Boeing has suffered economic setbacks, such as declining defense procurement through the US Pentagon, other firms in the Seattle area have not been as affected as if they had depended only on Boeing contracts.

Overall, Boeing may be considered most powerful in its role as a regional agglomerate, specifically in its capacity to influence the regional economic infrastructure and labor pools. For example, many engineering and supply firms have located within the Seattle area in order to tap into the regional labor pool, specialized business services, and the business opportunities provided by Boeing employees' affluence (Gray et. al, 1999a). Additionally, the presence of the Seattle aerospace hub has influenced the development of the quickly growing software hub. Boeing Computer Services (BCS) established in 1970, provided internal services to Boeing as a whole, and by 1989, it was the region's largest software developer with around 6,000 employees (Chase, 1991). From a regional development perspective, BCS was most influential in providing a critical mass of highly skilled software professionals, who were recruited nationally and bolstered the regional labor pool with a critical mass of expertise. Thus, these recruited software professionals provided a local labor pool to draw from for hundreds of smaller software companies established in the 1980s, which included the now software giant, Microsoft Corporation.

Microsoft Corporation is perhaps the most well-known 'hub' high-technology firm associated with the Seattle metropolitan economy. The enterprise gained its lead in the industry by tying its product, the operating system MS-DOS for IBM and IBM compatible microcomputers, to the sale of microcomputers themselves. The firm then took an international lead in the software industry through product innovation, through purchasing other competitive firms and their products and through the aggressive use of the courts to protect its patents (Gray et al., 1999a: 277). Today, Microsoft Corporation has matured beyond its era of expansive innovation and focuses more on market penetration, cost control, and service. Similar to the aerospace industry, its primary contribution to the region is through the formation of a highly skilled labor pool (ibid.). This labor pool has not only contributed to the development of the region's software industry, but has also provided an array of professionals that the emerging regional biotechnology cluster can draw from, especially since computers are an essential tool in biotechnology research. In an effort to secure regional Canadian talent as well as international talent, Microsoft Corporation established a development center with three different sites of operation throughout the greater Vancouver, Canada area beginning in 2007, and these facilities employed a total of roughly 300 high-tech employees by the mid-2010s. As of 2015, Microsoft Corporation formally established a Microsoft Canada Excellence Center in downtown Vancouver with plans to eventually accommodate over 700 high-tech professionals, both foreign and domestic, and plans to consolidate Vancouver development operation to this one location (Levy, 2016).

Finally, Amazon.com, a newly emerging e-commerce Seattle start-up in the mid-1990s, has surpassed Walmart in market capitalization rates, being valued at over 300 billion dollars in 2015. As of late 2015, Amazon.com employed approximately 25,000 people in Seattle, and was historically headquartered in the old Veterans' Hospital in south Seattle. The company has plans to grow to over an estimated 70,000 employees, primarily based within its new campus situated in the South Lake Union area of Seattle proper by 2019 (Forshee, 2015; Demay, 2015). Similar to Microsoft Corporation, Amazon.com has leased considerable real estate in downtown Vancouver, BC in late 2013 with plans to develop a major R&D facility that will eventually employ over 1,000 professionals as part of its regional corporate enterprises (CBC, 2013; Parkhurst, 2015).

The following subsection provides a synopsis of Seattle's growing biotechnology cluster, and ends with how the region has recovered from the dot-com bubble bursting in 2000 and the subsequent 2008 financial crisis, and its response to the needs of a post 9/11 world.

3.2.2.1.1.2 Seattle's emerging biotechnology economy   Over the past 15 years, Seattle has emerged as a leading national cluster of biotechnology firms with over 60 firms within the area in addition to a complementary medical instrumentation industry. The literature review in Chapter 2 revealed the importance of regional institutions. Here the University of Washington and the Fred Hutchinson Cancer Research Center (the 'Hutch') have been the two lead institutions in the biotechnology industry, employing over 1,700 professionals (Gray et al., 1999a). Approximately 700 of these people are faculty with joint appointments at the University of Washington. There is a strong cluster effect within the biotech sector with approximately 30 percent of newly created firms being spin-offs from the University of Washington and/or the Hutch. However, as of late 2013, the majority of the top five Seattle biotechnology firms for employment were headquartered outside of Seattle with only Bio-Rad Laboratories, Inc. based in the area (Puget Sound Business Journal, 2015).

3.2.2.1.2 Seattle's recent booms and busts   Since the bursting of the dot-com bubble in late 2000 and early 2001, Seattle's labor market was severely impacted with job losses of over 10,000 up to 2003 and firms closing in every sector. Overall, Seattle was one of the most heavily impacted cities after the bursting of the dot-com bubble, with unemployment rates still around 7.7 percent in 2004 while the national average was around 5.88 percent (Office of the Forecast Council cited in Jones, 2004). Yet, by the end of 2005, Seattle's software industry was beginning to rebound, but at that time, it was below the levels of growth in the late 1990s. Some of this relative decline has been attributed to Microsoft Corporation continuing to offshore work and expanding its software campuses in India and other offshore destinations, while curtailing expansion plans at its headquarters in the Seattle suburb of Redmond, Washington (Mahapatra, 2005). However, Seattle's rebound, beginning in 2005, was short lived by the onset of the 2008 global financial crisis. Although not as severe as the 2001 dot-com bust, the 2008 financial crisis did lead to the unemployment rate in Seattle surging to 8.2 percent by late 2009, and housing prices falling by an average of 25–30 percent. As well, Washington Mutual, the largest savings and loan company that collapsed as a result of the 2008 crisis, was based in Seattle for over 100 years.

By late 2005, the Seattle economy was beginning to show signs of a rebound, with Boeing setting a record for commercial airplane orders, beating its previous record set in 1988 (Linn, 2006). Interestingly, by 2008, the company had high cash reserves, very little debt, and airplane orders backlogged with international clients that had access to financing not affected by the US banking crisis (*The Economist*, 2008). Thus, Boeing was somewhat unscathed by the 2008 financial crisis, with record plane deliveries and, like much of Seattle's economy from 2012 onward, surged ahead (Gates, 2016).

In fact, in early 2016, all of Seattle could be considered back in a 'boomtime' economy with unemployment levels at 3.3 percent for August 2015. As well, the median King county housing prices have surpassed their 2007 peak of $481,000 to $508,000 for early 2016 (*Seattle Times*, 2016). Some have cited the salaries and stock options found within the tech economy, and especially Amazon.com, to be the main driver for rising housing prices and subsequent housing affordability and declining quality of life issues in the Seattle area (Demay, 2015). However, after the tough and difficult recession of the early 2000s, the region still encourages growth and diversification of major high-tech firms by supporting the establishment of the headquarters of Redfin, a technology savvy real estate company situated in trendy Belltown; Zillow.com, also based in Seattle; and facilitating a Facebook office in Kirkland, just across Lake Washington from Seattle.

Despite the growing sense of economic optimism found in early 2016, there appears to be a sense of caution that comes when a city begins to mature. Historically, Seattle has always been a 'boom bust' economy since the late 1800s, so its inhabitants may be somewhat used to these dramatic economic swings (MacDonald, 1987). However, until late 2001, Seattle's economy accomplished an astounding 15-year boom. Oliver Morgan of *The Observer* newspaper captured the more cautious post dot-com spirit and aftermath of 9/11 with the following quote:

> Five years ago the city was celebrating a modern-day gold rush. Jobs in IT multiplied as Bill Gates's Microsoft soared, and the boom was fueled by the likes of Jeff Bezos' Amazon.com, which sucked in talent from California and the east. Internet whiz kids fueled by Starbucks coffee flew round the globe on Boeing jets. Seattle's glitter began to fade with the infamous World Trade Organization meeting in 1999, marred by anti-globalization protesters. Three months later the dotcom boom ended, and IT jobs were flushed away. Washington State now has the second highest unemployment rate in the US – 7.3 percent compared with the national 5.8 percent. Seattle is still a dynamic, optimistic and highly attractive city, bordered on one side by Puget Sound and on the other by spectacular mountains. But the economic realities are unavoidable. (Morgan, 2002: A8)

Johnathan Raban, an award winning British writer, who now makes Seattle his home, summed up the cultural realities of post dot-com and 9/11 Seattle. In an interview with the *Seattle Times* in September 2003 about his novel, *Waxwings*, a book about the lives of two immigrants grappling with the American experience in post 9/11 Seattle, Raban expressed the following:

Seattle Times: You've lived in Seattle for 13 years. How has it changed?

Raban: It's come down (from the dot-com boom) with a bump. To me that's a good thing. There was a sense of everyone being wildly over promoted; the waiter (at your favorite restaurant) should have been a dishwasher; the owner should have been a waiter. There was a kind of inflation of roles. I like the mood of chastened realism that's crept into Seattle life. Seattle is a much more realistic city now. (Gwinn, 2003: A8)

Perhaps as Seattle begins its second century as a leader in the new economy and well situated on the Pacific Rim, its labor market may grow and excel with a mature sense of cautious optimism, which may be more similar to its northern sister city of Vancouver, BC. As MacDonald (1987) states, both Seattle and Vancouver emerged as cities around the same time in the late 1800s, but Vancouver grew more slowly and cautiously, with heavier government intervention in its development and planning processes as compared to Seattle's developer dominated culture of growth. Although the more mature industries of timber and fishing compete against one another in a regional context between British Columbia and Washington State, it is unknown if the newer economies, such as high-technology and biotechnology, are competing or complementary economies between Seattle and Vancouver. In fact, this particular conundrum is something the empirical work from this study will help to provide more factual information on in Chapter 4. The next section covers the economy of the city of Vancouver. It has been, perhaps, more successful than Seattle in the past 30 years in attracting outside investment and immigrants primarily from the Asia Pacific region, although its new IT sector has not generated the large number of stable high paying jobs that Seattle has. Indeed, despite the fact that the Vancouver economy was not as heavily impacted by the dot-com bust and post 9/11 fallout, the regional economy still has experienced setbacks as well as successes over the past 16 years (2000–16). However, many commentators believe that the new economy of Vancouver has much to offer in the future especially with the telecommunications sector, software for electronic gaming, and world-class biotechnology development. The economic profile of Vancouver is where the study now turns to.

3.2.2.2   The Vancouver economy – from peripheral hinterland to growing new economy

Vancouver began its identity in the late 1800s as the western most point of the Canadian Pacific Railroad, a port city for exporting commodities for all of western Canada and the entry point of goods coming from the Asia Pacific (MacDonald, 1987). The greater Vancouver area was based in a tradition of resource-exploitation, with timber exports and, to a lesser extent, mining exports producing the major thrust of growth. These two hinterland staples helped to set the economic culture of the region for over 75 years, or what Innis (1962; 1999) describes as a classic staples economy. However, the robustness of natural resources began to wane in the early 1980s (Barnes, 1996). This required that Vancouver begin to diversify its economy to high value added services such as tourism in addition to encouraging foreign direct invest and immigration from Asia Pacific economies such as Hong Kong and Japan (Edgington and Goldberg, 1992; Edgington, 1995; and Hutton, 1998). Vancouver emerged as a world-class destination point by hosting the World's Expo in 1986. In addition to notoriety and international attention, the city at this time also received enormous infrastructure upgrades. These funds, primarily from the Federal Government of Canada, allowed the city to clean up its old polluted lumber yards and harbors (e.g. False Creek), and transformed these areas into what some consider post-modern sites of entertainment and human habitat, contributing greatly to Vancouver's international reputation as a 'Livable City' (Ley et al., 1992).

3.2.2.2.1 Vancouver as a site for immigrants and foreign direct investment Compared to Seattle, immigration and foreign investment have been more important to Vancouver. Canada, generally, has always been a draw to foreigners and overseas workers wishing for a new and better life in North America. In fact, Canada is the one of the few remaining developed countries in the world that still provides reasonable access to foreigners wishing to immigrate permanently. At a national level, Canada used its open immigration policy to its advantage in the 1980s and 1990s by aggressively advertising Canada as a place to live in Hong Kong and East Asia as the 1997 China takeover deadline loomed (Ley, 1996; Mitchell, 1996; and Waters, 2000). This national recruitment strategy helped to lure wealthy Hong Kong residents to Vancouver as a new home, and Canada, more generally, as a country ripe for their foreign/domestic direct investments and a depository of their vast amounts of personal wealth. The so-called 'business migration plan' worked reasonably well with many Hong Kong residents moving to Vancouver and other large urban centers over the course of the late 1980s and 1990s (Waters, 2000). For example, people of Chinese or South Asian ancestry make up more than 60 percent of suburban Richmond, BC residents. In fact, over 40 percent of the population of Richmond, BC speak Cantonese as their original language (City of Richmond, 2016). Additionally, Hong Kong investments have found their way into condominium developments, helping to transform parts of the skyline of Vancouver, which is now often known to resemble the urban architecture of Hong Kong (Hutton, 1998). However, Canada has not been as successful in convincing these new Asian residents and citizens to invest a significant amount of their personal fortunes in Canadian business due mainly to Canada's high personal and corporate tax levels and limited investment returns at a domestic level (Ley, 2005; 2011). In fact, this is a growing area of frustration for Revenue Canada and Citizenship and Immigration Canada to the point that immigration officials have often stripped new permanent residents of their status when they attempt to reenter Canada from abroad, citing the fact that they have not truly immigrated to Canada.

Perhaps a more acceptable form of recent direct foreign investment into Canada from Asia is from the country of Japan. Japan has invested in the natural resource economy of western Canada for over two decades with relatively positive financial returns on their areas of interest. Over the past 20 years or so, these investments have also focused on tourism in the Canadian West (Edgington, 1995). In the late 1980s, Japanese *sogo sosha*, or the foreign trading companies component of the massive *kereitsu* business groups, invested in hotels, ski resorts, and other travel amenities that were popular with Japanese tourists, hoping to recoup these Japanese expenditures in BC when their citizens traveled to Canada. Despite the fact that Japan has a world-class electronics industry and a burgeoning biotech industry, Japanese firms have chosen to not invest in these industries within the Vancouver area, favoring Silicon Valley and the greater Los Angeles area as major North American destinations for R&D based investments (Florida and Kenney, 1994). Nonetheless, high-technology production and biotechnology in Vancouver are fast growing industries, with high-technology and biotechnology having combined higher employment levels ($\sim$ 84,000 people) than timber, mining, and oil and gas in 2012 (KPMG, 2014).

3.2.2.2.2   Vancouver's fledgling industries of high-technology and biotechnology   The development of the high-technology sector in BC in the 1980s was seen as an opportunity for the province to move away from the cyclical resource industry of timber to an industry which provided longer-term employment for an increasingly highly skilled workforce. The sector has gone from employing 23,000 workers in the late 1980s to about 84,000 workers in 2012 (KPMG, 2014). Revenue for this industry has grown from approximately $5 billion Canadian in 1997 to over $23.3 billion Canadian in 2015 (BC TIA, 2015). Although the bursting of the dot-com bubble in 2000 impacted growth on the BC provincial revenues, the industry could be described as volatile even before 2000, with growth rates varying from $7.6 billion Canadian to $4.1 billion Canadian in 1998 (Rees, 1999). However, despite the volatility in corporate revenue, the industry has moved from a stage of infancy in the early 1990s to one characterized by gaining a stable critical mass of growth through firms and employees by the late 1990s. Although the industry suffered from the post dot-com shakeout in 2000, followed by a post 9/11 economic slump, the Vancouver region did not suffer through the 2000–2001 recession as severely as its southern neighbor, Seattle, in terms of comparative losses in employment and revenue (BC TIA, 2003). This may be attributed to the fact that the Vancouver based firms did not have such easy access to US based venture capital as the Seattle firms enjoyed before the dot-com bust, nor was the high-technology sector as developed as its southern neighbor. Thus, Vancouver firms were not as highly leveraged compared to their Seattle counterparts when the bubble bust, and so they could 'ride out' the dramatic economic restructuring after 2000 since they did not have the higher debt loads of Seattle based firms (Hudson, 2000).

By the early 2010s, Vancouver's tech industry experienced a revival of sorts with recent locally grown firms such as Hootsuite, Global Relay, and Avigilon receiving international attention for their global growth potential, and the region of Vancouver continued to develop a reputation for its highly skilled local talent and its ability to draw and retain international talent within the tech sector (Richardson, Florida, and Stolarick, 2012; Richardson 2016). This city is also becoming known for its innovative new economy firms (such as gaming) that contribute to the rising cultural economy (Hutton, 2015). Nevertheless, despite the fact that there were over 9,000 technology focused firms in BC in 2014, Vancouver's technology sector could still be characterized as a grouping of small technology firms, with a majority of its firms employing less than 50 people (KPMG, 2014). Thus, growing the average size of Vancouver's tech firms in addition to facilitating the growth and permanency of medium and large size anchor tech companies in the Vancouver area still remains one of the greatest challenges for the Vancouver tech sector. Despite the boom time of growth that the Vancouver technology sector was experiencing by early 2016, observers and experts stress that if Vancouver's tech sector is going to achieve some sort of maturity as an industry, it must grow, nurture, and sustain medium to large sized anchor firms (KPMG, 2014).

Unlike the software side of high-tech, Vancouver's fledgling biotechnology industry was even less affected by the bursting of the dot-com bubble, 9/11 fallout, or 2008 financial crisis. In fact, biotechnology has gained substantial ground over the past 20 years with over 159 active firms as of late 2011 (Park and McCaffrey, 2013). However, the industry may be characterized as being comprised of small enterprises with over 65 percent of these firms having fewer than 30 employees, and the largest firm employing almost 500 employees in 2014 (Lifesciences BC, 2015). Overall, the biotechnology industry may be considered a key component of the high-technology sector in Vancouver, and employed just over 4,000 people in late 2011(Park and McCaffrey, 2013).

In the last 15 years, Vancouver has developed a positive reputation for its emerging world-class biotechnology research and development cluster (DeVol and Bedroussian, 2006). Many factors have contributed to the BC biotechnology industry's success as a whole, such as close ties between the university and local commercial activities (Cortright and Mayer, 2002; Holbrook et al., 2004; Rees, 2004), world-class medical research, and ease and availability of venture capital for later stage firms (Wolfe and Gertler, 2004; Niosi, 2003; and Niosi and Bas, 2004), and the region's ability to attract and retain international talent (Richardson 2006b, 2016).

Nevertheless the Vancouver biotechnology industry is not immune to volatility over the past ten years. In fact, some of Vancouver's largest and better known biotechnology firms, such as Angiotech, QLT, and Cadiome Pharama Corp., have either filed for bankruptcy or laid off almost their entire research staff in the past five years. Importantly, much of these firm failures could be attributed to corporate missteps, competitor threats, and chocked off credit rather than a particular economic crisis (Lawrence, 2013; Richardson, 2016). There was much concern about the overall health and viability of the biotechnology industry in the early 2010s as a result of these large firm failures. However, Richardson (2016) found that this crisis proved to be a good thing for Vancouver's biotechnology industry since it has propelled key executives and senior scientists to begin to start their own firms, similar to what occurs in Silicon Valley. Thus, what emerged are many new start-ups and small and medium sized companies within Vancouver's biotech cluster. Unlike Angiotech and QLT, two Vancouver based biotech firms that were able to conduct initial public offerings without the influence or takeover of large international pharmaceutical companies, many of these newer biotechnology companies focused on niche products that are eventually sold to larger US based firms. Thus, the landscape of Vancouver's biotechnology sector may now be fitting a model of outsourcing research and development for international pharmaceutical giants (Lawrence, 2013).

3.2.2.2.3   Vancouver's new economy – all ring and no core   Overall, the BC high-technology sector is much more diversified than just software and biotechnology, which describes much of Seattle's situation. Vancouver's diversification within the sector helps make it much more resilient to industry slumps and product failures. For example, as of 2015, Telus, a telecommunications firm, was the largest IT sector BC based firm based on revenue, followed by MacDonald, Dettwiler and Associates, Ltd., a global communications company, and third, Sierra Wireless, Inc., which specializes in device hardware and software (Business in Vancouver, 2015).

However, unlike Seattle where a few large corporations dominate much of the economic activity in the region, the high-technology industry of BC continues to be characterized as having many very small firms and few large firms as Rees (1999) described in the late 1990s. Contrary to Seattle's hub and spoke structure, the Vancouver high-tech industry may be described as operating as what Storper and Harrison (1991) define as an 'all ring, no core' manner (Rees, 1999). This may be characterized by a lack of a core lead firm, such as Boeing and Microsoft Corporation in Seattle, and a horizontal production network system of products, as opposed to a vertical and hierarchical system. Its system of governance may be similar to the Marshallian industrial district of Italy, where there are many highly creative local firms (Piore and Sabel, 1984). However, Rees (1999) stressed that these firms are different from their Marshallian counterparts in the sense that there is an absence of intraregional collaboration between firms within the greater Vancouver area, which mitigates against the development of a true regional innovative network. Thus, the mix of innovation in high-technology coupled with fragmentation may be deemed as being 'territorial innovative, but without milieux' (Camagni, 1995; cited in Rees, 1999). This all ring, no core structure characterized by predominately external collaborative linkages best describes Vancouver based firms as they continue to seek complementary access to basic research, testing, and marketing-oriented activities. This is especially true for the biotechnology sector. The broader high-technology industry has significant external linkages derived from increasingly foreign ownership/major investments and information flows extending beyond the local Vancouver area and Canada, generally. A majority of these external linkages for both high-technology and biotechnology continue to lead to California (Richardson, 2006a). However, there is growing evidence of emerging connections leading to Seattle (Richardson, Florida, and Stolarick, 2012). The eastern US and western Europe also had strong linkages with Vancouver's biotechnology sector (Richardson, 2006b).

3.2.2.2.3.1   Vancouver's ring – external linkages and the need for access and mobility of the internationally highly skilled   The crucial external linkages for Vancouver's high-technology and biotechnology industry introduced in the preceding subsection are heavily dependent on the movement of internationally highly skilled professionals and executives in order to continue to grow these locally developed industries (Richardson, 2011; 2016). High-technology is dependent not only on sending qualified Canadian professionals over the Canada–US border for sales meetings, service delivery, job promotions, and general contact with the parent firm, but it is also dependent on the hiring of international professionals, especially Americans, in order to fulfill its growing professional employment demands. Biotechnology, for instance, is dependent not only on the hiring of world-class scientists and executives, but also on the movement of professional personnel back and forth across the Canada–US border for clinical trials, partnerships with pharmaceuticals, and general collaborative research efforts with US firms and institutions (ibid.). Although a majority of these connections expand beyond the region of Cascadia, a growing number of activities within the high-tech sector can be found within the Vancouver–Seattle corridor. For example, both the aerospace and software industries of Seattle have always hired considerable numbers of Canadian software professionals, and there is growing activity with Microsoft Corporation and now Amazon.com and Tableau Software, Inc. establishing development centers in Vancouver over the past ten years. Thus, the need to move personnel back and forth across international borders, especially the Canada–US border, has become more critical. Chapter 16 of NAFTA, which deals with professional labor mobility, seems like a crucial, and rather timely, mechanism to facilitate these movements.

The next section addresses existing arrangements that regulate cross-border flows of professionals and knowledge workers in Cascadia. It will first explore the impacts of broader scale regimes dealing with labor mobility embedded in the WTO/GATS Agreement, and moving to national arrangements, such as the US H-1B visas for foreign professionals. It concludes with closely examining Chapter 16 of NAFTA and its implications for the cross-border region of Cascadia.

3.3   CASCADIA IN ITS WIDER CONTEXT

The preceding section has provided an overview of the Cascadia region and its high-tech economies. It is now necessary to explore how exactly NAFTA has impacted labor mobility in the Cascadia region since this is a key question within the book. In addition, it is important to point out that there may be institutional apparatus besides NAFTA that also affect cross-border labor mobility within the Cascadia region. This particular section reviews these varied mechanisms including the labor mobility provisions under the General Agreement on Trade and Services (GATS) developed by the World Trade Organization; Chapter 16 of NAFTA; the US's H-1B visa; and general Canadian professional work authorization for foreigners. (See Tables 3.1–3.3, which show the different levels and major attributes of these foreign work statuses for the US and Canada.)

Table 3.1   US temporary entry statuses

Types of Entry Status	Description	Labor Certification	Length/Renewable	Strengths/Weaknesses
H-1B	Foreign professional with at least the equivalent of a baccalaureate degree. Must file through the DHS case-processing centers	Employer must ensure that foreign worker is not displacing US worker	Good for up to three years; can renew for three more years. Must leave US for one year after six years on an H-1B	S: Renewable and can lead to permanent work status (a 'green card'). W: Annual cap. Frequently requires the help of a lawyer (~ $5,000US). Processing time can take anywhere from two–six months
TN (Treaty NAFTA)	Canadian/Mexican nationals who meet the education and/or work requirements for 65 professional job classifications. Can file at port of entry. Applicant should usually not need legal help	No labor certification is required	Debatable. As of 2008, the TN statuses can be issued for up to three years. Attorneys/employers say that this status can be renewed indefinitely. US immigration officials say that the job the TN status is being granted for can take no longer than three years	S: Fast (ideally) and inexpensive. W: Port of entry officers are sometimes inconsistent with adjudications. Very little recourse for applicant if application is denied. Applicants frequently need the help of lawyers

Table 3.1 (continued)

L-1	Intracompany transferees-executives/managers/employees with specialized knowledge. Can file at ports of entry	No labor certification, but person must have worked for at least a year for company before transferring	Can be renewed for seven years for managers and executives, and five years for employees with specialized knowledge	S: Fast and inexpensive. Can lead to permanent residency status for managers and executives. Spouse can also procure a US work visa. W: Specialized knowledge employees have difficulty renewing the L status after five years
B-1	Business visitors who are traveling to the US trade shows, meetings, training, or conferences	No labor certification required	Allowed for up to one year (six months and renew for six months)	S: Easy and accessible at POE. W: Many foreigners do not know they need this type of visa. Cannot be paid by a US employer under this type of visa
E-1 and 2	Applies to foreign traders/investors that conduct considerable business between US/home country	No labor certification required	The status is good for up to one year. Can renew for up to five years	S: Accessible visa for serious traders and investors. W: Significant amounts of paperwork. Four-eight weeks to approve

Sources: US Department of Homeland Security (2016); research interviews for this study.

Table 3.2 Canadian permanent entry statuses

Types of Entry Status	Description	Labor Certification	Length/Renewable	Strengths/Weaknesses
Provincial Nominee Program (Express Entry is optional)	CIC program run by various provinces to 'fast-track' various professionally skilled foreigners that the province has a shortage in. Also open to foreign investors/entrepreneurs	Employer sponsors applicant. No LMIA	Leads to permanent residency status ideally within 5–12 months	S: Effective/efficient program for eligible applicants. W: Firms must spend money (legal fees) (~ $8,000) and human resource personnel's time to help foreign employee process application
Canadian Experience Class. (Must apply through Express Entry first)	CIC run program. 'Fast-tracks' a foreigner's permanent residency application. Must work full-time in Canada for at least a year in a managerial/professional/ designated skilled trades position before applying	Does not require LMIA	Applicant must work for at least one year full-time in Canada, and complete this work within a three-year window. Permanent residency is usually attained in a year after applying	S: Effective and efficient program for eligible applicants. Used by matriculated foreign university students able to secure Canadian employment. W: Moving yearly cap on total number of visas

Table 3.2 (continued)

| Federal Skilled Worker Program. (Must apply through Express Entry first) | Foreigners with suitable admission criteria. Must demonstrate interest through 'Express Entry' (EE). If applicant satisfies eligibility criteria through the EE ranking process, applicant then may be eligible to apply for permanent migration status | Applicants must demonstrate that she/he held a full-time position in Canada/foreign country for at least a year in 347 eligible occupations. Employers must conduct an LMIA if wanting to hire an applicant. EE screening process favors applicants who have arranged employment in Canada | Once invited to apply for permanent residency, it is usually attained within a year | S: Based on the screening mechanism of EE, highest ranking applicants are processed first. Applicants with a job offer or provincial nomination are quickly invited to apply for permanent residency. Processing time less than six months for those who rank high. W: Employers must conduct an LMIA. Applicants must first be screened via EE. Due to EE, some see the process as elitist/ misleading in speed and odds of securing good employment in Canada |

Sources: Citizenship and Immigration Canada (CIC) (2016); research interviews for this study.

Table 3.3   Canadian temporary entry statuses

Types of Entry Status	Description	Labor Certification	Length/Renewable	Strengths/Weaknesses
Treaty NAFTA (TN) – Temporary status that falls under International Mobility Program	Applies to US/Mexican nationals who meet the education and/ or work requirements for 65 professional job classifications. Can file at POE. Self-explanatory. Applicant should usually not need legal help	No labor certification is required	As of 2008, TN statuses are issued for up to three years. CIC perspective is that the TN may be renewed indefinitely	S: Fast (ideally). Also, no labor certification. W: Status is only for three years. Applicants are increasingly needing the help of lawyers
International Mobility Program – Temporary Status	NAFTA and GATS, intracompany transferees, young people seeking a working international experience in Canada, and foreign students who matriculated from a Canadian university seeking up to three years of professional work experience in Canada	No labor certification is required	These temporary statuses are usually good for up to two to three years. Many NAFTA/GATS applicants and foreign matriculated university students then apply for permanent residency after one year on this type of visa	S: Fast. Also, no labor certification. W: Types of professional positions allowed under this program are narrow

Table 3.3 (continued)

Temporary Foreign Worker Program	ESDC oversees program. Applies to a majority of professional job categories. Similar to the US H-1B	Must conduct LMIA. Employer must demonstrate deliberate effect to unsuccessfully hire a Canadian	Work status is good for up to three years with the possibility of renewal. Foreigner may also apply for permanent residency status after one year in job	S: Applies to most professional jobs. W: Must get ESDC approval, can take beyond six months. Time/cost involved to show that no Canadian could be hired. Program overhauled in 2014 due to claims of widespread employer abuse of program

Sources: Citizenship and Immigration Canada (2016); research interviews for this study.

3.3.1 Mode 4 of the General Agreement on Trade in Services (GATS)

Labor mobility across international borders was first incorporated into an international trade agreement through the World Trade Organization (WTO), established in 1996. An outcome of the Uruguay Round, negotiated by the World Trade Organization, includes the General Provision on Trade in Services (GATS). Essentially, the GATS had recognized four modes of service delivery: Mode 1 – cross-border supply; Mode 2 – consumption abroad; Mode 3 – commercial presence; and Mode 4 – the temporary movement of natural persons. Of these four modes, Mode 4 is the smallest form of service delivery in terms of both trade flows and the volume of scheduled concessions recorded under the GATS (Winters, 2002). Currently, Mode 4 really only applies to highly skilled professionals and executives, especially intracompany transferees that usually follow corporate foreign direct investment. Additionally, Mode 4 of the GATS is usually used by countries that do not already have separate labor mobility agreements with receiving countries, and is especially relevant for professionals in developing countries that seek access to work in developed countries, or, for other reasons, are not eligible under domestic immigration legislation and/or labor market policy. It is argued by some (Winters, 2002; and Chanda, 2001) that Mode 4 of the GATS does not serve developing countries well since their competitive advantages lie with medium and low skilled workers as compared to highly skilled workers. Thus, one strong argument with the further liberalization of Mode 4 of the GATS provision on service delivery is to allow for the international mobility of medium and less skilled service providers (ibid.).

Since the Cascadia region is primarily used as an entry point for movement of skilled professional labor between the western portions of North America and a gateway for the Asia Pacific, the GATS has been seldom used in this region (interview with Douglas/Peace Arch POE Port Director-Vancouver, September 2003). Reasons for this include the fact that other more accessible visas, such as the Trade NAFTA or TN status, the US's H-1B visa, and Canada's temporary professionals' labor entry programs, are used more frequently. These visas are easily accessible and can be considered more familiar to the professionals who work with labor mobility visas, for instance, immigration officials and attorneys. These and other types of visas used to facilitate cross-border mobility of knowledge intensive employees in Cascadia will be discussed in the following subsections together with how they are used by immigration professionals, such as attorneys.

3.3.2 Various US Visas for the Admission of Foreign Professionals into the US

The US, often deemed as the strongest economy in the world, relies not only on the labor of its citizens for such a robust performance, but also on the capabilities of foreigners, both high and low skilled (Tichenor, 2002). In explaining the rather complex immigration and visa procedures for cross-border labor, the key discrepancies between permanent and temporary labor visas and migration regulations are discussed below.

NAFTA has made a significant contribution to the US's demand of highly skilled foreign workers. It is estimated that over 250,000 Canadians have secured a TN status since NAFTA's inception in 1994, and approximately 7,000–9,000 new TN statuses are issued yearly with occasional drops in numbers, most likely due to the economic impacts immediately following 9/11, and economic downturns such as the dot-com bust of the early 2000s and the 2008 global financial crisis (US DHS statistics, various years; interview with US Policy Analyst, January 2005). However, as one can see from Figure 2.6 in Chapter 2, the NAFTA statuses issued to Canadians are rising for the most part since 2011, most likely due to the North American economy rebounding.

However, there is also a need for the US to attract foreign labor originating outside of North America. Thus, the US immigration system allows for the admission of foreigners with executive, professional, and technical skills for both permanent and temporary immigration. However, this admission of foreign professionals can be somewhat unbalanced when one considers permanent versus temporary workers. The certification process for admitting permanent immigrants is slow and costly, whereas the process for highly skilled temporary workers or immigrants is fast and relatively inexpensive (Martin, 2001). Nevertheless, both avenues provide options for US employers looking to hire non-US employees, but both options are numerically limited.

3.3.2.1 US temporary immigration – the H-1B program

By the year 2001, there were 14 types of non-immigrant visas for foreigners seeking work in the United States (Martin, 2001). Beginning in the early 1990s, the US developed a number of these foreign worker programs. Each visa program has been designed for a very limited area of the labor market, with the H-1B program being the largest when it comes to admitting highly skilled foreign workers into the United States. Overall, all non-immigrants seeking temporary entry into the US for purposes of work must demonstrate that she/he will leave the US when the visa expires, and show ties to their country of origin. Most non-immigrants may bring their family members, but family members are usually unable to work in the US unless the spouse attains his/her own work status/visa. Finally, there are usually no limits for the majority of these non-immigrant visas, except for the important H-1B visa type, since it is used so frequently. Over the past ten years, US Congress has continued to set its limit annually with a minimum ceiling of 65,000 visas, not including 20,000 H-1B visas which are issued to foreign nationals who have attained master's degrees or PhDs from American universities. There are a number of other exceptions to this minimum ceiling, which include universities, non-profits, and governmental research facilities in need of professional foreign labor.

Essentially, the H-1B program allows US employers to admit foreigners into the US as professional employees. The current program was established under the Immigration Act of 1990, although its roots go back to the 1950s (Martin, 2001). Under the H-1B program, the potential applicant must have at least the equivalency of an undergraduate degree. The prospective employer does not have to submit a labor certification, unlike the case of a permanent immigration visa requirement for foreign professionals, as discussed in the preceding section. In this case, the employer must attest that he/she is offering the H-1B visa worker prevailing wages within the workplace; that the working conditions do not adversely impact, or undercut US employees' working conditions; and also that the foreign employee does not fill a position caused by any strike or lockout (ibid.). If issued, the H-1B visa is valid for three years, and this can be renewed for another three years. Finalizing of any application usually takes anywhere from two to four months to process. The H-1B program visa is limited in its duration though. Thus, after six years, any visa holder must apply for permanent immigration, usually through being sponsored by his/her place of employment or must return to his/her country of origin for one year. In the recent past, it usually took anywhere from three to four months to process a more permanent 'green card' application. Beginning in the late 1990s, a prospective employer could pay an additional $1,000 to 'fast-track' an H-1B application, and if successful, the visa will then be issued in two weeks (ibid.).

By comparison, the Canadian federal government has not had the same concerns or negative perceptions relative to other western countries regarding the use of foreign workers and immigration in general. Canada may be considered unique in this regard since it still allows, if not encourages, over 250,000 immigrants annually. Over 65 percent of these new immigrants usually must have at least a bachelor degree in order to be considered for immigration to Canada. In regards to this concept of being open towards foreigners, Bloemraad (2012) discussed the notion of Canadian Exceptionalism when it comes to understanding why Canadians are perceived as more accepting of foreigners than citizens of other western countries. The author stressed that the notions of immigration and multi-culturalism were instrumental to Canada's nation building in the 1960s and 1970s and have subsequently become part of the modern Canadian identity. The chapter now turns to a brief review of the Canadian immigration policies that are dedicated to professional immigration.

3.3.3   Canadian Professional Immigration

Canada is one of the few countries in the world that has a relatively open immigration policy relating to recruiting skilled workers. This more open immigration system extends to the family members of Canadian citizens, and also refugees fleeing political and/or religious persecution from their countries of origin. Importantly, 65 percent of Canada's annual intake of immigrants is made up of skilled workers (Tolley, 2002). Thus, professionals seeking permanent entry into Canada have a relatively easier time as compared to foreign professionals seeking permanent entry into the US for purposes of work. This section provides a review of Canada's permanent immigration policies for skilled workers as well as foreigners seeking professional work in Canada on a non-permanent basis. It also examines trends and possible future directions for the recruitment of foreign skilled professionals.

3.3.3.1   Permanent migration for foreign professionals

The Canadian Immigration and Refugee Protection Act, implemented in June 2002, encourages foreigners seeking permanent residence who are capable of becoming economically established in Canada. This program emphasizes the broad human capital attributes and flexible skills of intending applicants as opposed to the traditionally narrow range of allowable occupations. Significantly, Tolley (2002) argues that this broader approach is more reflective of the needs and demands of the current flexible labor market. The process of seeking permanent immigration as a skilled worker is based on a points system, with education, language proficiency, employment history, age, arranged employment in Canada, and general adaptability, all being important factors.

Canada along with Australia has led the way with a skills focused approach to immigration over the past 15 years. Other countries appear to be following this approach. For example, both Germany and the UK have just instituted highly skilled migrant programs in order to attract global talent (McHale, 2003; Beaverstock and Hall, 2012). In addition to innovative design elements, such as giving points for past earnings, both the German and UK systems emphasize speed of application processing.

This was in direct contrast to the updated Canadian system where some applications, especially for applicants originating in India and China, literally took years to process (McHale, 2003).

In a response to the growing backlog of permanent migration applications, the Government of Canada instituted a new 'expression of interest' or 'Express Entry' for highly skilled foreigners wanting to immigrate to Canada in early 2015. The thrust of the Express Entry program requires that all applicants who would normally apply directly to a permanent immigration program, such as the Canadian Experience Class or the Federal Skilled Workers Program, now must file a profile expressing an interest in migrating to Canada. Based on the applicant's ranking of various points awarded for level of education, English and/or French proficiency, age, Canadian work experience, and perhaps most important, arranged employment in Canada, only then are high ranking applicants 'invited' to apply to a particular permanent immigration program. Although the system has only been operational for a little over a year, Express Entry has been lauded for its ability to avoid application backlogs and its flexibility when responding to the actual demands of extremely high skilled applicants (Desiderio and Hooper, 2016). However, the majority of the 'arranged employment', which is crucial to a high score regarding Express Entry, must still be subject to a Labour Market Impact Assessment (LMIA). This stringent requirement has received an outcry from many small and medium sized enterprises that stress that the LMIA is a too time consuming and expensive test when it comes to hiring a highly skilled foreigner. This is especially true if an applicant intends to apply to the general Foreign Skilled Workers Program, since both the Canadian Experience Class and the Provincial Nominee Programs do not require a labor market impact assessment. Specifically, the Canadian Experience Class allows foreign nationals who have been working in Canada full-time for at least a year as a trades person or as a professionally skilled foreigner to apply for permanent residency. The program does not require a job offer or a subsequent LMIA, and the foreign applicant usually attains Canadian permanent residency status within a year. The Provincial Nominee Program (PNP) is run by a number of provinces, such as BC, to 'fast-track' various professionally skilled foreigners that the province has a demonstrated shortage in (e.g. IT professionals and health care workers). Similar to the Canadian Experience Class, the PNP program does not require the employer to request a labor market impact assessment, and the foreign applicant, once hired, usually attains Canadian permanent residency status within a year.

Under the updated immigration provisions beginning in 2002, a status change from a temporary worker to a permanent worker is allowed.

Previously, there was tremendous ambiguity as to likely success when it came to moving a foreign worker from temporary work to permanent work status.

Despite a more flexible approach in addressing the permanent migration of skilled worker applicants, Canada has not been as flexible when it comes to temporary workers compared to other countries such as the US, the UK, Germany, and Australia. Specifically, Canada's system for temporary work authorization is becoming increasingly reliant on a labor market test conducted by Employment and Social Development Canada (ESDC) in order to guarantee that the job could not be filled by a domestic worker. The process usually takes anywhere from three weeks to six months, which represents critical time lost when it comes to recruiting highly skilled foreigners. As will be discussed in Chapter 4, the empirical research for this study revealed that this issue was of primary concern for many Vancouver based high-tech and biotechnology firms, leading to the conclusion that if the Vancouver economy continues to grow, a slower visa process could impede the local region's labor market and economy. Although Canada's immigration system is perceived to be quite permissive when allowing the entry of highly skilled foreigners, it is not without its problems. The text now turns to a short review of these temporary foreign worker programs that are dedicated to the entry of foreign highly skilled professionals.

3.3.3.2   Temporary foreign worker programs

The Temporary Foreign Worker Program allows Canadian employers to hire foreign nationals on a temporary basis when the employer is unable to recruit and hire a Canadian citizen or permanent resident for the position. For most employers seeking a foreign hire, they often have to request a LMIA from Employment and Social Development Canada (ESDC) to ensure that they have tried but have been unsuccessful in hiring a Canadian or permanent resident; demonstrate that the job offer is genuine; and the employer must have a positive record with job offer commitments regarding temporary foreign workers they have hired in the past (Citizenship and Immigration Canada, 2016). While a majority of these foreign workers are hired to perform a short-term employment contract, some of these temporary foreign workers are eligible to transition into Canadian permanent residence through the Canadian Experience Class and the Provincial Nominee Program.

For example, the International Mobility Program oversees all non-permanent work permit applications for foreigners that do not require a labor market impact assessment. A majority of these types of positions that do not require a labor market impact assessment are covered by free trade agreements such as NAFTA or the GATS. Beyond job classifications included in the NAFTA and the GATS, the other major category of positions governed by the International Mobility Program are for young people working as a part of experiential exchange programs in seasonal positions such as camp counselors and ski lift operators. However, many have argued that these types of positions that are exempt from labor market review are becoming increasingly narrow, and do not reflect the growing global hiring needs of many high-tech and biotechnology firms found in BC. Interestingly, in September 2014, as part of a provincial-federal agreement, Microsoft Corporation's new Centre of Excellence, located in downtown Vancouver, was allowed to bring in foreign professionals from around the globe who would be exempt from the labor market impact assessment. The decision was met with considerable outcries from legal experts and industry professionals questioning the fairness and transparency of such an action for a single firm (Elliott, 2014). Interestingly, the Information Technology Worker Program,[6] which allowed for eight different types of foreign professionals to enter Canada without a labor market impact assessment, was shut down in early 2004 for the very reason that the policy discriminated against smaller firms, which was deemed unacceptable under the Canadian Immigration and Refugee Act passed in June of 2002.[7] It was noted in interviews for the study that a majority of Vancouver based firms had to turn to NAFTA visa provisions more and more when looking to hire American workers, whether temporarily or permanently. However, the NAFTA status cannot be applied to foreigners who are not US or Mexican citizens. Chapter 4 of the text provides a more thorough examination as to how these increasingly limited short-term visa options have affected the Vancouver IT industry. The next section explores Chapter 16 of the NAFTA.

3.3.4 Chapter 16 of the North American Free Trade Agreement

The NAFTA established in 1994 was the first continental-wide trade agreement to contain labor mobility features. Chapter 16 of the NAFTA allowed for the preferential visa/status treatment of (1) business visitors; (2) traders and investors; (3) intracompany transferees; and (4) for 65 specific professional categories listed under the NAFTA. (See Tables 2.2 and 2.3 for a listing of permissible professions.) This class of professionals are called Treaty NAFTA (or TNs) which allows free movement of these particular professionals within the territories of Canada, the US, and Mexico.

NAFTA is, of course, only applicable to Canadian, US, and Mexican citizens. Spouses who accompany NAFTA status entrants are allowed to work if the spouse is entering on a trade, investor, or intracompany transferee status. Currently, there are no pre-entry labor certification screens nor any numerical limits to any of these four categories of highly skilled labor.[8] As of 2008, NAFTA work statuses are usually granted for three years, with the possibility of renewal according to some. This is especially true for Canadians and Mexicans seeking entry into the US. However, this is seen as a source of contention between US immigration attorneys, the US Department of Homeland Security, and foreign firms seeking entry into the US, and this issue is explored further in Chapter 5 of the text.

Overall, in the past 20 years since NAFTA has taken effect, it has undeniably been beneficial to many North American industries and their professional staffs by lowering trade barriers in capital, goods, services, and by facilitating the entry of certain types of highly skilled professionals. (Again, see Figure 2.6 for a graph regarding how many NAFTA statuses have been issued and flows over the past 20 years.) However, in some of the more innovative and cutting edge sectors, such as high-technology, biotechnology, and now the creative industries, the implementation of NAFTA has not kept up with the rapid pace of technological change and innovation (Vazquez-Azpiri, 2000: 805; Richardson, 2011; and Cryne, 2013). In fact, NAFTA may be argued to be an imperfect mechanism for the facilitation of Canadian high-tech and biotechnology professionals into the US. Thus, a major thrust of the study is directed at what are possible constraints of NAFTA provisions by exploring firms in Vancouver and Seattle in an effort to better understand to what extent the NAFTA status system has possibly impeded the free flow of professional workers in the Cascadia labor market.

3.3.4.1   NAFTA and labor mobility

The previous subsection provided a brief introduction to Chapter 16 of NAFTA, which allows for labor mobility of professionals and other business people throughout North America, namely Canada, Mexico, and the United States. However, the final interpretations of the impacts of NAFTA on its signatory nation states and each country's respective socio-economic classes of citizens are far from over. Still, one interpretation of the NAFTA provisions regarding cross-border movement of labor is that it allows more and more North American professionals to cross the Canada–US border with relative ease.

Since the signing of NAFTA in early 1994, Canadian scholars in particular have dedicated serious efforts to discussing the fact as to whether or not there is a brain drain of Canadian university educated professionals being lured to the United States in pursuit of better, higher paying jobs. These seemingly more lucrative job opportunities, coupled with the new more easily accessible NAFTA work statuses, give the impression to many Canadians that a much better future lies south of the 49th parallel.

However, despite the fact that NAFTA has been enacted for over 20 years, current literature suggests that regardless of these 'open borders', a majority of citizens in one country do not easily move to the now more open 'other' country, despite the relatively permissive labor mobility provisions. Helliwell (1999) notes that the highly skilled are much more mobile than the less educated. However, his research suggests that the highly skilled are, by an order of magnitude, more mobile within their own country of origin than between countries (Helliwell, 1998). DeVoretz and Iturralde (2001) found that most highly trained Canadians remained in Canada during the 1990s, exclusive of Canadian nurses. Their research presented a life cycle model that predicted staying patterns, which were consistent with the thesis that changes in life cycle events in a household conditioned the movement for highly trained Canadians' movements to the US. Thus, the most likely potential mover to the US is likely to be young, have a low discount rate, and expect an immediate and rapid gain in earnings. DeVoretz and Iturralde (2001) concluded by stating that this was exactly the profile of the knowledge worker who received payments in the form of stock options, physicians entering their specialties, and star academics.

The above review of previous research demonstrates that even with relatively open borders the majority of people tend to remain in their country of origin for purposes of work, as is also demonstrated by evidence from the European Union, as discussed in Chapter 2. Nevertheless, the labor mobility provisions under NAFTA are designed, ideally, to allow the freer movement of certain categories of business executives and certain categories of professionals, which include knowledge workers, without the bureaucratic problems of its predecessor, the H-1B visa. The general premise behind the NAFTA TN status is that it has potentially helped to create a more fluid North American border for working professionals. In fact, the TN status category now accommodates 65 specific classes of professions, most of which require an undergraduate degree. Vazquez-Azpiri (2000) argues that the newer TN category in NAFTA offers Canadian professionals wishing to work in the US four advantages over the H-1B visa. First, the applicant need not file a non-immigration petition with a US DHS Service Centre before entering the US; she or he can present all material/documentation at the POE or pre-flight inspection station. Second, Canadian TN applicants are not required to obtain approval of a labor condition application from the US Department of Labor (US DOL), which was mandatory for the H-1B visa. Third, unlike the H-1B visa, the TN category does not impose a maximum period of stay of six years, and TN status may be held indefinitely. Fourth, there is no limitation to the number of Canadian nationals who may be admitted to the US in any one year. Currently, the H-1B category imposes a limitation of 65,000 new admissions overall for fiscal year 2016, which began on 1 October 2015. Regardless of all of the perceived gains that the TN category was thought to bring, the H-1B visa was never phased out of existence since it is still one of the few temporary US work visas available to all other foreign nationalities other than Canada and Mexico.

3.3.4.2 NAFTA and the Cascadia region

Despite its claims that the NAFTA status facilitates 'preferential' entry into the territory of a state party, it has actually proven to be an imperfect and unpredictable mechanism for the entry of information technology (IT) knowledge workers to the United States (Vazquez-Azpiri, 2000; Richardson, 2011). From a regional perspective, this imperfection of the TN status may have tremendous impacts on the US cross-border area between Vancouver, BC and Seattle, Washington (namely the more northern geographical portion of Cascadia) since the high-tech sector continues to be an employment growth area for high-technology and related industries despite the cyclical nature of the regional economy. A well-regarded US immigration attorney, James Vazquez-Azpiri (2000: 807), based in the San Francisco Bay area stated:

> One development that has gone largely unnoticed in the national dialogue with respect to the IT industry's unsatisfied demand for knowledge workers is the emergence of Canada as an important repository of such knowledge workers. No one should be taken aback by this; Canada's geographical proximity, its cultural affinities to the US, the high level of technological education available at its universities, and the fact that it has its own well-developed IT industry make it seem quite natural that US IT companies struggling to meet their hiring needs should view qualified Canadian professionals as particularly attractive resources.

The above quote sets the tone for the future of North American labor needs especially when it comes to high-technology and biotechnology. Even though the citation is slanted towards the US economy, there is also a growing need for Canadian firms to tap American professionals, especially if the firm in question is highly integrated in the form of markets or monetarily with the US economy (Richardson, 2011). However, despite the growing demand for Canadian high-technology workers over the past few years, immigration attorneys residing along the more northern portion of the US west coast (Seattle and San Francisco) have seen a rising denial rate of TN admission applications for IT workers at US POEs since 2008 (Richardson, 2011). For instance, entry of Canadian software engineers into the US for employment under the TN category has proven to be quite a challenge. Specifically, it appears that one of the great obstacles for software engineers, and the attorneys writing the TN status application, has been demonstrating to the US DHS official at the POE that 'software' engineering is actually a true engineering activity and that it is recognized as one of the 65 professions allowed under NAFTA provisions. Although the number of NAFTA admission applications being approved at US POEs remains constant, there is still a concern among immigration attorneys in the Seattle and San Francisco areas that DHS POE inspectors do not allow a particularly flexible interpretation of job descriptions, especially to the degree required for software engineers and related professions (Richardson, 2011). Consequently, many Canadian software engineers and related professions have been refused entry into the US with what on the surface appeared to be a valid TN application, which was usually written by an experienced US immigration attorney.

Although records are kept regarding why TN applications are denied, they do not remain in the DHS's computer system for more than seven days (Richardson, 2006a). Indeed, there is a need for further research in order to determine the actual numbers of TN applications being denied at the POE and reasons why. Regarding some of the actual reasons behind these continued excessive denials at the US POEs, Vazquez-Azpiri (2000) argues that the US INS's stance towards software engineers, for example, may be explained in part from a deeply rooted belief by border officials as to a more traditional notion and definition of engineers as someone who builds tangible products and structures, employed typically in twentieth century manufacturing industries. This lies, of course, in stark opposition to a software engineer who usually writes code and designs whole systems of computer applications for many new, smaller, and relatively unknown firms. As well, the US DOL's Occupational Outlook Handbook states only engineers recognized by professional societies are the touchstone of true engineers, all of which have professional associations and licensing requirements. By contrast, many of the software engineers are extremely flexible in the type of work that they do, and job requirements evolve so quickly that it is difficult to reflect this in a handbook that comes annually (Vazquez-Azpiri, 2000; Richardson, 2011).

Additionally, from an educational perspective, NAFTA does not require that a person crossing a border on a TN status has exactly the same educational background as the actual TN profession being sought. NAFTA's provisions regarding labor migration state that the person in question must be in a discipline or field *germane* to the job duties typically performed by members of that profession [Appendix 1603.D.1 of NAFTA] (Vazquez-Azpiri, 2000). However, in the context of software engineers, Vazquez-Azpiri (2000) stresses in practice that TN applicants must show there is a complete congruence between the relevant engineering specialization and the degree being sought. Thus, holding a degree in computer science or for that matter, English, and requesting TN admission on one's baccalaureate degree as a software engineer opens the person up to a high likelihood of rejection by the DHS, and possesses great risk for US companies wanting to hire Canadian software engineers.

Overall, the TN category of Chapter 16 of NAFTA may be argued to have been a limited failure for Canadians seeking entry into the US, in the sense that it is not a wholly reliable, predictable, or consistently administered method through which to secure the services of Canadian IT workers (Vazquez-Azpiri, 2000). Specifically, Vazquez-Azpiri (2000) states that the TN category is deficient in three basic respects. First, it fails on policy grounds, especially due to the lack of an unambiguous policy inherent in the NAFTA to promote and facilitate the mobility of citizens of one state party into the next. For example, the provisions of NAFTA state that US DHS officials are to allow the mobility of legitimate North American professionals across the boundaries of said signatory countries, whereas, at the same time, to protect American jobs for the domestic labor force [Article 1601 of NAFTA]. Second, on structure, the TN category provides an over-rigid framework that lacks the elegance required to consider the heterogeneity of the IT industry's professional occupations. For example, there is no listing in the US DOL's Occupational Handbook for 'Web God' or 'Systems Genius', which are surprisingly common job title listings for many firms that work in the IT industry (Vazquez-Azpiri, 2000). Finally, on process, the internal rigidity of the reading of the TN category on the part of the US INS officers at the POE has become the most significant hazard involved in applying for TN admission. What this means is that the US DHS POE officer has an unfettered right to deny or approve TN applications at the US POE. Thus, the biggest contradiction of the TN category's new benefit, 'POE Adjudication', which was lauded for its presumed speed and efficiency and elimination of long months of waiting for either a visa approval or denial like that of the H-1B, is now proving to actually become the TN category's greatest obstacle.

3.3.5 The Canada–US Border: a Sieve or Shield under NAFTA?

This chapter has drawn attention to one particular characteristic of the Cascadia region, namely its growth as a corridor of knowledge driven industries, which includes high-technology and biotechnology. This is especially true when compared with the auto industry economy that drives Toronto–Detroit–Windsor and Buffalo–Niagara Falls. However, the study argues that inflexible implementation of NAFTA visa provisions has actually created an adverse impact on future possible growth of the region. In an era of an internationalized economy based on free trade, knowledge, and information, some nation states are clearly intensifying their efforts to tighten the cross-border movement of people, and the US may indeed fall into this category. Such a circumstance appears to be especially true not only for Canada's experience with the US in a post NAFTA era, but more importantly for the cross-border region of Cascadia. If this situation continues it could have tremendous repercussions on IT and biotechnology worker cross-border flows. Although Chapter 16 of NAFTA, in theory, allows for more fluid flows of professionals, NAFTA's actual range of comprehension and its rigidity is, in part, based on a previous age of manufacturing and more predictable employment structures. The adjudication process for TN admission issuances appears to not allow for any flexibility, which is often paramount in the IT and biotechnology industries. Since this is perceived as an impediment to Canada's perceived 'Brain Drain', relatively little official action has been taken on the Canadian side, for example, by using Articles 1606 and 2007 of NAFTA which focus on disputes settlement mechanisms (Vazquez-Azpiri, 2000; Richardson, 2010). Clearly, some additional professional classification could facilitate the movement of IT professionals as has been argued by the American Immigration Lawyers Association (Vazquez-Azpiri, 2000) and also Richardson (2011) and Cryne (2013).

3.4 CHAPTER CONCLUSION

The purpose of this chapter was to explain the growth in high-technology and biotechnology industries and labor in both Seattle and Vancouver as well as the many institutional apparatuses that regulate cross-border labor mobility. These institutional apparatuses range from the General Agreement on Trade and Services, to NAFTA and also domestic policies, such as the Canadian Provincial Nominee Program and the International Mobility Program, which may affect cross-border labor mobility within the Cascadia region. A fundamental to understanding the characteristics in Cascadia is the realization of how it is different from the other more traditional goods and trade oriented border zones, such as Detroit–Windsor, Hong Kong–Shenzhen, and the San Diego–Tijuana, Mexico, border regions. Cascadia may be characterized as an advanced service-based economy, which has developed rapidly over the past 30 years. One of the key characteristics of this so-called new economy is a continued need for foreign professionals and an unhampered ability for firms to move these professionals across borders.

The continued growth of the Cascadia region as a center for world-class high-tech and biotechnology commercial development draws attention to the key research question as to whether or not the Canada–US border is a constraint or facilitator to the symbiosis of more interactions between these industries in Vancouver and Seattle. Thus, this chapter helped to set the parameters for this key research question and leads into a focus of how key actors – high-technology and biotechnology firms, Canadian and US regulators, and immigration lawyers – all play influential parts in the possible development of this international high-technology region.

These actors and their various relationships will be explored more completely in Part II of the text.

NOTES

1. The book was originally published privately in 1975. The rights to publishing were bought out by Bantam Books in 1979.
2. The Inland Empire is centered around Spokane, Washington, and its region includes much of the Columbia River Basin, northern Idaho, northeastern Oregon, and northwest Montana.
3. It is essentially a connected chain of mountains, but each adjoining political territory calls its portion of the range by a different name.
4. The Canada–US softwood lumber dispute was originally settled under NAFTA dispute resolution proceedings in late 2004, although the US did not recognize the official arbitrators' ruling, which favors the Canadian position.
5. Although Boeing's main headquarters are located in Chicago, Illinois as of early 2001, Boeing's commercial headquarters still remain in Seattle, Washington.
6. The Information Technology Worker Program was commonly referred to as the 'Software Pilot Program' by the Canadian firms and government employees that were interviewed for this study.
7. This finding is based on a memo sent by Greg Anstruther, Corporate Service Manager at the downtown Vancouver office of the then HRSDC in January 2004 to three of the larger Vancouver firms included in this study. Essentially, the memo stated that the High Tech Project of 'fast-tracking' these firms' applications for foreign IT professionals would cease as of February 2004. The reason for this action was that it was deemed that this policy discriminated against smaller firms, which was now unacceptable under the then new Canadian Immigration and Refugee Act passed in June of 2002 (see appendix 5 in Richardson 2006a).
8. Initially, the US restricted Mexico to 5,500 professionals, which could enter under NAFTA per year. The US eliminated this quota in 2003. It should be noted that Mexico never reached the upper limits of this quota before 2003.

PART II

The empirical work

4.　The firms

4.1　INTRODUCTION

Chapter 3 ended by providing a three-part research approach to studying the role of the international border in Cascadia, focusing on the activities of firms, trade regulators, and immigration attorneys involved in cross-border labor movements. This particular chapter is the first of three that explores the results of the empirical data for this study. Specifically, the chapter reviews and assesses 30 interviews conducted with human resource executives and vice presidents of primarily high-tech and biotech firms based in Vancouver and Seattle as well as key R&D facilities of Seattle and San Francisco/Silicon Valley firms situated in Vancouver, Canada. It focuses on their experiences moving professionals back and forth across the Canada–US border as part of a growing continentalism under NAFTA and in light of a post 9/11 world. The chapter closes with reflections on the overall findings and ends with a brief conclusion.

4.2　THE TYPES OF FIRMS SURVEYED AND THE QUESTIONNAIRE

A total of 25 firms were interviewed for this study. Specifically, eight large firms (four based in Vancouver; two based in Seattle; and two based in greater San Francisco/Silicon Valley[1]) were included that had over 200 employees or more at the time of the interview; seven mid-sized firms (all based in Vancouver) that had between 100–200 employees at the time of the interview; and ten small-sized firms (nine based in Vancouver and one based in greater San Francisco/Silicon Valley[2]) were included that had between 1–99 employees at the time of the interview. Additional material came from the web pages of the surveyed firms, company reports, and published materials on the high-technology and biotechnology industries of Vancouver, BC, Seattle, and the Greater San Francisco area, which included Silicon Valley. The focus of the firms interviewed ranged from electronic gaming, to aquatic equipment, to financial software, and even timber production. The variety of Vancouver firms (both headquarter firms and R&D facilities) reflected the region's character of supporting a diversity of new industries, which include environmental and marine technologies, software, new media, and biotechnology. Over the past 20 years, there was a growing interest on behalf of major high-tech firms headquartered in both Seattle and San Francisco/Silicon Valley to access the domestic talent associated with these Vancouver industries as well as to make use of the facilitative Canadian immigration policies when securing foreign talent. This was accomplished by establishing major R&D centers in the greater Vancouver area. Vancouver firms (both headquarter and R&D facilities) were selected primarily from *Business in Vancouver*'s listing of 'top high-tech and biotech firms in terms of employment' over select years from 2002–15. Dr. David Edgington, the author's former PhD advisor, facilitated initial contacts for four of these Vancouver firms. The Vancouver based firms were approximately three to four magnitudes smaller than the Seattle and San Francisco/Silicon Valley based firms interviewed. Specifically, the Vancouver based firms included in this study ranged from employing 2 people to over 2,000 people worldwide.

In contrast, the Seattle and San Francisco/Silicon Valley based firms employed between 10,000 to over 50,000 people worldwide. Importantly, the two Seattle based firms had only recently been operating in the greater Vancouver area for less than 20 years. The first firm acquired the holdings of a major Canadian based company in the late 1990s, and the second firm made a deliberate strategic investment in the greater Vancouver area in the 2010s by establishing R&D facilities within the city region. A foreign trade specialist with the then Department of Foreign and International Trade, Government of Canada, procured initial contacts within both Seattle firms. Dr. Richard Florida of the Martin Prosperity Institute, Rotman School of Management, University of Toronto provided access to one of these Seattle firms. The two San Francisco/Silicon Valley based firms, by contrast, acquired formerly Vancouver based firms over 25 years ago, remaking these firms into their 'Vancouver' R&D facilities. For the most part, both California headquartered firms encouraged the autonomy of the acquired R&D facilities by wanting to facilitate and capture a particular 'creative spirit and culture' unique to Vancouver. Thus, the chapter will categorize all Vancouver based and San Francisco/Silicon Valley based firms as 'Vancouver Firms', and all Seattle based firms with R&D facilities and activities as 'Seattle Firms'.

The questionnaire was administered to senior managers and covered a range of areas relating to each firm's experiences with operating in a North American space, and included a range of questions. These questions focused on the background information of each firm; whether or not the firm was mobile throughout North America and/or the world; the levels of international personnel within the firm; the firm's experience with attaining visas and work statuses; the employees' experiences with crossing the Canada–US border and attaining visas/statuses, especially in light of post 9/11 security measures; overall reflections on the Canada–US border in relation to the firm's activities; what would happen if cross-border mobility was impeded; and how important is the region of Cascadia to the firm's success.

These topic areas explored three of the four areas of the general literature covered in Chapters 2 and 3 of the study; specifically, how the concept of clusters and innovation applied to the Vancouver and Seattle urban areas, whether geographically they had a strong likelihood of being connected as a cluster, and would ideally contribute to greater innovation within the Cascadia region than if a firm operated just on its own (see Gertler, 2002). Additionally, a closer look at how and why the firms hired and moved employees around North America helped to provide a more refined understanding of North American labor mobility and immigration in addition to their experiences with the various institutions that are supposed to facilitate labor mobility and immigration. The next section explores findings from the interviews, categorized into various key themes and topic areas.

4.3 STRATEGIC CONNECTIONS BETWEEN THE US, CANADA, AND THE REST OF THE WORLD

This section will cover the many strategic connections that firms had within Cascadia, the US, Canada, and the rest of the world.

4.3.1 Sales Connections to the US and Beyond

This section will now explore the types of markets that firms had who were interviewed for this study. Question number 1 from the firm survey best addresses this topic area. Specifically, the question asked the following: Can you discuss the various sorts of activities that your firm engages in Canada/US or beyond? Do these interactions with firms on the other side of the border (sales, inputs, finances, joint research, and so on) require the movement of your employees? If 'yes', for what reasons, and what types of employees move across the border?

4.3.1.1 The Vancouver firms

Based on the responses to question 1 of the interview survey, all Vancouver firms (both headquarter and R&D facilities) reported that a primary component of their sales, client, marketing, and support services were dedicated to the US, but also European markets. Specifically, firms recorded that anywhere from 25 percent to 95 percent of their sales were found within the US market (this included California) as a whole rather than merely the local Cascadia region. In fact, crossing the international border to access markets was a key feature of their connections to clients. One human resource executive for Firm-V1 put it succinctly,

> As you know, we are involved in software sales. 95% of our customers are in the US. We visit our people [in the US] for pre- and post-sales. The entire development and implementation of our product is here in Canada, but our sales are in the States. Thus, our people move [across the border] for the purpose of sale. (Firm-V1)

However, in addition to targeting the whole US as a primary market, many firms had also stressed that they were really *global* in their outreach (Firms-V3, 4, 7, 8, 9, 10, 11, 12, 13, and 14). Some had operations in Germany and Japan (Firm-V3) and, as well, general sales and client bases in South America, Europe, and Asia. In fact, one firm (Firm-V4) explained that even the Vatican was one of their clients!

Due to the sophistication and high costs of some of the firms' products (running into the hundreds of thousands to millions of dollars), four firms (Firms-V3, 4, 9, and 10) emphasized that Western Europe was equally as strong a market for their products and services as the US. In fact, for Firm-V3's products, which included sophisticated alternative energies, Europe had the most active market as compared to other world markets due to Europe's advanced environmental laws and policies. Additionally, another firm (V8) noted that although it carried out a considerable number of projects with Microsoft (based in Seattle), the US market, overall, was very difficult to break into for a new Canadian firm of their type. For example, the interviewee noted that the culture of this firm's particular industry (banking) was based on very old connections with clients, which sometimes went back over a century. A vice president for this firm explained,

> . . . Our core is Canadian, but most of our revenue is international. We have four customers in the US – one credit union and three banks. The main banking firms in the US are mature firms with old [and loyal] connections. For example, we work with Microsoft to develop a PC based banking system. We have the market in Canada as the biggest service banking software system . . .
>
> We are doing a lot of work with Mexico and other firms in South America and South Africa right now. 90 percent of our people work with product development and professional services. Their job is to travel [internationally]. For example, we are currently implementing our products in Africa on behalf of American Express. We are also doing an extensive amount of work in Asia. (Firm-V8)

The above quote alluded to the issue that even though NAFTA had helped to eliminate trade and investment barriers between Canada and the US, cultural barriers found within various domestic industries still existed. The interviewee for Firm-V8 noted that they had a difficult time breaking into the US market not because the company was a 'Canadian Firm', but because the particular industry that they worked within went back over 200 years in the US and took pride in its strong culture of loyalty and tradition towards other firms that had been in the business a long time. Thus, this firm had found opportunity within the domestic market of Canada in addition to the emerging economic systems of Latin American and Asia.

However, the above firm (Firm-V8) was somewhat of an anomaly, having such a large client base domestically within Canada. For the most part, all other Vancouver firms stressed that they were strongly dependent on the US and Western Europe for much of their client base, significantly far beyond the local Cascadia region. Additionally, Mexico and South America were seen as promising emerging markets. Although Asia had considerable promise in the mid-1990s, two firms (V4 and V8) noted that at the time of the first round of firm interviews in the mid-2000s, the region was still recovering from the Asian Flu of 1997, and was seen as somewhat dormant, economically. Table 4.1 shows for all the firms interviewed percentage breakdown of sales, indicating the distribution of markets within Cascadia, Canada, California, the greater US, and the rest of the world.

As shown, these results reveal that the sales connections in the main lie far beyond the Cascadia region alone.

4.3.1.2   The Seattle firms

As discussed earlier, both firms interviewed could be considered large multinationals with global sales markets. Thus, the two Seattle firms usually had strong local nodes or clusters of sales team distributed in key locations throughout the world. However, for Firm-S1, with its significant Canadian operations, especially in BC, and its close proximity to Seattle, the human resource manager noted that there was a considerable amount of cross-border activity for sales personnel and knowledge workers connected to various Canadian projects within the firm. She explained,

> We also have something called commuters. These commuters move back and forth to work on projects that include technology and engineering. (These kinds of things.) They go for maybe a couple of days. Sometimes Monday through Friday, then they go home for the weekend. Driven by what the business needs. Sometimes the expert is in one country, and is needed in the other country. Sometimes these are business trips. If a person is going to fix something, then we need work authorization. (Firm-S1)

Table 4.1   Selected distribution of sales for firms interviewed*

Firm	Cascadia	Canada	California	Rest of US	World
Vancouver 1	<1%	<1%	15%	80%	5% EMEA, Philippines & Australia
Vancouver 2	Strategic partnership with Microsoft	13% includes Asia Pacific	NA	68%	19% EMEA
Vancouver 3	NA	NA	Strong partnership with urban localities	45%	55%
Vancouver 4	Regional management of services with Seattle	25%	NA	30%	25% EMEA 15% Asia Pacific 5% S. America
Vancouver 5	NA	NA	NA, but HQ in California	NA	NA
Vancouver 6	50%	>10%	40%	>5%	NA
Vancouver 7	NA	NA	NA	40%	38% Europe 18% Japan 4% Other
Vancouver 8	<10%	40%	20%	10%	10% EMEA 10% South America
Vancouver 9	<5%	<5%	NA, but HQ in California	50%	40% Europe, Australia, S. America
Vancouver 10	<5%	10%	NA	45%	45% Europe & Australia
Vancouver 11	<5%	<5%	NA	45%	45% Europe & Australia
Vancouver 12	NA	<10%	NA	40%	45% Europe & Australia 12% Japan
Vancouver 13	<5%	<10%	NA	50%	45% Europe & Australia
Vancouver 14	<5%	<15%	NA	40%	40% Europe & Australia
Vancouver 15	NA	NA	NA	NA	NA
Vancouver 16	NA	NA	NA	NA	NA
Vancouver 17	NA	NA	NA	NA	NA

Table 4.1 (continued)

Firm	Cascadia	Canada	California	Rest of US	World
Vancouver 18	NA	NA	NA	NA	NA
Vancouver 19	NA	NA	NA	NA	NA
Vancouver 20	NA	NA	NA	NA	NA
Vancouver 21	NA	NA	NA	NA	NA
Vancouver 22	NA	NA	NA	NA	NA
Vancouver 23	NA	NA	NA	NA	NA
Seattle 1	NA	>5%	NA	60%	20% Europe 10% Asia 5% Other
Seattle 2	NA	NA	NA	NA	NA

Notes: * Firms V-15–V-23 were early stage biotechnology companies that at the time of the interview and did not have active sales of firm products.
EMEA: Europe, Middle East, and Africa.

Source: Based on company reports and materials and interviews with author

4.3.2   The Hiring of Foreign and Domestic Personnel

4.3.2.1   The Vancouver firms

Question number 2 from the survey asked: Do you recruit employees from Canada/the US/around the world? If 'yes', from what universities or labor pools do you seek potential employees? The question helped to explore how Vancouver firms became more international in their products' reach. Additionally, as these firms increasingly faced global competition, they were often forced to recruit from outside the local labor market to obtain a professional workforce. Consequently, as indicated in Table 4.2, anywhere from 6 percent to 85 percent of professionally highly skilled staff within all Vancouver firms interviewed were considered 'foreign', or 'not Canadian'. This included general professionals, technical staff, and executives, who had developed considerable expertise and 'know how' outside of Canada, and these skills were vital to the firm continuing to succeed. To facilitate the recruitment of non-Canadian professional workers, Vancouver Firms-V2, 5, and 9 had even hired full-time immigration specialists to orchestrate the hiring and retention of foreign employees. This was in addition to dealing with immigration lawyers when these professionals were needed.

One immigration specialist working for Firm-V9 discussed its recent hiring practices,

Table 4.2   *Places of origin for the professionally highly skilled*

Firm	Cascadia	Canada	California	Rest of US	World
Vancouver 1	NA	NA	NA	NA	NA
Vancouver 2	35%	25%	15%	10% (US executive team)	15%
Vancouver 3	25%	35%	>10%	15% (US executive team)	15%
Vancouver 4	40%	20%	10%	20%	10%
Vancouver 5	20%	45%	20%	>10%	>5%
Vancouver 6	80%	16%	4%	>1%	>1%
Vancouver 7	10%	5%	25%	25% (US executive team)	35%
Vancouver 8	NA	70%	NA	7%	23%
Vancouver 9	40%	25%	20%	6%	10%
Vancouver 10	25%	20%	30%	10%	10%
Vancouver 11	<10%	25%	20%	20% (US executive team)	25%
Vancouver 12	<10%	40%	10%	20%	20%
Vancouver 13	15%	45%	NA	15%	25%
Vancouver 14	40%	40%	NA	8%	12%
Vancouver 15	20%	40%	NA	15%	25%
Vancouver 16	15%	25%	35%	15%	10%
Vancouver 17	20%	30%	NA	15%	35%
Vancouver 18	25%	25%	10%	20%	20%
Vancouver 19	55%	25%	20%	NA	NA
Vancouver 20	40%	30%	NA	10%	20%
Vancouver 21	45%	25%	NA	15%	15%
Vancouver 22	40%	30%	10%	10%	10%
Vancouver 23	35%	20%	15%	10%	20%
Seattle 1	80%	>5%	NA	15%	5%
Seattle 2	<10%	<20%	NA	<10%	70%

Source: Based on company reports and materials and interviews with author.

We have upwards of 1–2 international people coming into [Firm-V9] a week for work. For example, last year with 400 people hired, this included graphic designers, software engineers, producers, development directors, and language translators in quality assurance. Essentially, 25 percent to 35 percent of the firm is dependent on international hires. Our business is tied to being able to hire internationally. We cannot find these skill sets in Canada. Within this 25 to 35 percent, 75 percent of it is from the US. Many of these people are from southern California and they worked for our competitors as producers, directors, and top graphic designers. The other sources of our people are from

Great Britain, Germany, and France . . . We compete with the movie industry for talent . . . Basically, our recruitment model is 75 percent directly from
universities (green) that come in and grow with the company, and 25 percent
of the hires are at the higher end. For example, people with gaming experience,
entertainment, TV, people working for Academy Award winners etc., and senior
software engineers. Our head office, worldwide, is in California. We also have
studios in Tiberon, Florida. We have two studios in the UK one near London –
a large one, and one near Manchester. We also have affiliate studios in Germany,
Spain, and Australia. (Firm-V9)

The preceding quote also alludes to the hiring of top talent from around
the world for senior positions in addition to professional software develop-
ers. For this particular firm (Firm-V9), the elite international hires were
at the project manager level and included US Academy Award recipients.
The interviewee also noted that the majority of their executive staff was
from the US, which was a common theme for 7 of the 23 Vancouver firms
(Firms-V2, 3, 5, 7, 9, 11, and 16). In fact four Vancouver (Firms-V2, 3, 7,
and 11) interviewed had an entire 'US team', which made up their executive staff. The immigration specialist for Firm-V2 noted that American
executives had a much wider range of experiences than their Canadian
counterparts due to the larger US markets and a perceived stronger culture
of entrepreneurship than in Canada. Additionally, Firm-V2 reported that
the US executive talent pool provided ten times the number of applicants
as compared to the Canadian market. Other interviewees stressed that
almost all founders of firms interviewed were Canadian, but when the firm
had reached a particular point in its development, it often had to bring
in not only a seasoned Chief Executive Officer (CEO), but also a team
of executives who could continue to move the firm forward, and on to
the next level of development. A human resources manager for Firm-V7
explained,

All of our executives are now from the US. However, William Van Reikswick
is from Vancouver. (He's the founder of company, and he sits on the board.)
Essentially, the US executives have more experience within the industry. It is a
pretty tightly knit community, and we have to tap from other industrial clusters
[which are usually located in the US] if not the actual person we want [who is
usually from the States]. (Firm-V7)

The need to hire computer professionals and professionals in general was
a constant for all firms interviewed. Vancouver based firms stressed that
if they needed high-level professional staff then they were often forced to
recruit from other industrial clusters located throughout North America.
The largest 'clusters' that these Vancouver firms drew from was the greater
San Francisco Bay/Silicon Valley area and the Greater Los Angeles/

San Diego region when it came to hiring both high-tech and biotechnology professional and executive talent. However, one firm (Firm-V5) noted that they usually drew from Ottawa more than any other region since that is where the largest supply of appropriate professionals, in this particular industry, were located. The human resource manager for Firm-V5 noted,

> We hire some folks who are local. We often look at people with transferable skills. Also, we hire many people from Toronto and Ottawa. Regarding the tech labor pool, there are many more people with the skills that we need coming from Ottawa, than elsewhere. We DO recruit from the States, for example, California, Boston, Maryland, and Texas [and] in the past, from Europe and Asia. Now, with the downturn, it takes too long to get someone from Asia and Europe, and it costs too much. Nortel was our customer, but we also competed with them [for employees]. We also compete with other small firms for employees. For example, Alcatel is our customer, but we also compete with them for employees. (Firm-V5)

The above quote helps to emphasize that not all talent in the Vancouver high-tech sector was found outside of Canada. (See Table 4.2.) However, perhaps more appropriately, it was often stressed that it was very difficult to find seasoned talent from just the local Vancouver labor market. The immigration specialist for Firm-V9 explained,

> Overall, it is a lot easier to hire locally. For example, it cost about $25,000US to relocate people, even from Seattle. We would like to hire Canadians . . . it's less stressful, easier on the wife, etc. See, [when they relocated to Canada] everything is a question, groceries, banking, you name it . . . But all of my job is dedicated to our foreign employees [and helping them get situated in Canada]. Our business dictates that if we are going to grow and be the biggest and the best, then we need the world's best brains. We are a global company. (Firm-V9)

This quote reveals the truly global focus of many Vancouver firms interviewed for this study; and there were also reflections of this situation in the needs of the majority of the 23 Vancouver firms interviewed. The other Vancouver firms had a primarily North American focus, but needed to hire across the border, nonetheless. (See Table 4.2.)

The next subsection explores the Seattle firms' hiring practices. The next section then turns to the firms' reasons for moving their highly skilled professionals across international borders. The chapter then moves to understanding the firms' experiences with different types of visas and experiences at actual ports of entry between Canada and the US.

4.3.2.2 The Seattle firms
Seattle firm 1 (Firm-S1) reflected carefully on the hiring of local and domestic versus international labor. Despite the fact that Firm-S1 was a

large global company, the senior human resource manager for Firm-S1 stressed that they emphasized hiring locally first, before looking to other labor markets. She expanded,

> Lower down in the corporation [with more routine jobs], we can find [people] in the domestic workforce. In fact, we have a policy to hire locally! Only if we cannot find someone local, do we begin to look internationally . . . Occasionally, the best person for the job in the US may be a person in Canada. We also have people working on projects as teams. Hence, we need to move people around based on their abilities and the different stages of the project.
>
> With international assignments, the time period is usually five years, then they return. The reason is social security and taxes. A person cannot be out the country for more than five years. Certain countries have agreements with the US. It is allowed that that person pays US social security, but then after that, they must start paying into the host country's tax and pension systems. (Firm-S1)

In sum, the general skills needed for the success of this firm's operation could be found for the most part with local and regional labor markets wherever this firm had operations throughout the world (see Table 4.2).

For Seattle firm S2, (Firm-S2), it was a considerably different approach. Much of this firm's growth and future was dependent on being able to hire and retain the very best, wherever they may be found in the world. As mentioned previously in this section, Canada had a robust community of highly regarded high-tech professionals, so it was only fitting that this firm established an R&D facility immediately over the Canada–US border in the greater Vancouver area. One executive noted that it was sometimes hard to convince people to relocate, even from Vancouver to Seattle, so the R&D facility created career opportunities for western Canadians in Canada. Another driving reason for establishing an R&D facility for Firm-S2 was access to domestic and foreign highly skilled students that recently matriculated from computer science, mathematics, engineering, statistics, or a related discipline from the University of British Columbia and other highly regarded Canadian universities. Due to progressive Canadian immigration laws, many of these foreign students were able to remain in Canada after graduating. Similar to the findings of Richardson, Florida, and Stolarick (2012), there was also a strong element of west coast style multiculturalism found in Vancouver, and for many of the firm's new foreign employees, this element of Vancouver's character was a big draw. There was also a 'westcoastness' work culture found in Vancouver, which could be described as a laid back, yet productive, approach to getting things done (Richardson, 2006b; Richardson et al., 2012), unlike the apparent intense work culture found at headquarter operations in Seattle. Finally, it was noted by both firms that it was generally easier, faster, and more predictable to hire and retain the foreign highly skilled in Canada as compared to the US.

4.3.3 Reasons for Movements of Professionals across International Borders

This subsection summarizes the reasons why firms in Cascadia move their professional workers across the international border upon responses to the question posed on markets, sources of finance as well as recruiting practices. Overall, 13 out of the 23 Vancouver firms interviewed depended absolutely on some connections to the US (not Canada) as part of their global strategy, in addition to maintaining the lifeblood of the firm. Even during the aftermath of the 2008 financial crisis and post 9/11, all Vancouver based firms maintained strong links to the US. South America was important for three firms interviewed (Firms-V4, 8, and 9), with considerable growth potential slated for the next 20 years. However, links to continental North America were more dominant, overall. In fact, the responses of all the Vancouver firms interviewed revealed that anywhere from 10 percent to 35 percent of staff were traveling somewhere in the US at the time that interviews were conducted. Thus, these patterns suggest that international mobility, although not necessarily focused on the Cascadia region, per se, was an important part of the raison d'être of the Vancouver high-tech and biotechnology firms. The international focus for all Vancouver firms interviewed mandated that many of their key employees should be able to move legitimately across the international borders without complications and undue delays. However, as will be shown shortly, this was particularly difficult in light of certain NAFTA provisions and interpretations of NAFTA as well as post 9/11 security concerns.

Travel requirements of many key personnel from all firms interviewed ranged from anywhere from a half day meeting in the US to a permanent move abroad. The majority of reasons for travel into the US and other foreign countries were for the purpose of product sales and after sales follow-up (Firms-V1, 2, 3, 4, 8, 10, 11, 12, and 14). Other firms recalled that their employees crossed international borders for collaborative firm research, which required anywhere from a week to a few years of relocation (Firms-V3, 5, 6, 7, and 11). One firm (Firm 6) moved an entire team of employees when they had to complete a project in the US. Due to the nature of their work, it was always difficult to determine how long they would be in a foreign country. As expressed, many firms noted that they hired many foreigners, especially Americans, and they relocated permanently to Canada (Firms-V3, 4, 5, 7, 9, 10, 11, and 16). One executive explained,

We were all tired of living in Silicon Valley. Since the majority of our executive team was Canadian, we said, 'Why don't we move home?' There was a gaming industry coming on in Vancouver, and we figured we would be able to hire locally for a lot of the talent positions we were going to need. We were concerned that we would lose some of our people who would want to stay in Silicon Valley when we made the move, but everyone wanted to come to Canada, even the Americans. (Firm-V10)

The human resource manager for Seattle Firm-S1 stressed that for the most part only managers, executives, and highly specialized employees moved globally within the firm's operations. She stated that the need for experience and pay were big motivators for these executives and managers to want to move internationally within the firm, but there were also other reasons. She explained:

Most traffic is from Canada to the US, for reasons of career enhancement. The power is here [in Seattle], so those wanting to move up come here! Sometime people move for reasons other than money. For example, the health care system is better in Canada. Canadians do not have to pay out of pocket . . . We do not really have a Concept of the 'Citizen of the World', which you mentioned. I mean my parents never gave a shed of thought to living anywhere else in the world than America. Moving around is difficult and stressful so we put people through an acculturalization process, even with moving to Canada. (Firm-S1)

The above comment helps to paint a rather wide, but bounded picture of the range and opportunities offered to this Fortune 500 firm's employees around the globe. Most interestingly, there was a strong emphasis on the fact that this Seattle based firm could hire locally for much of their work that needs to be done in any part of the world. But, by contrast, a more specialized project, and a more sophisticated job, may require a foreign based professional to come to the US. Additionally, unlike the toy manufacturer, Mattel, or Levis Strauss, the jean manufacturer, this particular Fortune 500 firm did not move their professionals around the world on a routine basis. In fact, as the human resource manager stressed, Firm-S1 moved their employees internationally only once, noting that this particular practice was very often hard on the person and his/her family.

For Seattle Firm-S2 there were considerable efforts to move their newly hired foreign employees based at the R&D facility in Vancouver to Seattle for meetings and conferences on a weekly to bi-monthly basis. Thus, these Vancouver based employees frequently found themselves traveling across the Canada–US border for face-to-face meetings and engagements in Seattle. The next section will cover the many visas and work statuses that foreign employees had to attain before crossing the Canada–US border for purposes of work.

4.4 VISAS AND WORK STATUSES

While the firms interviewed for this study recruited from many different countries, and also sent sales employees to many countries, the analysis focuses specifically on problems encountered when crossing the Canada–US border. This portion of the chapter is meant to provide a greater understanding as to what types of visas a firm used to move international employees into Canada or the US as well as moving employees across the Canada–US border. Overall, firms reported that they used a range of visas and work statuses when moving people back and forth across the Canada–US border. This subsection explores these work statuses and visas types from both a Canadian and American perspective.

4.4.1 The Vancouver Firms

Firms in Vancouver reported that they used many different types of visas and work statuses when moving their employees into the US in addition to moving American hires into Canada. Most importantly, the TN status for NAFTA (explained in Chapter 3) was seen as one of many options for the Canadian firms interviewed. General professional immigration arrangements, the Provincial Nominee Program (PNP), Express Entry (EE), the International Mobility Program (IMP), which NAFTA statuses are a part of (for US and Mexican citizens), and short-term work statuses (up to three years) were all possible options for Vancouver firms looking to bring foreigners into Canada for purposes of work. The following paragraphs explore the pros and cons of these various visas and work statuses, as perceived by the firms surveyed. The chapter then turns to examine the firms' experiences with moving employees into the US for purposes of work according to various visas.

4.4.1.1 Recruiting employees from the US

Prior to 2005, a majority of the Vancouver firms interviewed used something called the Information Technology Worker Program, which interviewees referred to as the 'Software Pilot Program'. This program exempted the applicant from a labor market review and fast-tracked the foreigner's application in a matter of weeks. The program was highly lauded for its expediting nature, and the fact that the hires were not subject to the then Human Resources and Skills Development Canada (now the ESDC) review on an application-by-application basis. However, in February of 2004, this program was cancelled, which led to confusion, if not panic, for many of the firms. Two human resource specialists for Firm-V5 and the immigration specialist for Firm-V9 explained,

Sometimes we use the Software Pilot Program, but this does not cover all of our needs. It was fantastic! We once had fast processing, but it was nixed in February of this year (2004). In June, the HRDC [Human Resources and Development Canada] and Skills Canada merged to become the HR'S'DC [Human Resources and Skills Development Canada emphasis added], and now they require us to [specifically] post position and salary wages [when we want to hire a non-Canadian]. We cannot post salaries due to competition! . . . Historically, the HRDC has been very good, but now (ever since they got that 'S' in their name) they are slowing us down!

For example, we have several Academy Award-winning people on staff. In fact these people directed very successful movies, but their applications were rejected by HRSDC! They told me that I did not 'recruit' for this position. This [particular] person [that we want to hire] is being fought over by Americans [in the gaming and film industries] for him to work on their projects. They [former HRSDC] tell us, 'Oh well, you didn't search Canada for these credentials,' but there are not that many local Academy Award-winning people, let alone in Canada . . . or the world for that matter. *I am trying to work with them so that they understand our needs.* [emphasis added] . . . We want to hire these people, now we need to look at moving them in under NAFTA (eyes roll). (Firm-V9)

The software pilot program is cancelled. This was very short sighted on the part of the Canadian government. Also, spousal hires were attached to this. This was a broad and progressive approach, and they cancelled it. (Firm-V5)

We used to be part of a high-tech project, essentially, we could get the job done in 2 hours. They took this away in late February, and this hit us hard. Now, the person is delayed for about 8 weeks. This greatly affects the scheduling of our projects . . . (Firm-V5)

The above comments help to capture some of the desperation that the Vancouver firms experienced in 2003–2004 with the elimination of the 'fast-tracking' aspect of recruiting foreigners for some types of jobs within high-tech industries. Additionally, there was general frustration felt by the managers of the Vancouver firms regarding the complete lack of understanding on the part of the former HRSDC (now ESDC) towards the basic hiring needs and human resource compositions of these Vancouver high-tech firms. The immigration specialist for Firm-V9 noted that since the former HRSDC had eliminated this 'fast-tracking' system, his firm then had to use NAFTA TNs when bringing American citizens into Canada. However, NAFTA was seen as a secondary option when there was the more efficient fast-tracking system in place. The reason for NAFTA's 'secondary status' was that prior to 2008, NAFTA statuses were only good for one year, compared to the three-year visa given under the now eliminated fast-tracking system. Two other firms (Firms-V4 and 7) noted that NAFTA was perhaps more suitable if the firm needed to bring an employee from the US quickly. The firm would then change the person's status once he/

she was in Canada. Also, Firm-V7 hired American medical doctors, as researchers, and PhDs in the sciences. Due to their highly specialized areas of professional expertise and education, these professions were more easily admissible under NAFTA. Since 2008, NAFTA statuses can be issued for up to three years, so many firms are now using NAFTA statuses much more frequently. Historically, the use of NAFTA statuses for Americans coming into Canada was seen as a temporary 'fix' (due to the status's former short-term nature) until a firm could organize the paperwork for a longer-term visa, work status, or even permanent residency.

The longer-term Canadian visas for foreign workers included a three-year work permit, which was frequently subject to labor market review in order to determine if a Canadian citizen was equally qualified or not. This type of visa was generally avoided since it was subject to time delays in processing for up to six months and required a considerable amount of time and paperwork on the part of the firm applying. After the Immigration and Refugee Protection Act and Regulations (IRPAR) had been implemented for about six months in the early 2000s, Citizenship and Immigration Canada (CIC) received a number of complaints from Canadian firms and individual applicants that the new Act was too slow. It then became a concern that the new regulations were deterring possible foreign professionals from seeking work and/or immigration to Canada. The Provincial Nominee Program (PNP), created in 2003, was a response to this concern. (See Table 3.2 for a general description of some of the program's key attributes.) Essentially, the PNP is a provincially administered program, which fast-tracks the applications of predetermined professionals that provinces have a shortage of (e.g. certain types of researchers, scientists, business professionals with expertise in trade, and so forth). This program had been in effect for over ten years and three firms (Firms-V7, 9, and 10) said that it was fantastic compared to the old system, although the immigration specialist for Firm-V9 reported a number of criticisms. He explained at length,

> Well, we are now looking at NAFTA for Americans . . . We are also looking at the Provincial Nominee Program . . . The pros of it are that it is a good avenue for getting people into the country quickly based on our established relationship. The cons are that is it really necessary to become a permanent resident right away? It is almost too soon. The Reason: we get HRSDC approval, the foreign employee gets a three year work permit. After 2 years they want to stay in Canada. They begin to apply for permanent residency. However, it takes them about 1.5 years to figure it out – especially if they come from California. Whenever they come to Canada. In a sense, you know that American attitude of, 'Well I'm going to Canada, like I'm going to the colonies' . . . after a while, they get over it. They begin to like it here. This is when the wives start talking to the husbands saying. 'You know, it is a nice place to live, the schools are really

good, [it is] a great place to grow up. Why don't we stay?' However, with the PNP the person has to apply within three months of arriving. We, as the company, have to cover the application fees and the legal fees, which is between $5–$8,000 per couple. We like to see how they work out within a year and a half. It is hard to assess within three months. The company has to get them going on it right away. (Firm-V9)

Finally, many of the firms lauded the recently created 'Canadian Experience Class', which allowed for a foreign hire to apply for permanent residency after one year on the job. They noted that this took much of the anxiety away from the foreign hire regarding the eventual renewal process of the work visa (usually every three years). As well, it saved a tremendous amount of work and time for the human resource staff within the firm that employed the foreigner. However, one firm noted that once the foreigner acquired permanent residency, the person was able to work in Canada without a visa. Thus, the foreigner was no longer beholden to a particular firm for employment. This concerned three firms since they stressed that they go through considerable effort and expense to hire foreign professionals, and they would hate to lose the employee to another firm that did not put up the expense and time to successfully conduct and execute an international hire.

The above commentaries illustrate that the firms in Vancouver had a variety of visa options when bringing staff from the US to Canada, and that each visa type – fast-track, NAFTA, the PNP program, and the Canadian Experience Class – had varying levels of complexities. NAFTA TNs, historically, were often seen as a secondary choice compared to the much more comprehensive and longer-term options offered by other types of Canadian work and immigration statuses. However, when Canada's immigration laws were rewritten in June of 2002, NAFTA, by default, became a primary choice for many firms hiring people from the US, since all other immigration options were bogged down in lengthy applications, and there was a dearth of Canadian government immigration staff, in addition to closures of certain components of the fast-tracking pilot programs for foreign hires. Now that NAFTA statuses may be issued for up to three years, the status is seen as a primary choice for Americans employees rather than a 'Band-Aid' foreign work status, as was historically the case.

The next subsection explores the Vancouver firms' experiences with various visas and work statuses when sending their employees (and potential employees) into the US for purposes of work.

4.4.1.2   Sending employees to the US: the Vancouver firms' experience

The majority of Vancouver firms used a TN status when sending their employee to the US to work for the short term. They also used L-1 statuses, which were considered an intracompany transferee under NAFTA. Many found that sending the person as an intracompany transferee, rather than a new hire TN, was easier to administer through the US POE. The following are reflections by the firms on their experiences with various US work visas and statuses,

> We use L-1s,[3] T-Ns,[4] B-1s[5] (for US meetings), with proper letters they are not that tough. In fact, I have never had a rejection. However, I must include more and more evidence with the employees' applications. The US office is sales and marketing, and the Canadian office is R&D, we need them to move across the border for our raison d'être.
>   . . . In terms of the US, we have anywhere from 20–30 people crossing the border at any one time for purposes of [on-site] client R&D, services sales, etc.
>   Overall, I am fine with it. However, blanket L-1s would be easier. They (the US DHS port people) know us, so it is not that difficult when we apply for L-1s. It would be a lot simpler if we could have a blanket L-1 petition. But, a firm must have over 1000 people and generate a certain amount of revenue to fall into this category. We cannot do this due to our small size. (Firm-V8)

> If it is just for a meeting, then we need a B-1. If it is for work, then we need a TN. It depends on the individual and what he/she is doing. We always have to be asking ourselves if the professional fits into the category we are trying to use. (Firm-V4)

> Going into the US, we try and use the H-1B, since it leads to a green card. The TNs and the L-1s are temporary . . . with the B-1 visas, you need letter of intent if it is for a short conference. With a TN, the assignment needs a beginning and end date. With the TN the expectation is to try out the person in the States, and then hire long-term, which is the H-1B. (Firm-V5)

Overall, despite the confusion and anxiety of sending people into the US, all firms noted that on most occasions they succeeded in sending their people for work across the border and into the US. However, roughly 10 to 15 percent of the time, they experienced delays and possibly being turned back at the border and being sent back to the firm for additional information.

4.4.2   The Seattle Firms

The two Seattle firms interviewed had considerably different experiences than the Canadian firms when seeking visas and statuses for their foreign employees when recruiting and transferring them from Canada. As well, in certain circumstances, both Seattle firms had similar experiences when seeking statuses or visas for their foreign employees and at other times these two firms had very different needs and experiences. The following section shall explore these issues in detail.

4.4.2.1 Recruiting and transferring employees from Canada

Both Seattle based companies recruited and transferred many employees from Canada to the US. For the most part, there was nowhere near the visa or work status options for newly recruited foreigners entering the US as compared to Canada. Nor was there the relative ease and reasonable predictability in obtaining the visas or statuses such as the PNP or Canadian Experience Class. In fact, the American experience was seen as more limited, cumbersome, and anxiety ridden when it came to the Seattle firms seeking US work statuses for their Canadian and international employees.

For the most part, work statuses for the Canadian employees of both Seattle firms were temporary in nature, and ranged from anywhere from just one day to three years in time. Chapter 3 reviewed many of the visa and status options for foreign professionals seeking entry into the US for work. The US's H-1B visa was the most frequently sought after since it allowed a foreigner up to three years in the US, and this could then be renewed for another three years.

One Seattle based firm (Firm-S1) discussed that it used every type of visa or work status that it could when moving employees and new hires across borders. The human resource manager noted that her firm had a very good attorney that she turned to regarding these matters. She discussed at length the different types of visas the firm used when bringing foreigner employees into the US, in addition to the pros and cons of each.

> Regarding immigration into the US, if someone is coming in short-term, I look to see if I can use NAFTA. We also look at 'Ls' or intracompany transferees. For Ls, they must have one year of experience with the firm. I then look at the H-1Bs, but we have to get labor market certification. The reason is a hierarchy. If it is a project where the person is a commuter and working short-term, then I look at NAFTA. I can prepare a letter, explaining what it is we need, and the cost is less than $100.
>
> I feel that people abuse NAFTA for the longer term stays. In the last couple of years, everyone started bringing people in on H-1B, they maxed out [the capacity limit set by the US Federal Government], so we then had to start turning to NAFTA. . ..We had a guy I want to bring in from Uruguay, so NAFTA was not an option for him. We used NAFTA when we ran out of H-1Bs for Canadians. This is low cost.
>
> If I cannot use NAFTA, then I use Ls. We have a preference of 'Ls' over 'Hs'. With Ls for intracompany transferees and if a manager or executive to get a green card does not require a labor certification. If not a manager or an executive, they could still transfer in under an L-1A. They must have specialized

knowledge not found in the States. So it is not just a firm employee. Those people, under the L-1B, we must do a labor certification. So this is why we draw the line with localizing. We really only localized high-level executive managerial positions because it is so difficult to get a labor certification . . . We are also looking at controlling costs. Moving people around is very expensive. (Firm-S1)

The rather lengthy quote from Seattle Firm-S1 helps to demonstrate the range of options with US work permits, almost all of which are temporary in nature. Additionally, the yearly capacity set by US congress on H-1B visas was an issue; and since the US economy had slowed post 9/11 and after the 2008 financial crash, US Congress was somewhat skittish about admitting large numbers of foreign professionals into the US. Most importantly was that cross-border labor flows and the subsequent time and cost was a significant issue even for a large Fortune 500 firm; one with ample funds dedicated to expert immigration attorneys and lobbyists. Thus, these factors were not just a concern for small high-tech start-up companies.

The second Seattle firm (Firm-S2) only recently started moving employees between their R&D facility and their operations in Seattle. An executive noted that it was difficult to immediately move foreign employees based in Vancouver to Seattle, even for a meeting. So, due to this challenge, human resource staff developed complex plans for each Vancouver employee regarding possible US visa needs. Based on this strategy, the first visa acquired for almost all Vancouver employees who were not US citizens was a B-1 visitor's visa. He noted that the firm had the best success in securing 'B-1' visas, which were used for meetings in the US. He also noted if the person was skilled enough, after a year of working in Vancouver, the person might be eligible for an L-1 as an intracompany transferee. Finally, there was also the highly coveted H-1B visa, but this took anywhere from six months to two years to secure on average. In the meantime, the firm encouraged their Vancouver based employees to apply for Canadian permanent residency through the Canadian Experience Class after working for one year at the Vancouver facility, if they were not Canadian. This allowed a considerable number of their Vancouver based foreign employees to have the option of remaining in, or returning to Canada, as a permanent resident and eventually securing Canadian citizenship.

Overall, the results of the interviews focusing on Vancouver firms sending employees to the US, and the results of the Seattle firms recruiting and transferring employees from Canada, suggest that the US immigration system was more complex and less certain than recruiting employees into Canada. In fact, the US side of the border appeared to be a maze for all Cascadia firms, whether a large 100-year-old Fortune 500 firm or a small start-up firm, especially after 9/11.

The study now turns to exploring some of the strategies that the firms used in order to get across the Canada–US border despite the growing impediments in a post 9/11 world.

4.5 EXPERIENCES WITH CROSSING THE CANADA–US BORDER

All firms interviewed had at least one interesting story to tell about the experiences that they had moving their employees across international boundaries, especially the US.

4.5.1 The Vancouver Firms

Each firm remarked that they found considerable variability between the various US ports of entry along Cascadia when it came to their employees crossing into the US. Five firms (Firms-V1, 2, 3, 8, and 13) noted that they had 'problems', which ranged from having requests for additional information by border officials, to more intense questioning and longer wait periods than what was once the 'norm' (i.e. before 9/11) at the Pacific Peace Arch Land Border crossing; but that the Vancouver International Airport and the Pacific Highway Truck Crossing were almost never a problem. Firms-V2, 3, 5, and 7 even had employees turned back for various reasons ranging from 'not enough information' to particular scrutiny for 'darker skinned employees' and perhaps more interestingly 'white women'. This will be discussed in more detail in an upcoming section. In fact, a human resource manager for Firm-V5 summed up some of his many experiences well when it came to moving his employees,

> It is always an adventure moving across the Canada–US border. It is basically the roll of the dice, and it depends on what kind of day they are having. Our folks have been prevented from entering. Since 9/11 there is a lot more questioning regarding our products. There is a lack of understanding as to what we do. About 10% of our people experience lengthy delays and need to return to the company for another letter.
> . . . There was one of our employees who had to meet with a customer. She was waiting for a flight to the US and was rejected. She was sent back to Vancouver. There was no rhyme or reason for why the officer refused her. She was on a letter of intent [usually a requirement for a business visitor's visa]. So I was not sure exactly WHY she was refused. (Firm-V5)

The Vice President for Firm-V1 explained that his firm had difficulties moving his employees across into the US even prior to 9/11. However, following 9/11, the firm began to use a seasoned US immigration attorney, and subsequently they had not found any difficulties with the Canada–US border. He explained,

> Most of our crossings are at the airport. Where we had problems is at the Pacific Border Crossing. However, we have never had a refusal. There is a bit of a problem with [port of entry] supervisors giving [what seems to be] too much power to front-line employees. We use immigration attorneys. It cost us about $3,500 to $4,000 [per application], to make sure that everything is in order. (Firm-V1)

By contrast, another human resource manager exhibited considerable frustration towards the US immigration authorities and their seemingly arbitrary nature when it came to admitting some of her firm's employees into the US. She stressed,

> . . . This is also especially important for our sales people, we need to know that they will get across the border without a problem. Otherwise, we could lose a multi-million dollar deal. These deals and meetings take months to set up. The government gets caught up in the process, and does not understand how sensitive it is for our firm to move across the border. Like I mentioned, millions of dollars are at stake in us crossing the border without a hitch. There should be a level of support coming from the government. (Firm-V3)

Despite these indications of cross-border hindrances, and particular frustrations as to the apparent variability and even randomness of cross-border checks, many of these firms continued to grow and succeed as global companies. The older and relatively more established firms discussed the fact that the US immigration officials between Seattle and Vancouver were beginning to recognize each particular firm's name and their employees when they crossed the border. Seven firms (Firms-V1, 2, 3, 4, 8, 9, and 11) stressed that this 'familiarity' was a good thing, since this familiarity with company names and employees made passing across the border a little easier, although it did not guarantee entry into the US. However, one human resource manager reflected on the fact that since her firm had developed a 'good' reputation as a viable firm, with major Fortune 500 company firms as its competitors, it now had to do everything 'above board' since the firm's reputation was at stake. This included hiring attorneys to scrutinize visa and status applications, and to make sure that everything was properly in order before their employees attempted entry into the US. She explained,

> . . . being listed on the NASDAQ is a plus when crossing the border. We are a public company [and this gives us credibility with border officials]. Our clout gets bigger as we grow. However, as we grow, we must protect our relationship

with the border officials. We are becoming a large company and must protect our reputation. We cannot get away with errors like we used to. Now, we always use attorneys and myself for our employees when we send them over the border. Part of my professional role is to know when to go to our attorney [in these circumstances]. (Firm-V4)

All firms noted that, prior to 9/11, it seemed that everyone 'fudged' when it came to seeking entry into the US. An executive for Firm-V8 explained,

> We used to use B-1s [short-term business visitor visas rather than work visas] a lot when we went over the border. No one really enforced it [in the past], and everyone fudged a lot of the time when they were going to trade shows and conferences. (Firm-V8)

Firm-V6 was most articulate about taking radical approaches when seeking entry into the US. (See the quote from Firm-V6 in Chapter 1 of the book). This demonstrates the often clever and determined approaches that Canadian firms often have to take in seeking entry into the US for a contract with a US firm or governmental group. Additionally, a Canadian attorney (who was interviewed for the material on immigration attorneys in Chapter 6), who had many larger multinational firms as clients as well as smaller firms, summed up some of the differences between the two types of firms, and how large firms often use smaller firms when they need something done quickly. He explained,

> Not everyone deserves NAFTA treatment. I work with Blue Chip companies, and they want to maintain their good corporate image. So, they only hire people who are permissible under NAFTA. They are not going to jeopardize their due diligence. They also have the money to pay higher wages, so they get better people. However, they also have larger overheads. Smaller and mid-sized firms have not been in it long enough (nor do they have the resources) to worry about due diligence, so they are not going to care. Large firms know this. Hence, large firms subcontract out to smaller firms when they need to get things done quickly. It is essentially like what Wal-Mart does with its subcontractors. (C-A6)

4.5.2 The Seattle Firms

Despite the fact that both firms were large multinationals with considerable operations in Canada, both experienced difficulties and 'hold ups' similar to the smaller Canadian firms when their employees who are Canadian citizens sought entry into the US for purposes of work. The human resource manager for Firm-S1 explained,

> We have had our moments. We had someone turned away [from the border] this week. He was fairly high level and was seeking an intracompany transferee

status. The person at the border asked for some of our financial records and also a corporate hierarchy depicting how [our firm in] Canada was related to [headquarters in the] US. I pulled all of the materials together for him. He went through the next day to a different DHS officer with all of the materials requested, but he [the officer] did not ask for them. He just issued him the status [emphasis added] . . . We have had people stopped – especially if they cross the border frequently. They [the border officials] just say 'no' without an explanation. One [employee] did say that the officer was really nice about it, but still said, 'No.' (Firm-S1)

The above section helps to reflect on some of the experiences, in general, that the firms have had when crossing into the US. Although the vast majority of firms interviewed have not had major problems with their employees crossing into the US since 9/11 there was now a strong addition of anxiety, tension, and confusion for these firms and their employees when traveling into the US. For the most part, both Canadian firms and the two American firms had nowhere near the levels of frustration with the Canadian ports of entry when bringing in American employees, or executives, into Canada, although they did emphasis that the Canadian ports of entry were becoming more 'security and enforcement' driven after 9/11.

In part from differences in experiences in crossing into Canada and the US, firms also reported that there was variability and randomness to the interpretation of NAFTA rules by different POE officers, which the firms felt were not warranted under NAFTA. Additionally, some firms realized that there was considerable variability *across* different border crossings, and that firms would often use this to their advantage, based on the situation. Finally, firms stressed that they had to use attorneys more frequently, due to the POE officers' increased intensity towards the review of NAFTA applications, and supporting documents, especially after 9/11. All of these factors have caused increased time, work, stress, and money for these firms in their additional requirements. The following section explores in more detail the strategies used to move employees across the border and the types of visas and work statuses the firms reported using to achieve this as well as their outcomes.

4.6   FIRM STRATEGIES WHEN CROSSING THE CANADA–US BORDER

Firm strategies about how to cross the Canada–US border in a more closely regimented post 9/11 world ranged considerably. These strategies included more paperwork, the hiring of firm personnel whose job was solely dedicated to the recruiting of key foreign employees and moving existing employees across borders. Some companies adopted more 'rogue-like' strategies, which included using POEs to one's benefit and others even adopted what might be considered a strategy of using 'fraudulent entries'. This section explores these strategies in some detail.

4.6.1 The Vancouver Firms

Every firm interviewed stressed that over time, more and more paperwork was needed to document their employees' reasons for entering into the US, as well as recruiting employees into Canada. For instance, the immigration specialist for Firm-V9 noted that even if their employees were going to Seattle for a basketball game, they had to have letters from the firm stating their intention of entering the US if it was a firm-sponsored event. He noted,

> Borders are getting tighter in both directions. Everyone must have a letter and explain why they are traveling. Our people [who are] going down for a basketball game, even to a Washington town, everyone must have a letter as to why they are traveling. (Firm-V9)

Additionally, all firms stressed that they hire attorneys to go over all of their visa and work status applications. The smaller firms noted that this was very costly for them since an attorney would charge from $1,500 to $5,000 per case to prepare the necessary paperwork for a visa or work status application. The Operations Manager for Firm-V6 explained,

> We are looking at getting [our] people permanent work visas . . . It is very expensive! The attorneys, the permit . . . We need better and more detailed information. We started with an immigration lawyer in San Francisco who charged $350 an hour. So, we looked around closer to home, and found someone [in the area]. (Firm-V6)

The need over time to use legal advice led three firms (Firms-V2, 5, and 9) to hire a human resource professional whose sole purpose was dedicated to arranging the paperwork for the hiring of foreign professionals and helping them move across international borders (usually into the US) for purposes of work.

> All of my job is dedicated to our foreign employees . . . (Firm-V9)

It should be stressed that Firms-V2, 5, and 9 were mid-sized to large firms (total worldwide employees numbers ranged between 175–over 2,000 employees) with considerable budgets for such a professional person.

However, smaller firms often had to use an attorney, and many firms, as expressed by Firm-V6 above, noted that these immigration lawyers put a strain on the expenses of the firm. This circumstance led one of the smaller firms (Firm-V8) to use one of the firm's executives, who was a lawyer by profession, as a quasi-immigration attorney when a firm employee needed paperwork for a work visa or status application into the US. The Vice President for Administration for Firm-V8 explained,

> The law firm we use is expensive! They charge about $1,500 for an average US visa and $1,000 for a TN. Now I do a lot of the applications since I am an attorney by profession. (Firm-V8)

Vancouver based firms also talked about the difference between the POEs, and how they used the ports to their advantage when moving people back and forth across the Canada–US border. One human resource manager for Firm-V7 noted that there was a considerable difference between the rural and urban ports of entry which straddled BC and Washington state. For example, one of their professional employees had difficulties getting residency visas for his children at the Oosoyoos border crossing, which could be considered a rural port of entry in the interior of BC, so that they could attend school in BC. The family and the firm's human resource staff had to sort out the problem when the employee finally arrived at the Douglas border crossing, 40 minutes directly south of Vancouver, BC. The human resource manager stressed that if the employee had passed through the Douglas border crossing originally, rather than Oosoyoos, or come through the Vancouver airport, this problem would most likely not have occurred since the officials at these more urban border crossing dealt with similar family problems for foreign employees almost every day. Another interviewee noted that his firm (Firm-V8) sent their employees through the truck border crossing a day or so ahead of time to pick up their L-1 visas and then they fly out of Vancouver airport a day or so later. However, formal procedure required that one is supposed to be heading to the US for the designated (and only the designated) purpose of the NAFTA status upon seeking entry into the US. The interviewee responded as follows,

> When we have to send our employees out through the airport, we send them through the truck crossing the day before to pick up the NAFTA status. Then we send them through the airport the next day. No one asks (US port of entry officials). It has not been a problem. (Firm-V8)

This particular procedure, however, was not permitted under NAFTA, as will be discussed in Chapter 5 (The Immigration Officials). However, it was still done by Firm-V8, and it appears that it was a classic 'don't ask, don't tell' type of situation. Overall, Vancouver based firms have had to develop some sort of strategy in moving their people back and forth across the Canada–US border, and quite clearly, some of these strategies involved ingenious ways of using the geographic variety of border crossings in the Cascadia region.

4.6.2   The Seattle Firms

Both Seattle firms reported that their only concrete strategy to navigate the complexities of the Canada–US border was to work closely with their attorney. Both firms had considerable financial resources to pay expert immigration attorneys to work on cross-border matters. However, the human resources manager for Firm-S1 stressed in a previous section of this chapter that even their high-level managerial staff had difficulties with the border. Perhaps most interesting was the fact that Firm-S1's Canadian employee who was turned back at the US border went back the very next day to a new US DHS officer, and he did not even request any additional materials than those presented to the first US DHS officer from the previous day. The new US DHS port of entry officer just issued the work status. The human resource manager for Firm-S1 noted that she and executive financial staff went through a considerable effort to prepare the requested materials within a single afternoon, and she was somewhat surprised that these materials were of no relevance to the 'new' US DHS port of entry officer. This experience helps to bolster the attorneys' claims reported later in Chapter 6 that US POE officers' reviews and requests for additional information have been rather random and without consistent logic.

The next section explores what these firms would do if existing levels of cross-border mobility was impeded, or stopped – as many found out for approximately 24 hours immediately following the 9/11 attacks on the east coast of the US.

4.7   WAS THE CANADA–US BORDER AN IMPEDIMENT TO A HIGH-TECH CLUSTER BETWEEN SEATTLE AND VANCOUVER?

The above frustrations with the Canada–US border might lead one to think that the Canada–US border was a serious impediment to firms moving their people around North America and inferred that NAFTA acted more as a shield than a sieve. So, when asked the question: Is the Canada–US border an impediment to a high-tech cluster between Seattle and Vancouver?, surprisingly, many of the firm respondents, after a few moments of reflection, said that overall, it was not more of a shield than a sieve. Despite all of the negatives, reported earlier, that the border brought to moving people post 9/11, it was considered still relatively open. Importantly, NAFTA, overall, appeared to provide many more options for companies than before it existed. Some of the firms explained,

> No, because of NAFTA, it is now much easier to get across. There is the possibility of creating a cluster (in Cascadia). In fact, some of our people go to Seattle for new jobs. (Firm-V7)

> All in all, it [the border] is not really a big deal. The number of incidences are small. We could avoid many things if we knew what to expect ahead of time. Maybe under the new blanket of security, things will be more difficult. Will there be big problems if there was a special US visa requirement for Canadians? We need to think about how we facilitate trade without compromising security. (Firm-V1)

> Specific to Cascadia, many of our employees need to travel to Microsoft to work on joint projects (software integration projects). We also have employees based in Seattle who travel to Vancouver on a regular basis for meetings, etc. Some of these employees could be based anywhere, but they choose to be located in Seattle in order to be close to our Vancouver office and family and friends. (Firm-V2)

> To date I have not found that this is so. The border is keeping things in check. In regards to 'impeding', the Canadian side [not the US side] is slowing us down with approvals! (Firm-V9)

> Well, sometimes we do struggle when it comes to moving our people across. However, from a bigger picture, the border keeps Canada Canada, and the US the US. I mean, without the border all of that Canadian culture and creativity would be lost! (Firm-S2)

So, despite all of the misgivings about the border, and the perceived inadequacies of many of the visas, there appears to be ample opportunity for knowledge worker mobility, both within Cascadia and within continental North America. Overall, the findings may appear as somewhat of a paradox. Apart from the comments made above, in an upcoming section, Seattle Firm-S1 expressed the preference to have freer mobility throughout Canada and the US with its employees. Interviewees tended to be more critical of US border controls than those on the Canadian side of the border. Yet, it should also be stressed that seeking entry into Canada was not without its problems. In fact, throughout the study, interviewees often heralded Canadian border practices as an example for the US to follow, but some firms also stressed the fact that Canada could be just as difficult as the US; and, indeed, Canada was becoming more enforcement driven, especially after 9/11, as opposed to its frequently perceived facilitative nature.

4.8 WHAT WOULD HAPPEN IF CROSS-BORDER MOBILITY WAS IMPEDED?

Each firm interviewed was asked the question: What would your firm do if cross-border mobility was even more impeded than now between Canada and the US? This was used as a way of gauging the importance of the Canada–US border on firms' activities. As mentioned, this actually did occur between Canada and the US for about 24 hours immediately following 9/11. In the months following this catastrophic event, the mobility of people and goods often slowed to a crawl across the border due to tougher security and inspection procedures. These actions had considerable negative effects on both economies, and if at all, helped to remind both Canadians and Americans how important a relatively open border was between the two countries for trading purposes. This section explores the reflections and anxieties of just how firms would respond if they could not move employees easily across the Canada–US border.

4.8.1 The Vancouver Firms

As indicated by patterns of sales, financing, and technology, all firms interviewed were closely embedded in such a way between both the US and Canada to an extent that they depended on the mobility of their people across the border to keep the links and networks active throughout North America. Indeed, each firm had a special and unique arrangement with how it tied and engaged itself with the US. This ranged from having headquarters in Vancouver, but calling itself an 'American' company (as was the case with Firm-V5) to receiving considerable infusions of capital from the US and Germany, but being based in Burnaby, BC (Firm-V3); and finally to being a solidly anchored Canadian firm, but relying heavily on US and other foreign markets for firm accounts (Firm-V8). Thus, with 23 Vancouver firms interviewed, there were 23 unique ways to develop relations and networks throughout the US and the world. However, each firm was absolutely dependent on the US for firm survival, if not success. It could also be said that both Seattle firms depended upon their Canadian activities and the greater Vancouver area's unique attributes as global firms. Consequently, each firm interviewed noted that if cross-border mobility was impeded, it would have a very negative effect on their business. Surprisingly, even by 2015, the majority of the firms interviewed still did not know what they would do if they could not move personnel between Canada and the US for purposes of business. Three firms (Firms-V2, 3, and 4) reported that they would have to resort to video conferencing. However, in the same breath, they stressed that this strategy would only be partially successful since they really needed to send people over the border as part of their operation (for sales, R&D, meetings, and so on). The human resource specialists for Firms-V2 and 3 explained,

> ... I wonder about this myself, sometimes! We would have to rely on remote communications, such as phone and video conferencing; make better use of remote access tools; and hire more people locally (e.g. consulting and sales). (Firm-V2)

> Don't know. We try and be proactive. I have a spread-sheet with all of the people who are not Canadian citizens. We try and get them to be Provincial Nominees and permanent residents. I push our people to get going on this. We try and be more proactive, and do things in-house. It is very expensive to use attorneys. It will become more and more challenging if they keep tightening up the border. We might do video conferencing, but we need hands-on engineers [crossing international borders] for much of what we do. (Firm-V3)

Although one other firm (Firm-V4) noted that they would also respond with technology, the human resource specialist also stressed that they needed to have an international pool of applicants, since their types of work were global in nature. Thus, they had to be able to choose from the best people in the world. Firms-V5 and 7 were quite emphatic about how absolutely necessary international talent was to the success of the firm. They explained,

> We probably could not do business! We need face-to-face interaction. We could rely on video conferencing. We would have to hire locally, which would limit us since we thrive on the very best [from around the world]. We would probably have to relocate the company to the US or bring everyone to Burnaby ... (Firm-V4)

> Lobby the government and join forces with other high-tech firms in our HR needs. Some folks may want to hire domestically, but we will miss out on some world-class talent. For example, we hire people from the Middle East, which includes Israel, Saudi Arabia, and Iran, [as well] as Eastern and Western Europe, and the US. We experience this already when [Canadian] professors leave for the States and take their good students away [with them]. We can only develop to the point that we have access to intelligent qualified people. (Firm-V5)

> Don't know ... maybe a sales office in the US? We would then have to hire those [American employees] in the US. However, we must hire internationally

to do the types of work that we do. We are dependent on their knowledge. (Firm-V7)

Another interviewee for Firm-V8 noted that his firm had a worldwide reach with the firm's products and 'shutting down', or 'drastically impeding' the mobility of people across borders, especially the Canada–US border, would have dire consequences on his firm. He explained,

> We would be dead! We would have to break contracts that we are under. We would have to buy new companies and become a US firm, and do a majority of the work via email. However, product development and new customers must go with people! We would then have to find implementation US partners, and these Americans would have to come to Canada for training and company interactions. (Firm-V8)

Perhaps most emphatic is the response from Firm-V9 to this question,

> IT WOULD CRIPPLE US! (Firm-V9)

The above remarks help to uncover the anxious quandary that human resource professionals and executives continue to have over the tightening and possible closures of international borders, especially between Canada and the US. These quotes reveal that although firm managers had thought about these uncomfortable possibilities, there was little they could do in order to avoid the possible situation of a complete border closure without a complete restructuring of the firm, or extensive use of teleconferencing in certain cases. As some firms exclaimed, it would more than likely completely destroy their abilities to operate and execute their purpose.

4.8.2 The Seattle Firms

As stated, both Seattle firms were of considerable magnitudes larger than the Vancouver firms, and with this size differential, the human resources manager for Firm-S1 stressed that if the Canada–US border was seriously impeded or even closed, then the impacts would go beyond that of the firm and likely impact the entire North American economy. She explained,

> We would see an impact on the economies of Canada and the US. Essentially, it would be to the detriment of the economy! It would affect our ability to manage trade throughout North America. This would really impact the Canadians who work for us. We are partners together. We would have to become separate functioning entities. There would be a detriment on both sides. (Firm-S1)

The comments further reinforce the importance of the smooth operations of the Canada–US border for all Cascadian companies. As has been demonstrated, even larger firms would be impacted by border closures, and this would have a major impact on both the Canadian and US economies.

In sum, while the material from the interviews suggests that Cascadian firms' major linkages are well beyond the region's own borders, the international Canada–US border plays an important role in the success (or otherwise) of these companies. The next section explores some of the specific impacts of 9/11 on the ability of firms to move their employees and new hires across the border.

4.9 MOBILITY OF NORTH AMERICAN PROFESSIONALS IN A POST 9/11 WORLD

The event of 9/11 had a direct and lasting impact on the mobility of all people crossing international borders. The question: Have the incidents of 9/11 affected your employees' experiences in crossing the Canada–US border?, tried to capture these experiences. This section focuses on some of the impacts from this catastrophic event on the firms interviewed, and how they responded.

4.9.1 The Vancouver Firms

All Vancouver firms interviewed felt the effects of 9/11 in different degrees. The firms stressed that, for a few months following 9/11, travel for their employees was impeded considerably. Additionally, the negative economic impact was perhaps even more detrimental to the firms since, as mentioned previously, all conducted a significant portion of their business in the US. From a more technical perspective, all firms interviewed stressed that there was more attention to paperwork for visa applications. For example, small details about their employees' applications that were never a problem before 9/11 could sometimes now prevent the employee's entry into the US. This additional scrutiny sometimes led to missed flights for some of the employees of the firms (Firms-V1, 5, and 6). Overall, there was considerable anxiety for all firms and their employees after 9/11 when seeking entry into the US. The immigration specialist for Firm-V2 explained,

> I had two employees turned back with deficiencies in their application for things that had never been an issue before. One was assessed by a very inexperienced [port of entry] officer, and the other employee was assessed by a senior officer who was training a new officer. Very recently I have experienced some additional problems with credentials, e.g. employee reference letters and university

transcripts. I am not sure if this relates to a general 'stepping up' of processing enforcement. Overall, I have few examples of employees running into problems, but there is always a threat, so employees tend to be anxious about applying for visas [at the border]. When something goes wrong, it tends to go very wrong! (Firm-V2)

Also, since 11 September 2001, the firms experienced increased scrutiny when they moved Americans through the Canadian POEs between Vancouver and Seattle. One human resources manager for Firm-V4 explained,

We have problems with Canadians coming across the US land borders. In addition there is confusion between the [former] HRSDC [Human Resource Skills Development Canada] and the CIC [Citizenship and Immigration Canada] as to what is acceptable. For example, service engineers coming into Canada. They ask very intense questions about their backgrounds. This primarily takes place at the Peace Arch–Douglas Crossing. This is a recent phenomenon. We have had two such incidents in the past month. The person was coming up from the Seattle branch office to service a Canadian customer. We do not have the human resource capabilities here to provide the services needed for our Canadian customers. There is a depth of knowledge and experience that our US engineers have over the Canadians. Thus, we need to pull staff from Seattle. However, there is a growing inability to predict what will happen on both sides of the border when we are moving people back and forth. (Firm-V4)

In regards to the vexed issues of racial profiling, the comments from firms were mixed. All firms interviewed thought it was going to be a problem, but for many, the post 9/11 border was not as severe as expected. However, four firms (Firms-V3, 4, 8, and 9) stressed that they had found additional attention being focused on their Iranian employees and Firms-V8 and 9 noted that there was always some anxiety with South American employees. Firm interviewees explained,

Within the last six months, it has become much tougher to move across the border. Just this week, one of our employees who is Muslim and with darker features tried to cross at the Windsor–Detroit border. He is a permanent resident, but they went ahead and took his fingerprints and mug shots, and said he did not have the correct paperwork. He stayed the night in Canada at a hotel near the border. I faxed him additional paperwork and he managed to get through the next day. If he did not get into Detroit, Michigan, our whole IT system might have come down. (Firm-V3)

Yes, we feel a lot more scrutiny than prior to 9/11. For example, we have an employee who was born in Iran. He is a mechanical designer for the company, and a Canadian citizen. However, he must explain every time he goes back and forth across the border. He usually goes though the airport, but he finds the questions to be intense and inconsistent. We always say to tell them the truth. (Firm-V4)

Now after 9–11, [everyone] must be cautious when crossing the border. Our people born in Colombia [and South America], and possibly people with pilots' licenses [have attracted attention]. Regarding Arabic people, it is not as big a problem as I thought. If they hold a Canadian passport, then it is easier. (Firm-V8)

We have had a few people turned away or delayed. Don't know why. For example, employees not included in our visa waiver program have a hard time. We had to get clearance from either the US Consulate or go to the Canadian Consulate. This slows things down. For example, an Iranian has to go to the US Consulate to get into the States to go to the Canadian Consulate, but they must get clearance through the US Consulate here in Vancouver to enter the US. This also happens a lot to South Americans. For example, Colombians and Brazilians come here for film school, or for Emily Carr. If we hire them, they then have to temporarily enter the US, which is hard to do. It is very hard to bring them into Canada. We have to change their study permit to work permit. Regarding the Middle East you ask? We do have some Israelis. (Firm-V9)

Additionally, one firm noted that immediately following 9/11 they hired about a dozen foreign professionals who were working in the US and were afraid that their work visas would not be renewed due to the current 'climate' in the US. The human resource manager for Firm-V5 explained,

After 9/11 we brought people here from the US who were concerned about renewing their work visas in the States. These were primarily Indians and Chinese. We landed 10 people as a result of this. (Firm-V5)

Perhaps most disturbing are the actual physical searches that have occurred after 9/11. Two firms (Firms-V2 and 7) explained that they have had employees searched before they boarded flights bound for the US. One of the firms (Firm-V7) noted that their employee who was traveling to the US for a clinical trial was actually strip searched. Most interesting to note is that both of these employees were women of northern European heritage. The immigration specialist for Firm-V2 commented,

. . . I didn't receive any feedback that employees were being scrutinized more closely, except for one, who was very embarrassed when she was searched at an airport gate prior to getting on her plane. She was sure it was because she held a Canadian passport. (Firm-V2)

Finally, the project manager for Firm-V6 stressed that the difficulties along the border were not just related to 9/11, but often much more closely tied to the North American economy. He frequently found US POE officers denying entry to Canadians in order to protect local US employees and their jobs. He stated,

> ... The reason being is that the [North American] oil industry is very competitive. For example, the Gulf of Mexico is full of divers, but they cannot get jobs due to the slump in the oil industry [up to 2004]. This started long before 9/11; much of this is related to the economy. However, the bulk of our problems have happened after 9/11. This may be due to training and awareness after 9/11. It seems like they are checking things more thoroughly. However, 9/11 is not just the reason that these things are happening. (Firm-V1)

The above comments paint a broad and somewhat mixed picture as to the varied experiences that the firms have had as a result of 9/11. Interestingly to note, although many have experienced increased scrutiny when seeking entry into the US many ethnicities and groups that had nothing to do with 9/11, for example Iranians, women, and South Americans, had received the most scrutiny and invasions of privacy compared to other groups. Additionally, although 9/11 slowed movements of people considerably, one firm reflected that increased scrutiny of non-US citizens across the border was also directly tied to a slowdown in various sectors of the US economy. Hence, although 9/11 did have an impact on the movements of people across all North American borders the increased security towards 'targeted' groups associated with 9/11 was not apparent in the interviews. The effects of 9/11 appeared to create more of a 'dragnet' effect, with repercussions for all crossing international borders, perhaps for those who may be seen as not being able to defend themselves.

4.9.2 The Seattle Firms

The two Seattle firms had different experiences and reflections on the Canada–US border in relations to their personnel. Firm-S1's reflections were those of a larger mature company with a strong human resource and legal presence to draw from. It had some negative incidences, but overall, it had not had any major problems, post 9/11. The human resource manager explained,

> Nothing that I can specifically cite, but I feel that things have tightened up. I cannot define how. We continue to have a good relationship with the border. We have had a few incidences, but it is working! (Firm-S1)

In contrast, Seattle Firm-S2 noted that they sometimes did have difficulties moving their Vancouver based employees across the Canada–US border. An executive noted that negative experiences could frequently be attributed to a level of overconfidence exhibited by their employees when questioned by US POE officers. He explained,

> For many of our foreign employees, this is their first real job. For some of them, this leads to a sense of overconfidence sometimes when engaging with border officials. We try and encourage them to be as polite as possible with the US border people. Sometimes the border officials will make them wait for an hour or more before they allow them into the US. (Firm-S2)

The next section shall explore various ideas proposed by firms interviewed as to how to make the experience of crossing into the US (and Canada) more predictable and less anxiety ridden.

4.10   RECOMMENDATIONS FOR IMPROVING THE EXPERIENCE OF CROSSING BORDERS

A summary of policy implications for the study will be set out in Chapter 7, the Conclusion. However, the comments of the firms on border issues are presented here. Indeed, all firms had comments and recommendations for improving their experience with crossing the Canada–US border. This section shall review these comments in some detail, and explores how effective these recommendations might be in creating a more predictable yet secure border.

4.10.1   The Vancouver Firms

The firms, above all, wanted clarity in the process and access to 'up to the minute' policy updates regarding the movement of people across the Canada–US border. Five firms (Firms-V2, 3, 4, 5, and 6) all stressed that they usually experienced some confusion when compiling the foreign worker applications for their employees, and would have liked to call the POEs or have access to a '1–800' number (with a competent person at the other end) in order to seek additional information. The human resource and immigration specialists for these firms explained,

> As an employer, clarity around the process would be good. We are a business and we do not have time to keep up with these things. It would be good to know what the changes are. It would be great if they could keep us updated with bulletins and memos. (Firm-V4)

> It is less than ideal right now. I would like to move back to the expedited process. For example, the Information Technology Workers Program and make it easier

for spouses to work and study here. More informational seminars would be useful. (Firm-V5)

> We should have 100% predictability with NAFTA, especially with TNs. However, we have changing and moving standards. With immigration, no one ever gives a straight answer. Nothing is documented [as to what we need to provide]. Thus, it is very difficult to plan. If our people are denied, there is no rebuttal. Essentially, we are told, 'It's the law!' The immigration people know us, and our patterns, so I don't understand why they make it so difficult. Essentially, they are building a process for the lowest common denominator. Once, again, we need to know what the rules are so that we can follow them. After 9/11, it became more difficult to move people over the border, and now it is becoming even harder still. NAFTA should be a slam-dunk, but it is not. (Firm-V3)

The above comments first point to a need for a 'help line' to assist firms when they send people back and forth over the Canada–US border; second, more continuity to various Canadian programs, such as fast-tracking firm applications for highly skilled high-tech workers, which has recently been eliminated; and third, greater access to expediting programs in the US, which due to the Vancouver firms' relatively smaller sizes, they were not eligible for. An additional finding was that the firms interviewed had a strong level of respect for the role and purpose of immigration officials, and wanted to do everything they could to cooperate with these branches of government. However, they also expressed their own needs as firms, which included a certain level of predictability in crossing the Canada–US border. Firm-V3, for instance, expressed that it found the US DHS to have a climate of changing and unpredictable standards, which was hard to comply with. At best, the material in the chapter suggested that firms had to use a 'coping strategy' to address border issues, and some firms had developed rather elaborate strategies in order to deal with what was perceived as constantly changing and seemingly unpredictable standards.

4.10.2 The Seattle Firms

The Seattle firms had different yet similar needs as the smaller Vancouver based firms. Although both firms had the resources to hire and move foreigners across the Canada–US border, the human resource manager for Firm-S1 stressed that it would be a lot easier if their firm could move their own people freely throughout North America without any labor certifications or work statuses, similar to the European Union and its citizens. She explained,

> I would like to see when it [the movement of employees] is between two firm affiliated companies, that it be easier to move employees, and that a labor certification requirement would not be needed, for example, the L-1B. I know that

this is different for getting them across the border. We are restricted when using some of our talents when it comes to this. (Firm-S1)

The comment demonstrates that as this firm operates its business seamlessly throughout North America, the firm would also like to be able to move their employees accordingly. Although the firm was perfectly willing and able to cooperate with the government officials at the Canada–US border, it would be much easier for firm operations if they were allowed to move their people without the stop-check measure at the Canada–US border.

4.11   CONCLUSION

Overall, all firms included in this study had a strong demand for hiring and sending employees across the Canada–US border. However, the region of Cascadia itself was a minor destination point for the majority of these firms' personnel. California was, in fact, the most frequent point of origin/destination point for employee movements of Vancouver firms. For Seattle Firm-S1, it tended to hire from all over Canada, and send their employees to Canadian regional offices or into the field, which were in locations frequently well outside of the greater Vancouver area. Seattle Firm-S2 hired a mix of both local Vancouver talent and international talent for its R&D facility. There was a complexity of visas used, each with their own advantages and disadvantages. There was a perceived problem with 'visa ambiguity', meaning uncertainty in what exactly was required to successfully obtain a work status or visa and frustration over seemingly changing standards implemented by POE officers. In order to deal with the seemingly randomness of NAFTA visa interpretations, especially in light of 9/11, the firms surveyed employed a number of strategies to better navigate the cross-border system. This included hiring in-house immigration specialists, using attorneys more frequently in the preparation of visa applications, and engaging in the activity of port shopping, which will be discussed in detail in Chapter 6. Although the events of 9/11 slowed down the process of moving personnel across the Canada–US border by approximately half a day, in addition to the added expense and time of hiring a professional immigration attorney to prepare and review visa applications, the security aftermath of 9/11, overall, did not appear to stop the movements of firm activities and their personnel across the Canada–US border.

NOTES

1. Both the Seattle firms and the San Francisco/Silicon Valley firms had considerable R&D facilities in the greater Vancouver area.
2. This smaller San Francisco/Silicon Valley firm established an R&D facility in Vancouver and was in the process of moving a majority of its headquarter operations to Vancouver at the time of the interview in the early 2010s.
3. Intracompany Transferee status, permissible under Chapter 16 of the NAFTA.
4. Treaty NAFTA professional worker status, permissible under Chapter 16 of the NAFTA.
5. Business visitor status, permissible under Chapter 16 of the NAFTA.

5.   The immigration officials

5.1   INTRODUCTION

This chapter examines the varied roles of Canadian and American immigration officials in administering the Canada–US border in Cascadia. Officials were interviewed at various ports of entry (hereafter POEs), primarily within the Seattle–Vancouver corridor, as well as key Canadian and American policy officials who had developed and overseen the policies surrounding Chapter 16 of NAFTA. As argued in Chapter 2, immigration officials are key to not only the facilitation of North American professionals across the Canada–US border, but their role also as gatekeepers served a broader function in protecting and securing the boundaries of the nation state for varied purposes and reasons. The study found that officials who developed the actual policies and laws that govern the management of the borders were critically important to the process of border management. Hence, it is the effective implementation of these ideas that contributes, ideally, to a consistent management of the nation state's borders. Thus, it is at these individual border crossings that there should be a smooth flow of information from policy development to implementation at actual POEs. In the case of a common continental-wide program such as NAFTA, it might be assumed that a common harmonious approach to administering status/visa applications might be in force, especially after the 20 or so years since its inception in 1994. However, for a variety of reasons explored in this chapter, evidence suggested that this was arguably not the case. Indeed, as argued in the literature review of Chapter 2, local norms and values, together with issues such as institutional history, training programs, and separate national legislation, have influenced substantially the interpretation and implementation of NAFTA *on either side* of the Canada–US border in Cascadia, as well as *along* the border at each POE.

5.2   METHODOLOGY

A total of 27 government officials were interviewed for this particular component of the research. Twelve participants worked for Citizenship and Immigration Canada, two worked for the Canada Border Services Agency, and thirteen participants worked for what is now called the US Department of Homeland Security (US DHS) (formerly the US Immigration and Naturalization Service). Twenty-two of those interviewed worked in the capacity of front-line supervisors or port directors at the various POEs, and five people worked in the capacity of policy development officers in either Ottawa (3), Washington DC (1), or British Columbia (1). The sample, of course, is not necessarily representative of the entire US/Canada immigration staff that worked at all Cascadia POEs between Vancouver and Seattle, which, for the US was about 220 people, and for Canada was about 200 people in the mid-2000s (interviews with US legacy INS Seattle Region Assistant Director-Seattle, Washington, May 2001, and CIC Senior Policy Analyst-Vancouver, BC, June 2004). However, this purposive sample can be considered a fair representation of the supervisory and management staffs at the targeted Cascadia POEs. In regards to the research issues covered in this study, each interviewee was asked a series of approximately 19 questions. These 19 questions can be grouped into the following themes: (1) the impact of NAFTA on labor mobility between Canada and the US, and the Cascadia region specifically; (2) types of high-tech professions and job classifications that are difficult to interpret under NAFTA status provisions; (3) the particular 'cultures' and histories of immigration officers, and the institutions that they form a part of; and (4) the impacts of 9/11 on the movement of professionals across the Canada–US border and on the interpretation of NAFTA.

The interview results revealed a wide array of findings and information on the administration of the Canada–US border; how labor mobility fitted into the overall regulation and facilitation of entry at the border; and the culture and histories of the immigration officials and their institutions. The following sections first review the overall findings from interviews with immigration officials, and the chapter ends with a conclusion.

5.3 THE CANADA–US BORDER AND NAFTA STATUS PROVISIONS

Immigration officials were first asked about the day-to-day mechanisms of obtaining NAFTA statuses, and also what they thought made the Canada–US border between Seattle and Vancouver unique compared to other crossing points. This section covers these particular themes.

5.3.1   Background Comments by US Immigration Officials

The US immigration officials interviewed stressed the fact that the Cascadia region was the third busiest point of crossing after Detroit, Michigan–Windsor, Ontario and Buffalo, New York–Niagara Falls, Ontario. In particular, in the US, the Seattle District had all three elements of entry, that is by air, sea, and land. The Vancouver Airport preclearance facility was the sixth busiest in the US regarding the handling of immigration in the US at airports. In fact, only John F. Kennedy (New York City), Los Angeles, Miami, Chicago, and LaGuardia (New York City) were larger. The Seattle area also had a cruise ship terminal with visa inspections for foreign travelers heading to Alaska. Thus, the Vancouver International Airport preflight US POE provided an all round level of experience for US immigration officers. Because the US and Canadian land POEs were located directly on the Interstate 5 (I-5) corridor between Seattle and Vancouver, and because part of the Cascadia regional economy was still dependent on natural resources, these land POEs were important for controlling cross-border trucks moving seafood and lumber as well as tourists. One port director (US-IO 1) stressed some of the unique qualities of this region's ports of entries, and how it differed from the US–Mexico border.

> The amount of fraud and smuggling [along this border] is much smaller than the US–Mexico border. However, this region still has problems with imposters and the smuggling of people and goods. In regards to the US–Mexico border, many more people are US citizens passing through this border, in fact, roughly 60% or higher. The other major group of people is Canadian – they do not need visas when crossing into the United States. Thus, this area [Canada–US border] is not document intensive. For Mexicans, there is the I-94 and the border-crossing card (in lieu of a visa). Both of these forms of identification take more time to process than what is required for the majority of people moving across the Canada–US border. However, in regards to the US–Mexico border, it is now becoming more biometrical.[1] The idea here is that it is not only more secure, but also easier to process people. (US-IO 1)

The above comments reflect that US authorities are aware of the balance between security and the need to process people quickly and efficiently. This balance in the Cascadia region will be explored further in later sections of the chapter.

5.3.2   Background Comments by Canadian Immigration Officials

Canadian officials also drew attention to the distinctive nature of Cascadia's international border crossings. The Canadian POEs between Seattle and Vancouver were part of the larger BC/Yukon Territories for the Citizenship and Immigration Canada (CIC), which had its regional headquarters located in downtown Vancouver. From a regional perspective, the amount of immigration flows using NAFTA statuses was only around 30 percent of the total border crossings compared to those in the Toronto–Detroit area (interview with CIC Regional Policy Advisor, C-IO 3). For example, the largest array of Canadian companies could be found in the Toronto area, and consequentially, this was where a majority of the highly skilled foreigners working in Canada were located. However, the Vancouver–Seattle corridor had the largest forest and mining companies in Canada, and these industries provided a substantial draw for the US knowledge workers and other internationally highly skilled employees with relevant expertise. One port director and another port supervisor both stated succinctly some of the main features of the Cascadia POEs.

> We are the only port of entry open 24 hours a day west of Windsor, Ontario. We deal with cars and commercial trucks. We are not the busiest, but close. We are not nearly as big as the US–Mexico border. This southern border is massive with eight-hour line-ups. People (Mexicans) would stream by and the US officials would single people out. One of our challenges is getting the Customs officials to screen for us[2] . . . We see many business professionals and management consultants coming through these particular land ports of entry. (C-IO 4)

> We do not have that many IT people crossing across the land border. This is mainly found at the Vancouver Airport. We do not see a lot of American film crews coming through the land ports of entry. Additionally, one must remember that we have other programs (apart from NAFTA) for software engineers, which facilitates labor mobility from around the world. NAFTA is merely one of many ways to enter Canada. (C-IO 5)

5.3.3 NAFTA Statuses: the View of US Immigration Officials

US immigration officers provided their own insights on how the special NAFTA statuses had operated in practice for high-tech employees wishing to cross from Canada (Vancouver) into the US (Seattle). In regards to how NAFTA influenced labor mobility across Cascadia's Canada–US border, there was a wide array of responses from those interviewed. One port director (US-IO 1) noted that the Vancouver–Seattle corridor comprised a cluster of high-tech industries (e.g. aircraft, software, and biotech) and that because these industries were located in both Seattle and Vancouver it was only natural that well-educated people would be moving back and forth across the border. The same port director noted that the US preflight immigration clearance at the Vancouver International Airport reported many thousands of NAFTA applications a year. Consequently, the US staff at the Vancouver International Airport had become very familiar with NAFTA applications, especially so when compared to a more rural POE, such as East Port, Idaho, which might only process less than 100 NAFTA applications a year. It was also stressed however, that NAFTA did not allow completely unregulated access to the US. The particular jobs that Canadians coming to the US could apply for were listed under NAFTA (as described in Chapter 3). In most cases, the applicant had to meet the minimum qualifications specified for each job type and the job must not be a permanent position. Thus, immigration officers at POEs played an important role in determining whether or not a NAFTA applicant matched a particular professional category and the subsequent job description, as listed under NAFTA. There were alternative longer-term visas (lasting three years with an automatic three year renewal), such as the H-1B (NAFTA's predecessor), which might be more suitable for various types of jobs, but, as explained in Chapter 3, these types of statuses/visas took longer to attain and were more expensive. Consequently, NAFTA statuses were often more attractive as they were easier to attain. Indeed, one US officer (US-IO 1) interviewed noted that some Canadian applicants used the NAFTA status to circumvent the longer visa processes.

United States immigration officials mentioned that the larger firms in the Seattle region, such as Boeing and Microsoft Corporation, often used Treaty NAFTA statuses or 'TNs', in addition to the more traditional H-1B work visa, in order to bring prospective Canadian employees into the US. Two US immigration officers (US-IO 3 and 4) noted that if a firm wanted to hire a person for a short amount of time to 'see how the employee worked out' (which was a strategy used by Firms-V5 and 9 discussed in Chapter 4) then the firm usually used a NAFTA TN status due to its administrative ease and low cost; and until 2008, the status was good for only one year.[3] So, historically, if the employee did not 'work out', then this was an easy 'way out' for the firm after a year's employment. However, if the firm in question did wish to keep the Canadian employee, the firm would often switch the employee over to an H-1B visa and then to a 'green card' (i.e. permanent job authorization). Smaller firms also liked the TN status since it was not as expensive as the H-1B, which usually ran into the thousands of dollars due to US DHS processing fees and legal costs. As well, the employer was not obligated to renew the employment status. It was stressed, however, that the larger firms had to be legitimate in the way that they used NAFTA statuses, and not abuse the NAFTA status application system. One POE supervisor stated,

> The larger companies usually go for the H-1B since they are longer term, but Microsoft, Boeing, and Volts semiconductors (a subcontractor of Boeing) also

do many TNs. The idea is that the company brings a person in on a TN, and if it works out (with the person) the company switches the person over to an H-1B, and then they can move to a green card. The company usually sponsors the person when they move to a green card. The small firms like the TN since it is not as expensive as the H-1B, and it is short term, so that the employer is not obligated to renew the status.

. . . Overall, the larger firms are usually more legitimate [in the use of NAFTA statuses]. However, the smaller firms (which are usually subcontractors to the larger firms) are the ones we have to take a closer look at, as I explained earlier. This may be due to a lack of understanding of the application process, or the fact that the actual person may not qualify under NAFTA. (US-IO 3)

The above comments reflect a continuing theme of additional scrutiny applied by border officials towards personnel working for smaller, lesser-known firms who use the NAFTA status application procedure.

Two US immigration officers (US-IO 3 and 4) noted that rather than going through a particular POE adjudication, an applicant could send his/her NAFTA application off to a legacy US INS/DHS Citizenship and Immigration Services Center[4] for NAFTA status verification and the hopeful issuing of the NAFTA status. However, this application process would likely take up to four months to process. The applicant could also send a TN status renewal off to the same service center, with the renewal usually taking about a month to process. The same two officers noted that this might pose less of a risk to the applicant rather than renewing the status at a particular POE. Applicants seeking renewal through a Citizenship and Immigration Services center would not run the risk of being denied entry back into the US if the application was flawed. In regards to remaining in the US, then the applicant could stay in the US under TN status as long as the person received a paycheck from the same firm as the TN status was issued for. If the person were to lose his/her job, then, officially, that person was obligated to return to Canada, and usually had 10–30 days to leave the country. With an H-1B, visa holders had 30 days to leave the country.

So, in the experience of many US immigration officers interviewed, overall, the NAFTA experience had been a rather mixed one with some support for its facilitation procedures for Canadians, while others commented on its unforeseen disadvantages. Since 1994, inspecting and adjudicating NAFTA statuses was only one of many tasks that front-line immigration officials were responsible for. The past 20 years had provided these officials with some experiences regarding the NAFTA procedures and documents in addition to the patterns that applicants exhibited when applying for NAFTA statuses. Some of these policies and patterns of practices were acceptable to these officials. These were the clearer and more direct professional job categories and job descriptions listed in NAFTA Chapter 16, and the need for presentation of the actual individual seeking entry into the US at a POE. However, other components of NAFTA and applicant behavior were not so acceptable. These included rather ambiguous job titles and job descriptions in NAFTA; as well the penchant of some applicants attaining a NAFTA status at a particular land POE, but with the intent of departing from the Vancouver International Airport at a later time.[5]

The following section explores the Canadian immigration officers' experience with Chapter 16 of NAFTA and the flow of American professionals into Canada since 1994.

5.3.4   NAFTA Statuses: the View of Canadian Immigration Officers

In regards to US professionals moving across the Canada–US border, Canadian immigration officials provided their own set of comments during interviews. In general, they processed a large number of US business professionals and management consultants who wished to come to Canada and work in Vancouver and other parts of BC. As stated previously, the POE immigration officials considered forest and mining companies to have the biggest demand when it came to moving professionals within the Cascadia corridor. However, the quantity of immigration flows using NAFTA statuses was substantially smaller than in the Toronto–Detroit area. Nonetheless, despite these regional size differentials, there were similar sets of issues in both regions when it came to professional labor mobility. Essentially, professionals in the US workforce coming into Canada were well educated and sometimes known internationally for their expertise. They usually prepare 'superior applications' based upon comprehensive 'homework'.

However, the BC/Yukon District of Citizenship and Immigration Canada (C-IO 5 and 6) stressed that they did not have so many information technology (IT) people wishing to cross the land border into Canada from the US. They mentioned that US professionals came from all around the United States and usually entered Canada through the Vancouver International Airport or Pearson Airport in Toronto. In sum, flows of employees within Cascadia per se did not appear to be so important. Additionally, three Canadian immigration officers (C-IO 1, 2, and 3) noted that, apart from NAFTA, Canada had other immigration programs for software engineers that facilitated labor mobility from around the world (e.g. The International Mobility Program and the Provincial Nominee Program). Indeed, long-term immigration to Canada generally as a professional software engineer was usually more appealing to both the foreign engineer and the firm doing the hiring as compared to shorter term options such as the NAFTA status. In other words, acquiring employment statuses for computer specialists coming into Canada was not seen as quite the challenge that was reported by Vancouver firms moving employees into the US.

Canadian immigration officers noted that they had greater concerns with the actual management at POEs when it came to the initial screening of foreigners (usually Americans) seeking entry into Canada. One port director in British Columbia (C-IO 4) reflected on the experiences at one of the land POEs,

> ... One of our biggest challenges is getting the Customs officials to screen for us[6] ... I mean, one time I looked out my office window, and I couldn't believe that the Customs guy was actually letting this particular carload of Americans in! I was shocked! These people should not have been let into Canada! (C-IO 4)

The above comment highlights that NAFTA is only one of a number of mechanisms that the Canadian government and private sector interests can use to bring international professional IT workers into Canada, even from the US. The chapter now turns to how NAFTA statuses are interpreted, and the various norms and rules that US and Canadian immigration officials used when understanding, interpreting, and adjudicating NAFTA statuses.

5.4 THE INTERPRETATION OF WORK STATUS APPLICATIONS UNDER NAFTA

All interviewees were asked to comment on how high-tech professional employees were treated when traveling between Vancouver and Seattle for work or consulting. The following section covers the major themes and issues that emerged.

5.4.1 The US Immigration Officers' Experience

US immigration officers (US-IO 2, 3, 4, and 8) noted that due to the rather ambiguous job descriptions of people working in the IT industry, work status/visa adjudications under NAFTA could often be considered difficult and non-routine. For instance, in regards to professions that were hard to interpret under NAFTA provisions, US immigration officials all agreed that the job description of 'management consultants', in particular, was seen as often 'very tricky'. 'Software engineers' and 'systems analysts' were also problematic job classifications in the NAFTA regulations for a variety of reasons. For instance, many management consultants were hired 'to do' (i.e. to carry out work activities in the US) rather than merely 'to consult', which was the specified activity allowed under NAFTA regulations. The professions of 'computer systems analyst', 'scientific technician', and 'scientific technologist' also caused problems for a variety of reasons. For example, with the category of 'scientific technologist', these types of workers had to provide proof of at least three years of relevant work experience. The category of software engineers also was difficult to interpret due to the wide range of job activities that software engineers could perform. In fact, three officers (US-IO 2, 3, and 4) noted that the US DHS had difficulty interpreting this category. Two immigration officers (US-IO 3 and 4), interviewed at the same time, summarized well the broader challenges involved with interpreting Chapter 16 of NAFTA:

> Registered nurses and management consultants are tricky. Software engineers and systems analysts are also difficult. Many people, both the applicant and the immigration officer, have different interpretations regarding NAFTA. Basically, it is a definition problem . . .
>
> In regards to software engineers, they are tough to interpret . . . Essentially, it is hard to sort out the software engineers and what they do. They must do a lot of explaining, and we then must verify their credentials. So, with software engineers we look at 1. Education; 2. Previous experience; and 3. Wages . . . with scientific technologist, they must have three years of experience, and be able to prove it. (US-IO 3)

As demonstrated above, US officers noted that in this case they often examined a variety of evidence including the actual applicant. This included the following: formal education; previous experience; wages and offers for the job that was sought. Usually, the job category of a computer engineer earned significantly more than a computer programmer, which was sometimes the job that the US firm was actually hiring a Canadian for, but computer programmer was not allowed under NAFTA. Two immigration officers (US-IO 3 and 4) noted that computer programmers could not enter under NAFTA because they were not listed as a suitable job category in the NAFTA Chapter 16 schedule. Consequently, in these cases, often the applicant and the immigration officer had different interpretations regarding NAFTA, especially with how particular job categories were defined. Some applicants prepared the NAFTA applications themselves for even the more difficult job categories. This was especially so when the applicant was an independent consultant or a very small firm that had just landed a contract in the US, and could not afford an immigration lawyer to prepare the application. However, three officers (US-IO 2, 3, and

4) stressed that the application was usually more thorough if a qualified immigration attorney helped to prepare the application.

> Some people pull the NAFTA application together themselves. It is quite evident when this happen, but it is usually more thorough if an attorney helps the person with the application. (US-IO 4)

Chapter 6 explores in more detail the role of attorneys in the NAFTA process. The section now turns to the Canadian experience in interpreting NAFTA statuses.

5.4.2   The Canadian Immigration Officers' Experience

By contrast with the US immigration officers, three Canadian immigration officers (C-IO 4, 5, and 6) stressed that from their perspective, the NAFTA applications were rather easy and straightforward. They stressed that everything within the application fits together nicely. However, these three Canadian immigration officers agreed with US-IO 3 that the job category management consultants could be very difficult to process and interpret under NAFTA regulations. One Canadian port director (C-IO 4) stressed that they would often go out of their way to even contact the company hiring the NAFTA status applicant in order to obtain a better understanding as to what the proposed job actually required, especially if there were questions regarding the application. Canadian immigration officers also processed many US nurses coming across the land border for jobs in Vancouver. Yet with software engineers, it was more difficult for these professionals to explain the exact nature of their work in such a way that it was succinct and understandable to the immigration officer.

A possible reason for the misunderstanding of the category of software engineer for the immigration officials is that many times the job duties of software engineers were often abstract and even avant-garde, so that the job description was difficult to communicate to people outside of the software industry.

Overall, the Canadian experience with understanding and interpreting the NAFTA applications were seen as a relative nonevent. This may be compared to the American experience, and the comments of the US border officials who stated that NAFTA provisions could sometimes be seen as rife with ambiguity and unpredictability, as reviewed in the previous section. The next section further explores these geographical differences by examining how US and Canadian immigration officers have been trained regarding NAFTA statuses, and how differences in levels of training and sources of knowledge may have contributed to differences in attitudes towards NAFTA statuses, both between the two countries and also along the various border crossings in Cascadia found *within* each country.

5.5 TRAINING AND AVAILABLE RESOURCES FOR THE UNDERSTANDING OF NAFTA

The variability in interpreting NAFTA provisions between US and Canadian officials led the study to examine the training programs with both the DHS (US) and CIC (Canada). This aspect of the study revealed how officers were trained to understand and interpret NAFTA applications. Importantly, the officers' training came from a variety of measures, and these varied considerably between the US and Canada.

5.5.1 The US Immigration Officers' Experience

From a US perspective, four immigration officers (US-IO 3, 4, 5, and 6) noted that although they usually had some training in the academy,[7] there was more on-the-job-training. It was also stressed that the NAFTA status provisions were not taught in their basic training, but rather these skills were taught in the advanced journeyman's schooling. Two immigration officers (US-IO 3 and 4) commented on where and how they learned about NAFTA,

> In regards to inspector training, there is some OJT [on-the-job-training]. NAFTA is not taught in basic, but it is taught in the advanced journeyman's schooling. We have not had advanced classes in this type of status. (US-IO 4)

When there was a designated NAFTA Free Trade Officer at the US POEs (prior to 2000), this officer usually provided about 8–16 hours of NAFTA training to the other immigration officers working in the same POE. There were also manuals provided to the immigration officers with step-by-step instructions on how to interpret NAFTA status applications. Three US immigration officers (US-IO 1, 3, and 4) noted that up to 1999 there were specific NAFTA officers at each POE within Cascadia who adjudicated and facilitated questions regarding NAFTA job statuses. These NAFTA officers also provided 'preapprovals', which allowed NAFTA applicants, or their attorneys, to send the required application materials to the POE usually a day or so ahead of the applicant arriving in person. If everything was in order, the applicant would almost immediately receive his/her NAFTA status. However, this policy was stopped suddenly on 20 October

1999, with a memo from legacy US INS headquarters specifically from Robert Bach, legacy INS Executive Associate Commissioner, Policy and Planning in Washington DC, stating that it was contrary to the NAFTA to engage in prior approval procedures, petitions, and labor certification tests as a condition for temporary entry. Additionally, the policy memo also addressed the growing disparities which had developed between the various POEs in regards to the interpretation of NAFTA Chapter 16 and particularly specific job classifications listed in NAFTA. The memo, in effect, was sent out in an attempt to harmonize POE adjudications of NAFTA provisions. Although the memo did not explicitly state this, it was at this time that all POE officers began to adjudicate NAFTA statuses directly rather than just Free Trade Officers.

Two immigration officers (US-IO 3 and 4) offered an explanation for this harmonization policy, stemming from headquarters, that immigration attorneys tended to identify the traits and characteristics of this small number of NAFTA officers and consequentially tailored their NAFTA status applications to the various officers' specific preferences. This sort of activity then led to something called 'port shopping', which will be discussed more fully in the following section.

In sum, since late 1999, any immigration officer at a POE has been able to review and inspect any NAFTA status application. Four officers (US-IO 3, 4, 5, and 6) emphasized that this was a better method of preserving the integrity of the NAFTA application system. One officer emphasized,

> Now, everyone does NAFTA applications. They get some instruction in basic academy training. We used to have a NAFTA officer who gave us about 8–16 hours of training. (US-IO 5)

Another officer stated:

> . . . now that we all do them [NAFTA applications], it is much more random and fair. (US-IO 4)

As of late 2014, as part of the 2011 Beyond the Border Action Plan, and perhaps in response to the ongoing outcry of erratic adjudications of NAFTA applications at POEs from a number of immigration attorneys as discussed in Chapter 6, an option called Optimized Processing for NAFTA TN applications and L-1 status application now occurs at 14 designated US POEs. Similar to the Free Trade Officers of the 1999s, specially trained US DHS POE officers were now available during designated times to adjudicate NAFTA TN and L-1 applications. However, it should be noted that any POE officer can still adjudicate a NAFTA application regardless if he/ she was specially trained with NAFTA applications or not.

Beyond issues relating to immigration officer training in the US, many immigration attorneys stated in their interviews that the spirit of interpreting NAFTA applications rests more on a broader port culture in the US of restrictiveness (see comments in Chapter 6) more than anything else. This became apparent shortly after the pre-adjudications of TN matters ended at POEs in October 1999. For instance, after this time, the interpretations of computer professionals, in particular, began to be interpreted very narrowly by US immigration officers. Overall, the interpretation of computer professionals under NAFTA has been one fraught with difficulty and confusion, as was discussed initially in Chapter 2. Even with only Free Trade Officers adjudicating NAFTA statuses, the interpretation of Canadian computer professionals attempting to enter to work in the US was riddled with unpredictability since the inception of NAFTA. For example, legacy US INS headquarters in Washington DC issued a letter of response to one immigration attorney in San Francisco in May 1995 stating that computer engineers, did, in fact, fall under NAFTA (i.e. qualify for a NAFTA status) if the applicant had a baccalaureate or licenciature degree. This policy letter helped to clarify the issue for the (pre-1999) Free Trade Officers. However, beginning in late 1999, at the time that all POE immigration officers were allowed to review NAFTA applications, immigration attorneys, once again, began to see many computer professionals' NAFTA applications being denied into the US once more. Boos commented on the issue (2002) and stated,

> ... Shortly after termination of preadjudication of TN matters by trained Free Trade Officers, TN status for computer professionals became one of the subjects of INS rigidity on TN issues, with INS inspectors at POEs and PFIs [preflight inspections] frequently taking the position that computer engineers and software engineers did not qualify as engineers for purposes of TN status, despite previous guidance to the contrary from INS headquarters. Denials of TN status to TN qualified computer professionals by INS inspectors at many POEs became commonplace, forcing INS headquarters to subsequently issue instructions to the field reaffirming that software engineers could qualify for TN engineer status.
>
> However, the instructions from INS headquarters received narrow interpretations at POEs and PFIs [Preflight Inspections], and practitioners were soon circulating reports of INS inspectors denying TN engineer status to Canadians with baccalaureate degrees in Computer Science on the grounds that these individuals needed software engineering degrees to qualify for TN status as computer engineers.

The above quote helps to demonstrate a continuing unpredictability of interpreting various NAFTA job listings on the US side of the border in addition to the wide range of discretion that POE immigration officials have had over NAFTA applications on a day-to-day basis, despite seemly clear policy direction from legacy INS headquarters that attempted to standardize interpretations of NAFTA job regulations. An important finding was that this gap in policy, or rules, originating from legacy INS headquarters, and the interpretation of these rules at the actual POEs, rested heavily on the 'norms' or culture at each POE as discussed by Finnemore and Sikkink (1998) in Richardson (2010).

The intellectual context of the definition of what a norm is and where it might be found provides a framework for explaining why such variability existed in interpreting NAFTA as between Canadian and US border officials and as between the many US POEs. In other words, the Canadian POE officials commented that NAFTA status applications were becoming 'routine' because the Canadian policy regarding NAFTA status applications was standardized for each POE. By contrast, the ambiguity or 'non-routineness' mentioned earlier by US POE officials was due to the greater ad hoc status found in training and applications of NAFTA policy along the US side of the border. Indeed, although the actual 'rules' of NAFTA have been constructed and approved by each signatory country, there remained considerable leeway between each particular country in the interpretation and implementation of NAFTA. Thus, it was up to each country as to how its front-line officials understand and interpret NAFTA applications. Richardson (2010) argued that these domestic norms have then set the tone as to the actual interpretation of NAFTA applications.

The next section, 'The geography of port shopping' explores in more detail how the norm of interpretation varies widely between Canada and the US, and also among each US POE; whereas the Canadian POEs appear to be relatively consistent in their NAFTA adjudications. The study finds that much of these differences may be attributed to differences in nationwide training, as discussed in the forthcoming subsection; but there are additional factors that will be explored.

5.5.2 The Canadian Immigration Officers' Experience

The Canadian experience regarding implementing Chapter 16 of NAFTA may be considered somewhat different from that of the US. This subsection covers some of the major differences and ends with a brief conclusion reflecting on the overall variability (yet some seemingly growing similarities) in interpreting NAFTA between the two countries.

First, for Canadian immigration officers, NAFTA was seen within a broader area of their overall employment training for immigration officers, rather than being treated as a specialized area of immigration. In fact, the CIC operational bulletins and training manuals for border officials is public and can be found on the CIC's web site (CIC, 2017b). Rather than the somewhat limited hours of official basic training provided for US immigration officers, more specialized training regarding NAFTA was provided to all CIC officers. Indeed this type of training was regarded as ongoing as long as the officer was employed within CIC. With regard to training, there was also constant updating, and what were called 'complete systems of communication' from the officers at the POEs directly to CIC headquarters located in Ottawa, and then also back to the regional POEs. In other words, there appeared to be a more systematic and thorough approach to NAFTA status interpretations, one that involved clear, concise, and timely directives from policy headquarters in Ottawa to all individuals at Canadian POEs. For instance, three officers (C-IO 3, 4, and 5) noted that when an unusual case was found in Cascadia, its details were then transmitted to the regional program specialist at the CIC regional headquarters located in downtown Vancouver, and he/she would then channel this information on to CIC headquarters in Ottawa. After discussion in headquarters, a resolution was then channeled back to the regions, with updates and memorandums, if necessary. One senior policy analyst explained,

> NAFTA is included within the broader category of employment training. You can find the manual on the CIC's web site. You have to remember, the training for all CIC officers is ongoing, and there is constant updating. When we find an unusual case, we channel this to our regional program specialist, and he then channels all of this back to headquarters in Ottawa. It is then channeled back to use with updates and memorandums, if necessary. (C-IO 3)

In the Canadian system there were also special NAFTA trainers established for border control officers when NAFTA was first implemented in 1994. Immigration officers were obligated to undergo special training away from the POE office at least twice a year. One session in each training program was dedicated solely to covering updates/revisions to new types of associated legislation. The following quote from a supervisor (C-IO 5) reflects some of the required communications and training that all Canadian immigration officers had,

> We had NAFTA trainers when NAFTA first came on. Immigration officers go in for official training a couple times a year. They cover a wide scope of training, from updates/revisions to whole new types of legislation. All training is mandatory. There is much training up front, then experience takes over. (C-IO 5)

Concerning the interpretation of problematic job descriptions and classifications that were reviewed earlier in this chapter, Canadian officers noted that discussion on different types of IT professions, and the relevant type of job duties performed, were all part and parcel of the in-training process. Still, at times, it could be difficult to determine if a particular type of job and respective work activities fell under available NAFTA status provisions. For example, the job category of 'management consultant' was as particularly troublesome in Canada as on the US side; as has been noted, there were a variety of activities that could be performed by consultants. For example, a management consultant could work in all sectors of business enterprises, and was accepted under NAFTA provisions, just as long as the person 'consulted' rather than 'did'. Additionally, under NAFTA, the applicant did not need a bachelor's degree to attain the job category of management consultant. However, the fact that management consultants could possibly lack a bachelor's degree is where suspicion arose regarding the job category on the part of both the Canadian and US immigration services, since businesses frequently used this job classification to move employees throughout North America who did not have bachelor degrees or higher, whether they were proper management consultants or not. In fact, due to the way NAFTA was written, two Canadian immigration officer interviewees (C-IO 5 and 6) stressed that there was only a very narrow range of activities that CIC recognized as comprising a management consultant.

One officer (C-IO 5) noted that they had a 'cheat sheet' under the old legislation (the 1989 Canada–US Free Trade Agreement) in order to familiarize officers with what was and was not acceptable as to types of professional activities allowed under the then new NAFTA. However, the wider scope of NAFTA had still not resolved what was and was not acceptable under this particular job description, and in the interviews with Canadian border officials it was considered that it would take some time to resolve. Thus, despite the more extensive training that Canadian immigration officers underwent, one port director (C-IO 4) stressed that the NAFTA applications were still open to interpretation by individual POE officials, which could vary. She remarked,

> When NAFTA first came on, all we had were the Canada–US Free Trade Agreement guidelines within the three months of training that we have, and within this, we had three days of NAFTA training. Despite all of this training, there is still an incredible amount of variability with adjudicating NAFTA statuses. For example, one person went through two different ports of entry with the same letter and materials when seeking a NAFTA status. One POE approved it without a problem, the other port of entry almost denied it. (C-IO 4)

Despite the possible variability in interpreting NAFTA applications, Canadian immigration officers overall had a greater spirit of 'facilitation' towards NAFTA applications rather than the more 'restrictive' attitude of the US immigration officers. However, since the creation of the Canada Border Services Agency (CBSA), which now handles all initial POE engagement with NAFTA applicants, there appeared to be a growing culture of 'strictness' if not 'difficultness' for Americans seeking entry into Canada under NAFTA. This issue is discussed further in the forthcoming section, which deals with the geography of port shopping.

In closing, despite the view of POE officer, C-IO 4, quoted above, and the rise of strictness with the Canada Border Services Agency, the Canadian norms of interpreting NAFTA applications were still considered by interviewees as relatively consistent from one POE to another POE along the border in Cascadia when compared to the US experience. In other words, there was a smoother flow of policy over NAFTA 'rules', established by policy officials in Ottawa down to their interpretation across POEs along the vast Canada–US border. More, consistent nationwide training and education on the Canadian side had shaped the consistency of 'rules-to-norms' as well as more consistent norms at each POE. For example, the Canadians dedicated considerable effort to achieving nationwide training of immigration officers and updating the knowledge regarding the understanding of NAFTA statuses, job classifications, and other related issues as part of immigration officers' professional employment. The US, on the other hand, had relied less on the advanced stages of basic academy training; but depended even more on educating just a few staff (i.e. designated NAFTA officers prior to 2000 and now optimized processing at 14 POEs) at each POE, and then these designated NAFTA staff providing on-the-job-training to the other immigration officers.

However, this policy has changed since 2004, and the US DHS appears to be moving towards the Canadian example of mandatory ongoing training, although each particular US port director continues to have considerable influence in the training and education of individual officers, as compared to his/her Canadian counterparts.

In fact, by early 2005, one of the port directors (US-IO 10) interviewed stressed that all DHS officers were in a constant state of training. This was a very different mind-set compared to earlier interviews conducted prior to 2003. The port director explained,

> Now, we will always have on-going training. We are making sure that they have on-going training. We are in a constant state of training. For example, everyone will be required to go through the training of doing a personal search. Right now, we are working on professionalism training.
>
> On-going training is a key part of the new DHS . . . The training is established and the completion date is established [by Headquarters]. It is then left to the field manager to make sure that everyone completes the prescribed training

in the given time frame. Basically, we get direction and guidance from headquarters, and they leave it up to us to figure out how to implement the guidance and training within the specified timeframe. (US-IO 10)

These comments helped to demonstrate that a very different set of objectives and mind-set regarding training and consistency of NAFTA Chapter 16 interpretations was being applied under the new US DHS, as compared to the legacy INS. Now, constant and more uniform education is seen as a primary pillar of the DHS. However, as demonstrated, there is still leeway given to each port director as to how exactly the educational programs will be executed. Interestingly, Yale-Loehr et al. (2005); Meyers (2005); and Richardson (2006a) separately argued that this ongoing, mandatory, and extensive training that US DHS POE officers received beginning in the early 2000s was seen as a step in the right direction towards better Canada–US border management. However, the findings from Richardson (2011) revealed that these efforts towards continued professionalization and education were frequently overshadowed by each port's particular culture and attitude towards NAFTA applicants, and will be discussed in more detail in an upcoming section.

As will be shown in Chapter 6, US attorneys were still quite skeptical of this ongoing education in the US DHS, and its contribution to a more consistent approach with managing the Canada–US border. In fact, many of the US attorneys interviewed stressed that the port director's attitudes and perceptions of NAFTA still had a major influence on how NAFTA applications were interpreted on a day-to-day basis. In other words, the prevailing norms of NAFTA at each POE were directly influenced by factors other than just overall training and education surrounding the actual NAFTA document, and its official regulations.

5.6 THE GEOGRAPHY OF PORT SHOPPING

The above narrative has suggested that due to the inherent complexity of NAFTA status regulators, and the problem of rapidly changing job descriptions in the IT industry, adjudication of NAFTA on a day-to-day basis was potentially left to the discretion of individual POE officers. The US and Canada immigration systems differ in how they approached the problem; and Canada's approach was to emphasize more consistency across the board through more intensive training programs and better and more frequent communications between headquarters, regional headquarters, and individual POEs. Yet, while both sides had recognized the inevitable variability in NAFTA interpretations, it was likely to continue. This continued variability has led to the phenomenon of 'port shopping'. This section covers what exactly port shopping is, why it occurs, the efforts made to curb this activity, and how port shopping influences the geographical dynamics of NAFTA applications, especially for Canadians seeking entry into the United States. (Please see Figure 5.1 for a visual depiction of the many different POEs between the more western US states and Canada.)

5.6.1 The US Immigration Officers' Experience

From a broad perspective, port shopping may be considered the activity of seeking a POE that appears to be more facilitative towards allowing a foreign applicant into a desired country, usually for purposes of legitimate work or refugee status. This term can be applied to the Canada–US border in the interpretation of NAFTA status regulations in two ways. The first is when someone is denied entrance to either Canada or the US at a certain POE, and then the applicant has approached another port, trying to seek entry. The other form of port shopping is when an immigration attorney advises his/her clients as to which ports to go through, and even as far as which officers they should submit their NAFTA application to. One US supervisor (US-IO 2) stressed that port shopping was not illegal, but it tended to destroy an applicant's credibility, if found out. Disclosure was more likely in the US side of the border, since whenever a person was denied entry, the decision was registered into the US DHS's databases. This information could then be easily recalled when a second application was made at another POE. This same situation could occur on the Canadian side, but as will be explored in this section, Canadian immigration officers were more facilitative towards NAFTA applicants seeking entry to Canada compared to US immigration officers. In addition, there were more consistent NAFTA adjudications by Canadian immigration officials all along the Canada–US border.

Despite the use of computerized mechanisms, which should deter NAFTA applicants from port shopping, this phenomenon still occurred for a variety of reasons. As was discussed earlier in the chapter, when NAFTA was first implemented in 1994, designated Free Trade Officers in the US were the only immigration officials at POEs who reviewed NAFTA applications, up to 1999. Many immigration attorneys interviewed for this study emphasized that when only Free Trade Officers reviewed applications there was a much greater level of predictability and expertise focused around NAFTA applications. One immigration attorney stressed that she only sent her clients to two particular officers at the Vancouver POE since she was more confident that they would not adjudicate NAFTA status applications in an arbitrary or off-handed manner, and that they would be more professional in addressing her clients. She stated,

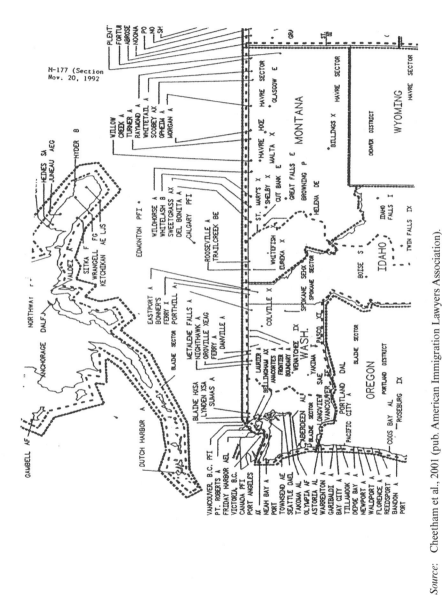

Source: Cheetham et al., 2001 (pub. American Immigration Lawyers Association).

Figure 5.1   All ports of entry between western-most US and Canada

I used to always send my clients through the airport. The Free Trade Officers knew what they were doing, and the port director expected professionalism from his staff. My clients were always treated well, and it was a pleasure to work with the [legacy] INS. (US-A3)

Although both US and Canadian attorneys praised the original NAFTA system of allowing only designated Free Trade Officers to review NAFTA applications, many US immigration officials stated that, over time, this began to erode the integrity of the NAFTA application process. One immigration officer explained,

What began to happen was that the attorneys began to write up the [NAFTA] letters with what the Free Trade Officers were looking for. They figured out what the various [Free Trade] Officers liked, then they would send their clients through at the time of day that that particular officer was working. This is called port shopping and it corrupts the procedure and integrity of the NAFTA system. Now any of our inspectors can review a NAFTA application. In fact, an applicant had the possibility of about 217 different officers reviewing a NAFTA application between Vancouver and Seattle when seeking entry into the US. (US-IO 1)

This comment underscores the attempt after 1999 to avoid port shopping and make the NAFTA adjudication more random and more equal along the border. Yet, despite the fact that the legacy INS tried to create more randomness towards the review of NAFTA applications (i.e. avoiding the targeting of specific US POEs and immigration officers) the activity of port shopping still occurs. In fact, the elimination of the Free Trade Officers in late 1999 gave way to what one US immigration attorney described as 'widely erratic' interpretations of NAFTA applications all across the Canada–US border (Boos, 2002; Cascadia Cross-Border Law, 2015). Rather than sending clients through one particular POE at a certain time of day, which was the case when Free Trade Officers were adjudicating NAFTA applications up to 1999, attorneys subsequently sent their clients through a wider range of POEs all along the Canada–US border. They even developed a rather sophisticated mechanism of written communication with each other regarding the various 'climates' at each particular POE, especially since the attitudes and interpretations of NAFTA applications now rested more heavily on the attitudes of the port director, rather than the professional expertise of a Free Trade Officer. In fact, after 1999, the smaller, more rural POEs became favorite access points for attorneys who had clients with marginal applications. One attorney elaborated on this phenomenon,

. . . Sweet Grass, Montana used to be the place to take it to if you were denied everywhere else. This has changed now. It knows now that it was seen as a soft touch, and it is now more difficult [with NAFTA applications]. (US-A 4)

In fact, port shopping involving sequential applications continued to be a game of 'musical chairs' all along the Canada–US border with respect to US POEs, well into the 2010s (Richardson, 2011). Despite the DHS's recent efforts to provide 'Optimum Processing' for NAFTA applicants at 14 designated larger POEs, there still remains a lack of a uniform, comprehensive, and ongoing educational program regarding NAFTA for all POE officers. In addition, there is a general lag time of NAFTA information circulating from Washington DC to the POEs and this continues to contribute to a wide variation in interpreting NAFTA status applications, especially in the case of problematic job descriptions such as 'management consultant', and 'software engineer'. This local variation was further exacerbated by many immigration officers relying heavily on local on-the-job-training and the expertise of other officers at their own POE. At times, this type of local 'knowing' could be subject to personal interpretations and attitudes as opposed to 'professional facts'. This circumstantial situation is what many immigration attorneys referred to as the 'culture' at each POE, and this could vary significantly from port to port.

From interviews conducted with US border officials and immigration attorneys from 2010–15, it was clear that a strong influence in the interpretation of NAFTA applications continued to rely on the attitude of each port director. If he/she understood NAFTA provisions and expected professionalism from his/her staff (i.e. a more consistent interpretation), then the NAFTA applicant was more likely to obtain a fairer (or more consistent) review. In fact, one of the US port directors emphasized that they (US DHS) were aware that some POEs were more 'lax' than others. However, during the interview, he focused on building up the reputation for his particular POE, stressing that it was 'difficult to get through' if an applicant had a less than accurate application. In response to the immigration attorneys' communication network of providing constant updates to other attorneys regarding the various ports of entries' cultures (see Chapter 6), it was the intent of this particular port director to be known as a leader of a tough, yet professional, staff at his particular POE. He stated:

At the Vancouver port of entry, I think we have a reputation that we are very conscientious, and we enforce the regulations. Although we do use discretion where appropriate. . .You might find a smaller port where they are laid back and do not get much traffic, so we started to hear things . . . For example, at Christmas time, we have people who are illegally living in the US as Canadian citizens, and they come home for Christmas. They do not know that there are a lot of them. It makes it quite evident when you see the [pattern of] travel in their passports. So, they do not get back in here [at the Vancouver Airport]. We refuse them. They withdraw [their application for entry]. Then they might try Lynden, or Sumas [smaller border crossings]. If they have a job in the US that they are uniquely holding, then they need to get back to that job. So they keep going! We have had people end up as far as Toronto, trying to get into the US. They hit the land borders and they say, 'Oh, that didn't work. So let's fly out of Toronto or fly out of Ottawa.'

It depends on the inspector that they get that day, but there are ports where there seems to be less of an interest on holding close to the regulations. So you can go to a port where the guy is actually not doing his job well that day, or people at the port are a little more laid back. But if people say, 'I don't like Vancouver because they really do their job well.' I can live with that. Versus, 'I don't like Vancouver because they humiliate people or treat people unfairly.' There is a big difference as far as why people complain. Or, 'I don't like Vancouver because they found out about my drug conviction. They didn't let me go.' I can live with that. (US-IO 10)

Overall, it is important for the reader to understand the power of the port's reputation that flows from the experiences at each POE. It was demonstrated in a number of interviews that the notion of a particular 'port's reputation' was a strong contributor to the variation in adjudicating NAFTA statuses and to the activity of port shopping along the US border with Canada. However, it should also be emphasized that this particular port director stressed the fact that he did not want his employees to be known as a staff that 'humiliated or treated people unfairly'.

This attitude of professionalism (i.e. treating applicants fairly and humanely) was a relatively new management concept for the US DHS, and will be more thoroughly explored in an upcoming section. Beyond the concept of port shopping, one immigration attorney emphasized that the use of rumors of border controls and port reputation about how 'tough' any particular POE was in adjudicating NAFTA applications was in itself a primary strategy used by the US DHS in keeping people away from the Canada–US border. He reflected on the backgrounds and culture of US DHS immigration officials at the various US POEs between Seattle and Vancouver, and compared these with those of similar Canadian immigration officers.

Overall, the border guards are underpaid. They are also undereducated, but rather intelligent. They know how to send out signals of deterrence. For example, they intentionally treat people with disrespect. From here a Canadian will send out a message to 20 of his/her friends that, 'The DHS is very disrespectful.' *Canadians do not like being treated with disrespect* [emphasis added]. The INS [now DHS] usually goes far beyond what is needed in regards to creating a climate of deterrence [at the border]. On the Canadian side, they [immigration officials] are much younger. They usually have some college education, and they are much less intimidating than the Americans. However, Canadian laws are much harsher for [foreign] people seeking entry into Canada who have committed crimes or who just are not admissible. Despite the fact that the Canadians have much tougher laws that they can apply to people seeking entry, you do not feel a military presence like the US side. (US-A11)

The above quote helps to pin-point some of the misconceptions regarding the often perceived relaxedness that Canadian officials have towards managing their Canadian borders. In fact, it is argued later in this chapter that since 9/11, the US border officials are becoming more like the Canadian officials in regards to the laws and rights that immigration officers have over foreigners seeking entry into the US. Yet, it is important to emphasize that prior to 9/11, the US relied not only on laws and policies but also on the use of rumors and impressions of intimidation to scare foreigners away from the border. Although Canadian immigration officials have more stringent laws when it comes to foreigners entering the country, the Canadian POEs have nowhere near the problem of port shopping, and in fact, some might argue that there was a spirit of facilitation when adjudicating NAFTA applications. Although others argue that the CBSA has begun to take on a tone of restrictiveness at times when adjudicating NAFTA applications for Americans seeking professional employment in Canada. The following subsection explores possible reasons why.

5.6.2 The Canadian Immigration Officers' Experience

Port shopping is something that also occurs at Canadian POEs, but nowhere near the levels that the Americans experience. Two Canadian immigration officials (C-IO 3 and 4) made specific comments on port shopping. They stressed that shopping for a POE typically did not work in Canada, although a considerable number of applicants and immigration lawyers engaged in this practice. The Canadian officers reported that they usually could see if a person was hiding something. Additionally, as in the US, once a person was denied entry, this decision was then registered on the Canadian CIC computer. This computer system also kept a record of criminal applicants' backgrounds. However, some officers were known to have let certain applicants in after they were denied entry at another port. 'Personalities get involved a lot of the time,' stressed one officer (C-IO 6). If an applicant did not understand why a particular decision was made at another POE, the reviewing officers would go over the decision with the NAFTA status applicant (unlike in the US).

As well, since the establishment of the CBSA in 2003, the screening officer at the POE became a CBSA officer, not a Canada Customs officer, as had previously been the case prior to 2003. Many immigration attorneys, both American and Canadian, noticed a strong change in tone (and experience) with their clients regarding these new CBSA POE officers. Surprisingly, these immigration attorneys noted that there was now a culture of 'strictness' and even 'difficulty' with these new CBSA POE officers. Attorneys also had a concern about these CBSA screening officers eventually becoming restrictive like their American counterparts, when it came to interpreting NAFTA statuses (Richardson, 2011).

However, Canadian immigration officials stressed, on the Canadian side of the border, almost every NAFTA applicant was eventually granted a NAFTA status, if there were difficulties initially. One policy advisor put it rather succinctly when asked the question about the particular process that an applicant went through when seeking entry to Canada under NAFTA. He stated,

> Essentially, it works like this:
> 1. Arrives
> 2. Asks
> 3. Gets
> . . . the majority of the NAFTA applicants are well prepared when they submit their applications. We also have addressed the process on our web site. (C-IO 3)

The above comment reflects not only a greater attitude of facilitation on the Canadian side compared with the US, but also the greater willingness of Canadian immigration officials to work directly with applicants by providing accurate and transparent information regarding the preparation of NAFTA applications. This was very different from the US experience at the border, which frequently emanated a feeling of restrictiveness, and deferred most professional advice and help with NAFTA applications to third parties, such as immigration attorneys. In fact, a policy analyst, and also a port supervisor, put it well with the following statements,

> Overall, most people know what is expected of them when they come across the border seeking work. However, they have the luck of the draw when it comes to the immigration officer who reviews the material. (C-IO 3)

> The process [of adjudicating NAFTA applications] is one of fact finding for the officers. We are facilitative in the way we see our work. However, we are also investigative in the process of our work. (C-IO 6)

These comments help to shed light on why there is a relative absence of port shopping for American applicants going through Canadian POEs. Canadian immigration officials tended to interpret NAFTA applications more generously and more consistently. As discussed earlier in this chapter, considerable time is spent formally educating Canadian immigration officials about NAFTA and other forms of professional work statuses. Additionally, CIC has developed its own detailed web site on how to prepare a successful NAFTA application (CIC, 2017a). This helps to alleviate the problem of incomplete and poorly prepared applications, which was a common problem for Canadians seeking entry into the US. Finally, the attitude or culture at Canadian POEs is one of facilitation, as described in the above section. The Canadian immigration officials are investigative in the process of their work, in addition to the fact that they have even stronger laws to fall back on if a foreigner is inadmissible. This is a striking difference when compared to the American immigration officials, who are generally more restrictive, and even vary in their attitudes of restrictiveness from port to port, which then gives rise to the activity of port shopping. Although many US immigration attorneys complained about this restrictive attitude, it also helped to secure their own roles as professional intermediaries in the movement of Canadian professionals across the Canada–US border, which is discussed in more detail in Chapter 6. The chapter now turns to immigration officials in a post 9/11 world, and how the NAFTA status procedures have changed in Cascadia as a result of increased emphasis upon cross-border security.

5.7 IMMIGRATION OFFICIALS IN A POST 9/11 WORLD

The events of 9/11, had tremendous impacts on the immigration services of both the US and Canada in addition to the day-to-day work of their respective personnel. These transitions ranged from the creation of entirely new institutions that oversee immigration into the US as well as Canadian border management, a rise of professionalism and ongoing training programs in the newly created US DHS, to a variety of new laws and policies allowing front-line immigration officers many more liberties on behalf of the state. In this section, it is argued that, in some ways, 9/11 has brought each country's implementation of border management closer to a common norm.

5.7.1 The US Experience – The Development of New Border Management Institutions

First, one outcome of 9/11 has been the creation of the Department of Homeland Security in the US. The US Department of Homeland Security (US DHS), established through the US Homeland Security Act of 2002, includes the merger of over 20 agencies and governmental organizations into one department. With the creation of the US DHS, the US Immigration and Naturalization Service, the US Department of Customs, and the US Department of Agriculture were merged into one inspections agency called Border and Transportation Security Agency. Within this merger was also the creation of two new bureaus, the Customs and Border Protection designed to manage the border and the Bureau of Immigration and Customs Enforcement, which is considered the investigative arm of the directorate (Meyers, 2005). In response to this, the Canadian government created something called the Canadian Border Services Agency (CBSA) in late 2003, which included the merger of Canadian Customs, Immigration, and Agriculture at Canadian POEs. Despite this merger, Citizenship and Immigration Canada is still responsible for enforcement activities regarding immigration, and has established a new admissibility branch in response to these larger changes regarding Canadian border management (Public Service Alliance of Canada, 2004).

5.7.2 The Rise of Professionalism in US Immigration Management

One interesting turn of events as a result of 9/11 and the metamorphosis of the US Immigration and Naturalization Service into the US DHS has been a rise of the culture of professionalism within the newly created US DHS. As discussed in the literature review in Chapter 2, a reoccurring theme for many people seeking entry into the US, whether legally or illegally, has been a rather 'hostile' one when encountering the US immigration officer responsible for inspecting the person seeking entry. Despite the fact that potential immigrants and foreigners have been seen as somewhat powerless and invisible when it comes to US federal political influence, enough stories and complaints found their way to US policy makers to the extent that a main architectural pillar in the formation of the US DHS has been the spirit of mandatory professionalism within all ranks. One port director elaborated,

> . . . We just completed our professionalism training . . . we keep it professional and impersonal. Even if you are a violator, you still have the right to be treated as a human being with respect. So, even if I have to have you carted off to jail, you will go with dignity.
> Yes, every person must now be greeted. This is something that has been mandated from the top. You have the right to be treated courteously . . . We are taking the time to do professionalism training. We try to make the port of entry officers aware of what we expect and not only expect, but demand. Because if we get complaints, this implies that we are not taking the necessary corrective action.
> So, 'Headquarters says that I have to be courteous and professional, or I'm going to be disciplined. I may lose some money.' I mean this is a *no-brainer*. 'It does not hurt me to say "Hello," even though I may not mean it. But I will greet everyone, otherwise I am not following established procedures.' With the interest of the Commissioner and Tom Ridge,[8] this is not optional. The [DHS POE] border culture, historically, was, 'Well, we own it, so we can do anything

we want.' This was especially true along the southern border, and even along the Northwest border ... Mr. Ridge has been here, our Assistant Commissioner has been here. The message you hear is clear, 'You will be professional, or we will try to make sure that we correct your behavior.' I think it is working!

If the person has been standing in line for 45 minutes, and the first thing they hear from the officer is 'Good Morning,' it diffuses much of any anger or frustration that they had from standing in line. This positive greeting makes the average person's experience a positive one. Whereas if the officer says, 'Give me a declaration!', and it goes from there. The idea is to start it off with a positive. If the response is not positive, so be it. We cannot control the public, and how people respond. But we do have to be in control of our employees, and how they interact with the public. This is the biggest change in my opinion. 'Be nice or else!' (US-IO 10)

This rather lengthy quote helps to demonstrate not only a significant turnaround of the US DHS that occurred in its attitude with the public, but also a change in the mind-set of front-line border officers, and how they perceive themselves in relation to the border. Although at times an inspecting officer may not be so sincerely professional, there has been a direct mandate from the former head (Tom Ridge) of the recently created US DHS in Washington, DC that all employees should conduct themselves in a professional manner with those seeking entry into the US. There were heavy consequences, such as deductions in pay, for those officers who did not behave in a professional manner. Perhaps more importantly was the effort to change the overall attitude of how US immigration officers saw their power and relationship with the border and people attempting entry. As will be explored in detail in Chapter 6, many immigration attorneys remained somewhat skeptical that the new professionalism training would sway front-line officers to an entirely different mind-set regarding their applicants at the border. However, the rise of professionalism within the US DHS did indicate a direct and conscious effort to change the driving perceptions about the institution's purpose and role in relation to NAFTA applications and foreigners, in general.

This section also helped to demonstrate the power that a particular port director had towards not tolerating the seemingly engrained older attitudes. As has been discussed earlier in this chapter, the port director at each US POE continued to have a considerable amount of influence, both professionally and charismatically, over each POE's employees. Thus, perhaps with the creation of the US DHS, the most important change was the port director's own embrace of these new attitudes and approaches towards managing the border. In fact, since the creation of the US DHS, more powers were given to the discretion of port directors in an attempt to provide devolution to front-line managers, which allowed for smoother flows of people at POEs, but without sacrificing security. The next sub-section reviews the new security priorities of the US DHS for all people seeking entry into the US, and their implications for Cascadia's border crossings. In addition, it examines how the Illegal Immigrant Reform and Immigration Responsibility Act (1996) and the US Patriot Act (2001) have allowed even more rights to US DHS officers on behalf of the state, and the new rights that port directors have as a result of the creation of the US DHS.

5.7.3   New Security Priorities for the US Department of Homeland Security

Since 9/11 the guidelines for admissible entry into the US have changed considerably. Before, there was a primary emphasis on illegal entry; now, terrorism is the main focus, criminality is second (drug smuggling, embez-zling, money laundering, and so on); and illegal (or fraudulent) entry ranks third. One port director (US-IO 10) explained:

> 9/11 changed everything, and how we look at the border! The directive is now the following: 1. Terrorism and bringing in terrorist weapons, 2. Criminality, and finally 3. Illegal immigration. Then we go to the NAFTA agreement. And what the three former agencies [Customs, Agriculture, and Immigration] covered. We then look to see if these people are representing themselves as legitimate business people. (US-IO 10)

The major transformation of the legacy US INS into the US DHS changed the experience of all who seek entry into the US. However, three officials (US-IO 3, 4, and 5) noted that, paradoxically, the change was perhaps not so important since the US DHS has always had a heavy veil of security when it came to admitting people into the US. Additionally, the experi-ence for people seeking NAFTA statuses has not changed drastically. One officer (US-IO 4) noted,

> Yes, overall, it has had an effect. The DHS has increased the scrutiny for all travelers. We are also using additional databases on people, which were not used in the past. For example, some people had past records for possession of marijuana . . . that did not come up under the old system, now they do. Thus, the person must get a waiver, which is usually done with the help of an attorney. (US-IO 4)

The above comment helps to situate the fact that although there were dif-ferent priorities for the newly created US DHS, there was also some level of consistency for professional business people. However, the newly created US Patriot Act (2001), coupled with the Illegal Immigration Reform and

Immigration Responsibility Act of 1996, allowed more extensive powers and rights to all levels of US law enforcement officers over applicants seeking entry into the US, as well as over US citizens. The following sub-section explores how this has been applied to front-line US DHS officers along the Canada–US border in Cascadia.

5.7.4 The Illegal Immigration Reform and Immigration Responsibility Act of 1996 and the US Patriot Act of 2001

The US Patriot Act was passed by Congress in late 2001, and gave more substantial powers to law enforcement authorities for security and political reasons primarily as a result of the events stemming from 9/11. Before exploring these new powers, it should be stressed that the Illegal Immigration Reform and Immigration Responsibility Act (IIRIRA) of 1996 provided the current foundation as to what constitutes 'entry' into the US for many non-US citizens. Much of what will be discussed in the next three paragraphs is based on the work of Ronald Zisman (2004), a practicing lawyer of Preshaw and Zisman.

The IIRIRA (1996), ratified by US Congress, significantly altered the definition as to what constituted an entry into the US, and so it has been an important benchmark in determining which constitutional protections were available to arriving 'aliens', or non-US citizens (Zisman, 2004: 1). First, the Act expanded the grounds for inadmissibility and narrowed the scope of constitutional rights applied to arriving non-US citizens, or aliens. A key issue here is the new distinction between 'admitted aliens' and 'applicants seeking admission', since admitted aliens had due process rights under the US Bill of Rights. However, these applicants seeking admission but who were found inadmissible during the inspection process at a POE might be subjected to 'expedited removal'. This program was administered directly at the POE. It indicated that there were no due process rights involving judicial review of such a draconian decision, and a person barred from entry in this way could be also barred from entering the US again for a period of up to five years. Added to these rather restrictive measures were other new laws developed within the guise of the creation of the US DHS, and these are found in the US Immigration and Nationality Act (US INA), Section 287 (Zisman, 2004: 1). After 9/11, all US DHS inspecting officers were able to use these more extensive powers of expedited removal at POEs on behalf of the state over the rights of the individual, whether a US citizen, permanent resident, or an alien. Some of the main powers that US DHS employees might use in connection with administering security along the US border included the following:

> The powers to search are unbound by warrant when a person is seeking admission into the United States. The power to arrest is based on the inspector's 'reason to believe that the alien so arrested is in the United States in violation of any such law . . .'and can also do so within a reasonable distance from 'any external boundary of the United States . . . and within a distance of twenty five miles from any such external boundary to have access to private lands . . .' (US INA 287 in Zisman, 2004)

The above quote helps to demonstrate that powers of US immigration officials were quite considerable. Accordingly, the rights of non-US citizens have been eroding for over 20 years (i.e. since the IIRIRA 1996 legislation), and this erosion began before the US Patriot Act of 2001. The findings from this study demonstrate that the process of expedited removal under the IIRIRA 1996 has had a strong effect on NAFTA applicants seeking entry into the US, and this concept will be returned to in Chapter 6. What is most surprising about the quote by Zisman (2004) in regards to the US Patriot Act is that the powers and rights afforded to US DHS personnel may not only be applied to aliens, but also to US citizens. The most well-known case of applying the US Patriot Act to a Canadian citizen is that of Maher Arar.[9] Perhaps the most disturbing aspect of this rather bizarre case is not the lack of rights given to a Canadian citizen but a deliberate refusal to return him to his country of citizenship.

One of the major components of the US Patriot Act is to 'beef up' security along the Canada–US border, aka the 'Northern border'. Specifically, the Act mandated that by 2005 there would be three times the numbers of personnel there as before 2001. However, in an interview with US DHS supervisory personnel in November 2004 revealed that the Vancouver International Airport, for the most part, had not received additional funding, nor additional personnel, as promised under the Act (interview with Port Supervisor-Vancouver International Airport, October 2004, US-IO 11). Importantly, even by 2013, during a second round of interviews with US POE officers, they continued to lack considerable funding and personnel as committed by the US Patriot Act. In fact, Harvey (2004; 2007) has done extensive research on the phenomenon of the promise of additional provisions for increased homeland security within the US, and the failure of these financial commitments to materialize.

5.7.5   The Power of Discretionary Authority

In closing, it should be stressed that the new legislative powers being handed down to US port directors occurred in a rather positive way. Specifically, since the creation of the US DHS, the devolution of discretionary authority from district offices to the individual port and assistant port directors has been a positive step for applicants seeking entry into the US under NAFTA. One port director (US-IO 10) stressed that he found this to be a very positive thing for Canadians who might be denied entry into the US based on a minor infraction of rules, or for purely technical reasons, such as when a person's passport was not machine readable. The port director explained,

> The DHS came into effect in March 2003. Prior to the establishment of the DHS, the district office could only OK a waiver. This has changed now. For example, a waiver of admissibility would now be handled at the local POE. For example, my status [as port director] allows me to make these decisions. Now with these new laws, I have local discretionary authority. I can give a waiver of admissibility for people who have violated the law. For example, a person convicted of marijuana. I can parole the person into the US for a certain amount of time. Also, even with machine-readable passports for countries that are visa exempt, some of these people were in transit when the law occurred. Due to discretionary authority, I am able to give a one-time parole to these people, which was not the case prior to 9/11. Before 9/11 they were refused entry. If the person does not represent a threat to terrorism or criminality, then I have the authority to make the determination to waive the requirement of a visa. This is a major benefit for the POEs. (US-IO 10)

Overall, the new powers of discretionary authority given to port directors was a key to each POE being able to better facilitate the movement of cross-border migrants. Port director, US-IO 10, stressed that knowing how to use this power properly was essential in using it correctly. He also noted that a representative from US DHS headquarters in Washington DC had come to his local office, to ensure among other things that his use of discretionary authority was being used properly. He commented on this at length,

> We are eager to take a much more conscientious approach to people who have minor problems versus the bureaucracy. Such as, 'Well, you have to have this visa, and you do not have it, so you don't get in. Bye.' . . . For example, if you are going to Mexico, and your ticket you paid $500 for and the ticket says you have to go through San Francisco, but now you are not allowed to go through San Francisco [due to a prior drug conviction]. So now you have to buy a $3,000 ticket to go directly to Mexico on the day of travel. With my discretionary authority, I can now allow the person to travel to San Francisco and then onto Mexico. So the discretionary authority is major. If used appropriately, there is nothing wrong with it . . .
>
> A perfect example is when I first got here, and it was before discretionary authority had been implemented. A gentleman and his wife, and his two small children were going to either Hawaii or Disneyland . . . All of a sudden, I heard a scream from one of the children. I went rushing over to the area, and it turns out that he had a minor conviction for marijuana, so he was inadmissible. The officer denied the husband. He said, 'The wife and the children can travel, but the husband cannot. He [the husband] can submit an I-192 for FUTURE trips,

but today, he is going to be refused.' Now with my discretionary authority, I can look at this and make a determination as to whether or not he should be refused based on that, who he is traveling with (his family), and where he is going. So it is a completely different situation. (US-IO 10)

The above section helps to demonstrate that since 9/11, with the creation of the US DHS and subsequent new legislation, controls along the Canada–US border have become stricter in some ways, such as the narrowing of rights for aliens through the IIRIRA of 1996 and the increased powers given to US DHS personnel under the US Patriot Act of 2001. However, there have been some efforts to soften the appearance of the front-line US DHS personnel through professionalism training, and perhaps more importantly through the increased powers of discretionary authority which have been given to port directors. On first brush, it appears that the US government has tried to be more lenient in the case of older minor criminal convictions, such as convictions of possession of marijuana, say 20 years ago, but much harsher on possible terrorists and people deliberately trying to commit fraudulent entries. Perhaps surprisingly, in a post 9/11 world, the study argues that the US system of law and border management has moved to more closely resembling the Canadian system in many ways, such as through more training and professionalism. The subsection now turns to changes in the Canadian situation.

5.7.6   The Canadian Experience and the Canadian Code of Conduct

The Canadian experience with 9/11 was initially a difficult one. Immediately following the attacks, Canada was accused of allowing four of the 9/11 terrorists into Canada, who then seemingly made their way into the state of Maine and then on to Boston (Andreas, 2003). However, despite these initial accusations, after careful investigation by Canadian Security Intelligence Service, Citizenship and Immigration Canada (CIC), and the US government, it was determined that all 19 terrorists entered directly into the US. Still, these accusations, although deemed incorrect after investigation, turned the American public's attention to Canada as a possible 'soft spot' of foreign entry into North America. This unwelcome focus forced the Canadian government to rethink its own immigration and border security systems. However, the author's empirical research tends to suggest that the Canadian system has long maintained professional and high levels of performance, in contrast to the US accusations. Moreover, since 9/11 it appears that the US system is actually becoming more like the Canadian system, as indicated by the US's effort to be more professional, establishing a more consistent and ongoing system of training and education, and creating greater powers of the state over individuals seeking entry into the US. This section explores further these growing similarities with a focus on the recent Canadian experience.

By comparison with the newly created US DHS's push towards professionalism in the US, Citizenship and Immigration Canada has always maintained that their staff should behave in a professional and non-intimidating manner when working with the public. One port director (C-IO 4) stressed that no matter what the situation, all officers shall treat applicants at the border with respect and dignity. In fact, she noted that each officer, while in training, had to read and sign a code of conduct, laying out the values, ethics, and behaviors that all officers should emulate as part of the CIC. She explained,

> We also have the idea of what is called Client Service. We are providing a service to our clients. We must treat people with respect. There is no other way to treat a person. We want our officers to be calm and professional, but thorough. There is the idea of values and ethics. We have something called a Code of Conduct and every officer must read and sign this. (C-IO 4)

This behavior was expected of all Canadian officers long before the events of 9/11 occurred, and it is more in line with the overall Canadian ethic of Good Government and good behavior, which in a large part has defined the Canadian culture and its people for over a century (Gwyn, 1985). By contrast, the US DHS has apparently only just begun training on how to act professionally, after a century of immigration management. This advanced management approach on behalf of the Canadian government is a strong indicator of other aspects of progressive professional management within the CIC. Despite the seemingly friendly and professional nature of Canadian Customs, Immigration, and now Canada Border Services Agency Officers at POEs, they have, in fact, many more powers over foreigners seeking entry into Canada, as compared to those of the legacy US INS prior to the IIRIRA of 1996.

Perhaps the most important characteristic following 9/11 from a Canadian perspective was that CIC immigration officers have for a long time been well educated and have always held professionalism in high regard, which is something that the US is only just beginning to embrace. Second, it should also be stressed that Canadian port directors have always had discretionary authority when it comes to issuing paroles or waivers of exclusion to foreigners not deemed as admissible into Canada, a power that has been just recently given to US port directors. Additionally, the CIC is as severe as the US with regard to powers of the state and the rights of law enforcement over people trying to seek entry into Canada. Finally, despite these strong and seemingly growing powers of the state, there appears to be a more human element of reflection in the case of the

Canadian officers, which the US officers seem to lack perhaps due to their traditionally more militant nature and strong reliance on the direct inter-pretation of regulations. The concluding section in this chapter explores the overall effect that NAFTA has had on the Cascadia border from the perspectives of both US and Canadian immigration officers.

5.8   HAS NAFTA FACILITATED CROSS-BORDER LABOR MOBILITY IN CASCADIA?

Both Canadian and US immigration officers were asked to reflect on whether the NAFTA status provisions had indeed been favorable in facili-tating the growth of the Cascadia corridor to cross-border labor mobility.

5.8.1   The US Immigration Officers' Experience

Two US officers (US-IO 3 and 4) noted generally that Canadians who entered the US under NAFTA provisions were regarded as a middle and upper middle class elite, and did not drain social services and possibly gave back to the US economy in the form of taxes and providing jobs to Americans. In fact, after reflecting on this question one officer (US-IO 3) expressed:

> This [NAFTA provision] is a nice quiet way to allow for immigrants. They are highly desirable. (US-IO 3)

However, with the adjudicating of NAFTA statuses, two port directors (US-IO 5 and 6) noted that there was potential conflict with the principle of 'enforcement' versus that of 'adjudication' coming from the same reviewing officer. There was also concern that as Canadians applying for a NAFTA status, they might be taking away a high paying job from a US citizen. Yet, under NAFTA provisions, immigration officers must uphold the spirit of NAFTA while also being careful to protect the viability of the existing American workforce. From an administrative perspective, two US port direc-tors (US-IO 5 and 6) noted that the reviewing officers needed a quiet place and time to review NAFTA applications, but under current working condi-tions, a busy POE could be a difficult environment to adjudicate a complex NAFTA application. Also, the immigration officers noted that they were required to shift from being extroverted and upfront, when first inspecting any applicant, to being quiet and introverted when reviewing completed formal NAFTA written applications. Overall, every US immigration officer interviewed noted that there had been an increase in Canadians coming across the border for purposes of work under NAFTA since the late 1990s.

5.8.2 The Canadian Immigration Officers' Experience

Canadian immigration officers, by contrast, were much more enthusiastic about NAFTA status provisions. All immigration officers interviewed stressed that Canadians, in general, gained from NAFTA. Canadian immigration officers interviewed saw NAFTA as a 'good thing', and 'not a bad thing at all'. Two officers (C-IO 4 and 5) noted that US applicants coming into Vancouver helped to keep the local BC economy sustained, not only in the major cities of Vancouver and Victoria, but also the more rural communities in BC where new investment was badly needed. This was especially true for those US personnel required to support the Vancouver film industry, and its operations in smaller rural communities outside of the greater Vancouver region.

In reflecting on the relatively stronger Canadian support for NAFTA, one Canadian supervisor (C-IO 5) stressed that the US was an employment hub for everyone from around the world. Thus, many people came through Canada as a transit point to the US. He went on to emphasize,

> The US receives many more people wanting to come in and work than is the case in Canada. Hence, Canada does not need to be so restrictive in protecting its borders as the US. This is one of the reasons that the US has such strict guidelines . . . Canada does not see the numbers of people that the US does. We do not see immigration as being that enforcement driven. However, at the same time, we are seeing more people wanting to come into Canada. Therefore, there is a growing need for a balance of enforcement and facilitation. (C-IO 5)

This comment helps to summarize the Canadian awareness of the US conundrum over balancing NAFTA entries with a high level of security when it comes to permitting foreigners past its borders. However, the quote also suggests the fact that Canada, in certain ways, may become more like the US as a desirable destination for purposes of work, professional advancement, and quality of life. In other words, as the Canadian side of Cascadia generates a demand for jobs attractive to potential foreign employees, then Canadian immigration officials may have to balance enforcement and facilitation. As mentioned in this chapter, the new Canada Border Services Agency, which now screens all people seeking entry into Canada at POEs, could be described by many of the interviewees as intimidating at times and, in fact, 'strict', if not 'restrictive', when it came to the initial screening of NAFTA applicants. Overall, it would appear that Canada and the US are becoming more and more alike in many respects when it comes to managing the Canada–US border.

5.9 CONCLUSION

This chapter has attempted to demonstrate some of the major differences between Canada and the US in interpreting the NAFTA Chapter 16 provisions and how these are administered at various POEs. It also pointed to possible growing similarities between Canadian and US immigration officials regarding the interpretation of NAFTA status applications and related matters. This closing section briefly reviews of some of these major differences and similarities.

In regards to how the interviewees understood labor mobility between Canada and the US border, most stressed in one way or another, that the Vancouver and Seattle areas had very similar advanced service economies, so it would be only natural for the flow of well-educated professionals across the Canada–US border to increase. All immigration officials stressed that the Cascadia region was a very busy area for the POEs between Canada and the US. Thus, both Canadian and US immigration officials emphasized that they were well versed with NAFTA and the movement of professionals back and forth within the Cascadia corridor of the Canada–US border.

Regarding NAFTA's impact on the national economy, the American POE immigration officials were a little more skeptical regarding whether Chapter 16 of NAFTA had helped the US economy, since they were concerned that Canadians might be taking jobs away from Americans. Surprisingly, American POE officers were much more tolerant and respectful towards US immigration attorneys, compared to their Canadian counterparts. Also, the US side was just beginning to introduce professionalism and ongoing training (meaning a more consistent approach) as a primary pillar to their new mission as the US DHS, whereas these two themes had already been a staple of the CIC. Additionally, 9/11 had tremendous impacts on both the American and Canadian immigration services. This resulted in entirely new agencies being created that were designed to more effectively manage both sides of the Canada–US border. Also, the US Congress and the Canadian Parliament created new laws that addressed national security and terrorism. Surprisingly, both the US and Canada have had very strict laws in place prior to 9/11 that pertained to alien rights (or an ever increasing lack of) and powers and authorities derived to the state in regards to border management. Additionally, this chapter suggested that Canadian law was in fact harsher than US law when it came to inadmissible foreigners seeking entry; yet the US was becoming more similar to Canada after the creation of the US Patriot Act of 2001. Table 5.1 helps to summarize these similarities and differences. Overall, it is a dynamic time for both Canada and the US when it comes to immigration

Table 5.1   *Types and characteristics of attributes which contribute to varying border management styles along the Canada–US border in Cascadia*

Type of Attribute	Canadian	American
NAFTA Adjudication	Seemingly consistent from port to port	Varies from port to port (based on port culture)
Mode of Communication of Problems/Issues	Iterative and deliberate	Top-down and seemingly inconsistent – post 9/11 more deliberate
Training	Mandatory 16 hrs/ annually	Eight hours in academy of on-the-job training – post 9/11 constant state of training
Education	Majority have 4 yrs of college or more	Majority have 2 yrs of college or less – military hiring preference. Post 9/11 becoming more culturally diverse and educated
Powers of Front-line Immigration Officers	Wide range of rights on behalf of the sovereign – more so than American officers	Wide range of rights, but less than Canadians. Individuals also have rights (either citizen or foreigner). Post 9/11, creation of DHS, heavy and deliberate security focus. Foreigners now have less rights beginning in 1996 under the IIRIRA
General Impression of Immigration/Canada Border Services Agency Officers	Immigration officers perceived as facilitative towards NAFTA, but new CBSA officers were seen as stern and sometimes difficult with applicant at POEs	Perceived as militaristic and restrictive towards NAFTA and disrespectful towards NAFTA applicants
Attitude towards Port Shopping	Not seen as a problem due to consistent interpretation of regulations from port to port – based on constant training and communication	Not illegal, but ruins a person's credibility. Based more on the culture of each POE, or attitude of individual officer. Post 9/11 – may become more consistent from port to port due to consistent and continual training of port officers

Source: Richardson, 2010 (pub. UBC Press).

and border management, and the interpretation of Chapter 16 of NAFTA is affected directly by both these changing parameters.

NOTES

1. This includes a transition from manual border crossing cards to a more sophisticated computerized crossing card, which included the computerized recording of all Mexicans traveling into the US. (See Chapter 3 of Nevins, 2002.)
2. Prior to the creation of the Canadian Border Services Agency in December 2003, Customs and Revenue Canada conducted primary inspections at the actual Canadian POE and Citizenship and Immigration Canada (CIC) conducted secondary inspections within the office at the POE.
3. As of 2008, the TN status can be issued for up to three years.
4. Lincoln, Nebraska is a US DHS Citizenship and Immigration Services/legacy US INS administrative center, which historically handled much of the administration of visas and work statuses for non-US citizens. Now there are a number of Citizenship and Immigration Services centers through the US dedicated to processing and adjudicating non-citizen applications. The Vermont Service Center is responsible for TN status applications.
5. As of 2015, the Blaine, Washington POE is allowing NAFTA applicants to apply for a TN status during any instance of admission to the US, even for tourist purposes. It is now claimed that a NAFTA application does not need to be made at the POE when the person is seeking entry into the US for purposes of work (Cascadia Cross-Border Law, 2015).
6. As stated previously, prior to the creation of the Canadian Border Services Agency (CBSA), it was the duty of Canadian Revenue and Customs Agency officials to screen all people seeking entry into Canada. One major concern that immigration officials had regarding this arrangement was the customs officer's inability to screen correctly regarding immigration matters. However, since the creation of the CBSA in 2003, all former Canadian customs and immigration officials are given the same types of training regarding both immigration and customs matters.
7. All US DHS officers go through an approximate four-month intensive training period at a school or an academy. This experience includes academics, physical endurance, security, operating firearms, and overall education dedicated to becoming a successful US federal officer.
8. The first Department of Homeland Security (DHS) Secretary.
9. US officials detained Arar, a dual citizen of Canada and Syria, as he attempted to pass through John F. Kennedy International Airport in New York City on his way to Canada. After days of interrogation about his alleged terrorist ties and despite his repeated refusal to concede to deportation, the US Government removed Arar to Syria (via Jordan), rather than Canada, where he reportedly suffered torture over a ten-month period. (Kerwin, 2005: 5)

6. The immigration attorneys

6.1 INTRODUCTION

This particular chapter examines the role of business immigration lawyers, primarily within the more northern portion of the Cascadia region, namely the greater Seattle and Vancouver areas. These attorneys helped to facilitate the movement of high-technology professionals moving across the border under NAFTA and associated regulations.

Consequently, understanding their part in how the Canada–US border operates in the Cascadia region is critical, and a key pillar within the empirical work of this study. It should be stressed that there was some hesitation and questioning by government immigration officials in both the US and Canada as to why attorneys needed to be involved in this particular study, especially as government agents saw the role of the attorneys as a very minor one in the overall process of cross-border labor migration in Cascadia. However, it is hoped that this chapter will reveal how important immigration attorneys were to this process, and the possible reasons why immigration attorneys were thought by governmental officials to not warrant a place in this study.

6.2 METHODOLOGY FOR THE EMPIRICAL RESEARCH

As mentioned previously in Chapter 1, a total of 23 semi-structured interviews took place with Canadian immigration attorneys (10) and US immigration attorneys (13) during 2002–15. In regards to the actual research, each interviewee was asked a series of approximately 15 questions relating to the Canada/US border, and could be grouped under the following themes: (1) the impact of NAFTA on labor mobility between Canada and the US and the Cascadia region specifically; (2) what types of professions are difficult to interpret under NAFTA; (3) how immigration officials are educated about Chapter 16 of NAFTA; (4) the issue of port shopping (i.e. choosing the 'easiest' port of entry); (5) how do immigration officials see the role of attorneys in the NAFTA application process; and (6) whether or not NAFTA has helped or hindered flows of professionals across the Canada–US border.

The interview results revealed a wide array of findings and information about the Canada–US border; how labor mobility fits into the regulation and facilitation of entries at the border; and more interestingly the relationship between the various actors that served as facilitators and/ or gatekeepers to the North American pools of human resources for the high-tech regional economy. The next section reviews the overall findings from interviews with the immigration attorneys. The results show significant differences in perception as to the effects of NAFTA between Canada and the US.

6.3   THE ROLE OF ATTORNEYS IN THE NAFTA STATUS APPLICATION PROCESS

Chapter 16 of NAFTA was written in such a way that an applicant, when assembling a NAFTA status application, would not need an attorney. It was deliberately created in this fashion as a response to the H-1B visa, NAFTA's predecessor in the US, which was seen as confusing for the average person, required a tremendous amount of paperwork, and an attorney was almost always involved in the process. Thus, the new NAFTA status was seen as 'liberating' and 'easy', and a reflection of the NAFTA as a whole, which, ideally, should embody a spirit of facilitation of movements throughout North America (Vazquez-Azpiri, 2000). However, as more and more Cascadian firms began to use the NAFTA status application in the mid-1990s, they began to realize that they did need the help of a professional, especially for the new types of job occupations found within the growing high-tech economy. The need gave rise to attorneys playing a stronger and stronger role in the NAFTA process, which is still the case today. This section examines the role of attorneys in the NAFTA process, both the American and the Canadian experiences, and the increasing distance that both Citizenship and Immigration Canada (CIC) and the new US Department of Homeland Security (US DHS) exhibited towards immigration attorneys.

Attorneys were questioned as to how useful or critical they considered their own role in the NAFTA process. All attorneys interviewed stated that, ideally, NAFTA status provisions should be rather straightforward and one should not need the help of an attorney. However, according to three US immigration attorneys (US-A2, 4, and 6) it appeared that about 15 percent to 20 percent of NAFTA applicants did need the help of an attorney, especially when applying for the professions involved in IT industries – such as management consultants, software engineers, scientific technician/technologists, computer systems analysts, and medical technologists. Three US attorneys (US-A1, 2, and 4) noted that the way these job and degree/experiences specifications were written under NAFTA, they were very 'tricky'. Yet as suggested in Chapter 5, for an applicant or human resource officer to write a proper and successful NAFTA application without professional and legal assistance was 'risky', according to attorneys. For example, one attorney (US-A6) discussed the fact that many Canadian professionals seeking entry into the US for purposes of work did not take the entry process seriously, neither did the human resource personnel understand the process of NAFTA. He stated,

> The Canadians are not taking entry into the US seriously. For example, Canadians say they are going to golf, but they are actually going to work. This is a fraudulent entry. Additionally, there are many human resource people trying to put materials together themselves in order to save some money. They usually do a half-baked job, and they then have to hire an attorney to unravel what they have done in addition to doing a correct application. This usually costs them more than if they hired an attorney in the first place . . . There is a terrible tension at the border [regarding NAFTA] based on these types of circumstances, and it is growing. (US-A6)

Additionally, three US attorneys (US-A1, 2, and 5) stressed that if an attorney was involved, the application process usually was much smoother. One US attorney (US-A2) also noted that from an ethical perspective, attorneys usually did not represent a prospective client who did not fall within one of the recognized professional categories permitted under NAFTA. Hence, the attorneys considered that they provided an unofficial screening mechanism for people seeking entry into the US. One attorney (US-A2) emphasized that since he began working with NAFTA applications, he had a 99 percent success rate. He said,

> I do not take clients that did not legitimately fall under NAFTA provisions. If I did, this would affect my professional reputation. (US-A2)

6.4 THE ROLE OF ADVOCACY TO POLICY ANALYSTS AND THE US CONGRESS AND CANADIAN PARLIAMENT

All attorneys interviewed had a clear understanding of the fact that certain key policy experts in the US and Canada, and to a lesser degree Mexico, held a certain amount of sway over how Chapter 16 of NAFTA was interpreted, officially, and how it has changed. Ideally, the US Congress, the Canadian Parliament, and the Mexican Senate had final authority over whether or not additional professions should be added to the 'NAFTA list'.[1] Still, the day-to-day management of the Canada–US element of Chapter 16 of NAFTA rested with two key North American government bureaucrats, one in the Canadian federal government and one in the US federal government. Both of these bureaucrats were found within the immigration component (CIC and the US DHS) of government, rather than an international trade department, and both could be considered experienced senior level officials. A more thorough analysis of the responsibilities of these two officials, in addition to the Mexican official, is explored in Richardson (2010).

As mentioned previously, part of these senior policy analysts' responsibilities included listening to all of the official complaints and the seemingly 'unfair' adjudications under NAFTA at various POEs between Canada and the US. In their capacity as members of the NAFTA Temporary Entry Working Group, these two policy experts had the ability to send memoranda of understanding to POEs for further clarification on the interpretation of Chapter 16 of NAFTA as a document. This legitimate power had led many immigration attorneys, and their associations, to directly contact and, in fact, lobby these two individuals regarding various issues and discrepancies in the interpretation of Chapter 16 of NAFTA. These issues ranged from discrepancies in the actual writing of the NAFTA document to the attitudes of border officials at various POEs. Overall, despite the fact that federally elected bodies of governments and trade ministers had the official final authority regarding Chapter 16 of NAFTA, it was these senior bureaucrats who were seen as being the most influential and knowledgeable. Thus, attorneys spent a considerable time e-mailing and telephoning these two policy experts and their offices on behalf of their clients, rather than federally elected bodies of governments (i.e. Congress or the Canadian Parliament), when they had problems or issues regarding Chapter 16 of NAFTA.

6.5   THE CANADA–US BORDER AND PERCEIVED OPPORTUNITIES AND PROBLEMS WITH THE NAFTA STATUS PROVISIONS

Both US and Canadian immigration attorneys interviewed for the study noted that NAFTA had helped tremendously with facilitating the movement of professionals across the Canada–US border. In fact one Canadian attorney (C-A2) noted the fact that over 70 percent of all Canadians lived within 90 minutes of the Canada–US border. Thus, Chapter 16 of NAFTA was one more avenue that could lure Canadians into the US. However, attorneys (US-A4 and C-A2) tended to suggest that NAFTA had not been as effective in opening the border to complete worker mobility in North America as the Schengen Agreement had been in the European Union. The opportunities and problems presented by Chapter 16 of NAFTA are now considered, according to the interview comments provided by both US and Canadian immigration attorneys.

6.5.1 US Attorneys

One US attorney (US-A4) stressed that there was no attempt to harmonize cross-border regulations for the three signatory countries (i.e. the labor mobility entry policies of Canada, the US, and Mexico), similar to that of the Schengen Agreement of the European Union. From the attorneys' viewpoint, therefore, it appears that, in theory, NAFTA was designed to maximize labor mobility, but, in practice, each NAFTA country had retained its own jurisdiction and standards for entry into its nation state. In other words, the attorneys' attitude was that there had been tremendous variability in how each respective country's immigration officials reviewed, interpreted, and adjudicated NAFTA applications. The variability between US POEs when it comes to immigration officials and their interpretations of NAFTA has been discussed in Chapter 5. This concept from the perspective of the attorneys will be explored in more detail in an upcoming section of this chapter. Another immigration attorney (C-A1) stressed that the US immigration officials often did not respect the NAFTA agreement, which is an international treaty, and they frequently defaulted to their own domestic laws and decisions when adjudicating and interpreting NAFTA statuses (i.e. falling back on immigration policy created by US Congress, which was not part of NAFTA). The key Canadian negotiator for Chapter 16 of NAFTA provided a good example regarding the many opportunities for variability regarding the interpretation of NAFTA from country to country (C-IO 9). For example, it states nowhere within the NAFTA treaty that TN statuses shall be issued for one year or less (Henry, 2003).[2] However, US immigration POE officers often decided that TN statuses would only be granted up to a one-year maximum when NAFTA first went into effect, and this arbitrary decision remained until 2008. The Canadian immigration officers followed suit, and so this is a good example as to how a somewhat arbitrary decision at the domestic level could hold sway over an international agreement like NAFTA.

6.5.2 Canadian Attorneys

Compared with the rather harsh and negative perception by US attorneys as to whether or not the border was open after NAFTA, Canadian immigration attorneys stressed that the more flexible NAFTA status provisions had been tremendously helpful. This was especially so in the way that NAFTA had assisted with circumventing the restrictive Employment and Social Development Canada (ESDC) (formerly the Human Resources and Skills Development Canada, or HRSDC) rules for foreigners seeking professional jobs in Canada. For instance, one attorney (C-A4) commented that prior to NAFTA, a foreigner seeking a job in Canada had to either obtain a validation confirming that he/she would not be taking a job away from a Canadian, or obtain a specific exception from the ESDC rules. After NAFTA, a foreigner (often assisted by an attorney) no longer had to experience the often cumbersome process of going through the ESDC in addition to seeking a work status/visa as noted in Chapter 3. This attorney went on to stress that although the ESDC is a Canadian federal government authority, the spirit or mindset of the ESDC regulators varied greatly from region to region. For example, in working with clients in both the Vancouver and Toronto areas, this particular attorney found the Vancouver region ESDC to be much more facilitative towards validating jobs for foreigners than the Toronto area ESDC. However, reference was also made to problems with immigration priorities for certain high-tech professionals due to their relevant shortage in the Canadian labor market. Thus, three Canadian immigration attorneys (C-A1, 4, and 5) lamented the loss of the 'Software Pilot Program' (discussed earlier in Chapter 3) in the mid-2000s that was designed to expedite the entry of international software professionals to work in Canada. To successfully complete a visa application for software professionals, 'All one needed was a job offer,' explained one attorney (C-A4). Now, besides NAFTA and the Provincial Nominee Program, almost all foreign tech professional visas must get a labor clearance from the ESDC. However, many of the attorneys noted that it is still easier to bring foreign professionals into Canada versus the US.

6.6 NAFTA STATUS REGULATIONS AND THE RANGE OF VARIABILITY IN THEIR ADJUDICATION

6.6.1 US Attorneys

Overall, US attorneys stressed that NAFTA had provided them with extra work since its inception. However, all noted there was tremendous variability in the adjudication of NAFTA applications among US immigration officers along the Canada–US border, not only between each POE but also between individual officers at each POE (as discussed earlier in Chapter 5). To specifically test this proposition, one attorney (US-A2) had prepared two NAFTA applications for a US firm for two Canadian engineers that the firm was hiring. Both applicants had the same degree and were being offered the same job by the same US firm. The attorney stressed that it indeed was exactly the same application except for the names of the applicant. Both applicants went through the US preflight immigration inspections at the Pearson Airport in Toronto at different times of day. One applicant was almost denied entry while the other NAFTA applicant went through the Pearson Airport in Toronto smoothly and entered the US without a problem. In fact, a US immigration supervisor at Pearson Airport notified the attorney to let him know that it was one of the best NAFTA applications that he had reviewed.

One US immigration attorney summed up the tension between how NAFTA benefits North American business mobility, but how there were also anxieties for Canadian businesses seeking access into the US.

> NAFTA and labor mobility help, but there are kinks. Some aspects of NAFTA have turned into a 'roll of the dice.' For example, L-1s and TN status adjudications at the border. It puts adjudications at the spot of the border. If it is a marginal case, it is left up to the POE reviewing officer to decide. If a person has been admitted 6–8 times, and then the 9th time his application is not 'OK'? How can subjectivity like this facilitate commerce? This deters Canadians from seeking entry into the US at the border. (US-A6)

There was considerable speculation that some of this variability in adjudicating Canadians' NAFTA status applications was based on how well the US economy was doing. Three US attorneys (US-A1, 3, and 4) stressed that in the late 1990s NAFTA adjudications seemed to become more predictable and that border officers in the US at this time had more of a spirit of facilitation towards NAFTA. In the late 1990s, the US information technology sector was booming. However, since about the year 2000 (right about the time of the dot-com bubble bursting) attorneys had noted that there was again more variability between the reviewing officers, both *within* each POE and, more importantly, significant variability *between* each POE, depending on the attitudes of each port's director.

Five immigration attorneys (US-A1, 2, 3, 4, and 5) stressed that each US port director had tremendous influence over how NAFTA applications were reviewed and adjudicated. This particular concept will be explored in more detail in an upcoming section. Finally, even before 9/11, there was a generally greater veil of enforcement and restrictiveness for all foreigners seeking entry into the US than into Canada. Two attorneys (US-A3 and 4) emphasized that this had not helped the average NAFTA applicant seeking entry across the Canada–US border into the US.

6.7   NAFTA AND PROFESSIONAL SKILLS

It should be stressed that NAFTA TNs rarely apply to professionals who did not have degrees or were not a practicing 'professional'. TN statuses were not designed to facilitate semiskilled or unskilled labor across the Canada–US border. One US attorney (US-A2) noted that the labor mobility requirement of NAFTA in reality did not provide many professional classification options for the business community. He stressed, 'One must be a "degreed" professional to come in under NAFTA, which excludes much of the existing business community.' He implied that there were many competent business people that did not fit under NAFTA's TN categories (e.g. business analysts, marketing experts, and so on). Hence, as has been demonstrated in Chapter 5 many companies in Cascadia have tried to fit their business personnel into the higher status 'management consultant' category, which is recognized under NAFTA. Yet this sometimes did not work, and immigration officials usually discovered this rather 'bogus' strategy when they began to question the actual work duties that the NAFTA applicant would be performing (i.e. 'doing' rather than 'advising'). The interpretation of NAFTA work status applications, and their limitations from the attorneys' perspective, is covered in this section.

As discussed in Chapter 3, NAFTA TN status applications may be applied for at a POE when seeking certain types of professional employment in either the US or Canada. When NAFTA was presented to the US Congress for approval, it was seen as a vast improvement over the previous H-1B visa (the NAFTA predecessor). The other attribute of the new NAFTA status was that the reviewing officer at the POE could review, adjudicate, and issue the actual NAFTA status as a 'one-stop' sort of process. However, despite the apparent efficiency involved, this particular step was also where there was the biggest controversy, or 'hazard', as Vazquez-Azpiri (2000: 820) notes.

Some of this hazard may be attributed to the internal rigidity of the TN category (i.e. the rather restrictive list of acceptable occupations) and the relative freedom of interpretation that the reviewing officers had when it came to applying NAFTA at the border area. Another problem was structural (Vazquez-Azpiri, 2000). As noted in Chapter 3, the TN category provided a very rigid framework when it came to job descriptions, as it arguably did not allow for the flexibility and heterogeneity often needed for a quickly changing range of professional occupations, like the H-1B visa, which did. This rigidity in NAFTA is particularly damaging for the high-tech sector in Cascadia, which is a rapidly changing industry. This section explores these concepts in more detail.

6.7.1 US Attorneys

Overall, all US immigration attorneys interviewed argued that NAFTA provisions should be read in a 'liberal spirit' and that the drafters of NAFTA presumably wished that the 65 professions listed should be interpreted as broad categories rather than narrow openings (see also Vazquez-Azpiri, 2000). Three US immigration attorneys (US-A3, 4, and 7) stressed that there was a broad disconnect between what the drafters of NAFTA envisioned and the actual interpretations at the POEs. All attorneys reported that many times their applications were 'picked apart' on details, and there was an apparent randomness as to how applications were interpreted. For example, one US immigration attorney (US-A10) noted that in his experience much of a successful NAFTA status application was based on semantics. For instance, on the day of the research interview, he was in the process of rewriting a person's job description as a 'management consultant' for a Canadian applicant's NAFTA renewal which was recently turned down at the US border. The attorney explained that he had to use the word 'advise' in the management consultant's job description as opposed to the word 'train', because 'advise' is more of a management or supervisory function as opposed to the word 'train' which is more of a 'doing' function, which is not allowed under NAFTA provisions. He noted, 'These fine details with the preparation of NAFTA applications have kept immigration attorneys busy.'

From a structural perspective, the TN status is written in such a way that the actual job position must be matched exactly with the NAFTA professional job description in order for a reviewing officer to issue a TN status. From about 1995 onwards, there were many problems revolving around the title of 'software engineer', since these types of engineers did not produce tangible engineering structures, nor were there accreditation boards or societies that recognized these professionals, which was frequently the case for other types of professional engineers. However, in 1995, Jacqueline Bednarz of the legacy US INS/DHS, and one of the key policy experts of Chapter 16 of NAFTA, issued a letter to an immigration lawyer based in San Francisco regarding the fact that a software engineer was in fact a legitimate profession under NAFTA status provisions, and if a person has a 'baccalaureate or licenciatura degree or state/provincial license would qualify under the profession of "engineer" as listed in Appendix 1603.D.1 of the NAFTA'. Subsequent memos were sent to all POEs with the intention of clearing up the confusion surrounding this new type of engineer. However, Michael D. Cronin, Acting Executive Commissioner, Office of Programs, US Immigration and Naturalization Service, issued a memo in July 2000 to all Regional Directors and Directors of Training entitled 'Guidance for Processing Applicants under the NAFTA Agreement'. Portions of the memo read as follows,

> . . . Appendix 1603.D.1 to Annex 1603 of the NAFTA includes the occupation of 'Engineer' within the list of professional level occupations. The minimum requirement for entry as a NAFTA engineer is a baccalaureate or licenciatura degree or a state/provincial license. There is no further delineation of the types of specialty engineering degrees (e.g. civil, mechanical, electrical, etc.) that qualify for TN classification. Since the appendix doesn't specify certain specialties, the three NAFTA partners interpret this to mean that all engineering specialties are included. Accordingly, an individual engaged in business activities as a 'software engineer' at a professional level that requires a baccalaureate or licenciatura degree or state/provincial license may qualify under the profession of 'engineer' under the NAFTA. The question is whether the individual possesses the requisite engineering degree or state/provincial license.
>
> The office has also been asked to provide guidance regarding the minimum educational requirements and alternatives credentials required for applicants for admission under the NAFTA. In addition to 'engineer', Appendix 1603.D.1 lists 60 occupations at the professional level with a corresponding list of education requirements. If there is an acceptable alternative credential in the education requirement it is also listed. The degree should be in the field or in a closely related field. Officers should use good judgment in determining whether a degree in an allied field may be appropriate. Returning to the 'software engineer' example, it is reasonable to require an engineering degree for admission as a TN to perform professional level duties as a civil engineer.

The above portions of the memo help to demonstrate the variability internally within the legacy US INS/DHS towards understanding and interpreting the profession of 'software engineer' as listed under NAFTA. In fact, many of the attorneys (US-A3, 4, and 6) found that software engineers still posed a problem for US border officials (unlike Canada). This was despite the fact that the US DHS/legacy INS had tried to recognize the university degree of software engineering as a valid degree for the profession of software engineer. Three attorneys (US-A1, 2, and 4) stressed that much of this had to do with the fact that many software engineers still did not have degrees in software engineering. Additionally, until recently, many Canadian and US universities did not grant degrees in software engineering. Many 'older' software engineers received their original degrees in physics, mathematics, and even in English. Accordingly, there was no perfect match between the university degree recognized between the US DHS and the particular job offered.

The above discussion leads to a third problem of interpreting NAFTA statuses and job descriptions. On the US side, there appeared to be an internal rigidity in the interpretation of the TN category, especially when reviewing officers expected a perfect match between the job title and description being offered and job title and description listed under Appendix 1603.D.1 of NAFTA (Vazquez-Azpiri, 2000). As noted in Chapter 3, in theory there should be considerably more flexibility to interpreting job applications and what is listed under NAFTA. However, two US attorneys (US-A1 and 4) stressed that current immigration practice and interpretations of NAFTA by US immigration officials led to confusion, if not deliberate rigidity and an unwillingness to be flexible with job descriptions. For example, software engineering jobs were at best abstract when compared to many other more 'traditional' engineering jobs such as civil engineers. Additionally, in the high-tech sector, the software engineering industry changed so rapidly that a job description written under NAFTA or the US Department of Labor's Occupational Handbook was usually outdated by the time it reached port of entry officials. This usually led to the prospective Canadian NAFTA status applicant having to explain his or her job description to the immigration officers beyond the facts of what was stated formally in the US company job offer. Two attorneys (US-A2 and 4) stressed that this could lead to the application being denied if the human resource department of the US company hiring the Canadian or the actual immigration attorney did not prepare the NAFTA status adequately beforehand.

Other attorneys argued that the way US immigration officers read and understood NAFTA applications was beyond the concept of internal rigidity, structure, and process, but based more on how well the US economy was performing. For example:

NAFTA has facilitated the movements of people. During the boom of the late 1990s, we saw that NAFTA was subject to very loose interpretations. Management consultants could get through without a problem. Anyone with a history or an English degree, or any related field could get through without a problem. However, after the collapse of the bubble the POE people [POE immigration officials] began to narrow the scope. Now, since 9/11 there is a strong sense of 'border protection'. (US-A5)

The US attorneys pointed to the ambiguous policy that Chapter 16 of NAFTA was cloaked in. Essentially, article 1601 stated that 'the desirability of facilitating temporary entry' and 'the need to ensure border security and to protect the domestic labor force', were two policy directives that 'deserve equal footing' (US-A4) with one another. These two conflicting directives apparently provided a sense of tension and confusion for many immigration officers, since one directive seemingly cannot be addressed without detriment to the other. Thus, POE officers were forced to side with one directive versus the other. From the attorneys' perspective, they frequently defaulted to the 'climate' of the economy and how other officers within the POE handled similar NAFTA applications, noting the lack of one guiding policy directive when it came to NAFTA. In light of 9/11, US attorneys confirmed that terrorism was yet another guiding directive that immigration officers had to screen for.

Overall, despite these contradictions in how NAFTA was written and the interpretations and culture of reviewing officers, education and training of POE officers was seen by US attorneys as a crucial component as to how officers understood the broader implications of NAFTA as well as the day-to-day adjudications of work status. The chapter now turns to the concept of 'port shopping', and offers comments on this phenomenon from US and Canadian attorneys.

6.8   PORT SHOPPING

As noted in Chapter 5, extreme variability in the interpretation of NAFTA status regulations along the Canada–US border (especially the US side) has led to 'port shopping', that is searching for a POE that might be more flexible in granting NAFTA statuses, despite the more uniform training and communication efforts coming from US DHS headquarters, which are discussed in an upcoming section. Port shopping comprised one of two events. The first was when someone was denied entrance either to the US or Canada, and the applicant then went to another port, trying to seek entry. The other form of port shopping was when a US immigration attorney advised their clients as to which ports to go through and which officers they should submit their NAFTA application to. Port shopping was much more common for Canadian NAFTA applicants seeking entry into the US than for US applicants seeking entry into Canada. This section covers a brief history regarding the adjudications of NAFTA applications at US POEs within the Cascadia region, and then focuses on what particular circumstances led to the activity called port shopping. The section concludes as to why port shopping still continues, despite efforts to stop it, in addition to why port shopping is not so prevalent for Americans seeking entry into Canada.

6.8.1 The Beginning of Port of Entry Adjudications under NAFTA in the US

All immigration attorneys were asked about the concept of 'port shopping' in the questionnaire. Essentially, when NAFTA was created in 1994, designated Free Trade Officers were installed at major US POEs, and were responsible for being a resident 'expert' and adjudicator of matters attributed to NAFTA. This was considered by attorneys to be a positive outcome of the NAFTA status arrangement and implementation process. The other positive attribute of the NAFTA application process was the 'preapproval' of NAFTA applications by Free Trade Officers at larger POEs such as the Vancouver International Airport. Essentially, an attorney could fax all needed NAFTA materials to the airport POE, and if everything was in order, the NAFTA status would be ready for the applicant when he/she went through preflight inspection. Attorneys stressed that the NAFTA application process was much smoother and predictable when there were preapprovals of NAFTA applications by designated NAFTA officers at various POEs, and especially at the Vancouver International Airport POE. For instance, many attorneys noted that the Vancouver International Airport Pre-Flight Clearance office was traditionally more 'Free Trade Friendly' than many other locations. Two attorneys (US-A2 and 3) noted, however, that in 2000 the experienced designated Free Trade Officer retired and the airport port director transferred to another POE. The input of these two individuals was seen as being critical to a successful NAFTA application, and contributed to the perception that the Vancouver Airport was 'friendly' to NAFTA status applicants in the Cascadia region. According to these attorney interviewees (US-A2 and 3), when the new airport port director arrived in 2000, the NAFTA preapproval process ceased, and he stipulated that any officer at the airport could review a NAFTA application. One attorney (US-A2) stressed that since this had happened, the airport was no longer considered so 'Free Trade Friendly'. Indeed, he reported that he once sent about 80 percent of his clients through the airport POE when it was seen as 'friendly'. However, beginning in about 2001, he started sending about 90 percent of his clients though the four land POEs, specifically, the Peace Arch or Truck Crossing POE. After 2001, he was more confident that his clients would have better success in attaining a NAFTA status at one of the four land POEs than at the airport. He stated:

> Yeah, I used to do lots of work at the airport [POE]. The reason is that it was 'Free Trade Friendly'. About three years ago, I could profile the NAFTA application and the I-94 form. It was painless. Now, the Free Trade Officer retired and the port director is gone. They did away with the preapproval process as well. Additionally, as lawyers, we were once allowed to go to inspections at the airport. This is no longer allowed. Sending people through the airport was once 80% of my work, now it is only 10%. I now send my clients through the land borders since it is more predictable than the airport. I should stress that now any officer can now review a NAFTA application. (US-A2)

Another attorney (US-A3) stressed the loss of professionalism now (at the time of the interview in early 2003), which was once almost mandatory with the old port director at Vancouver International Airport. She stated,

> In the late 1990s, there was a fantastic team at the Vancouver Airport when it came to NAFTA applications. They understood NAFTA and the importance of moving people within North America. They had a lot of integrity, and it was a pleasure to work with the INS. They also went above the call of duty when it came to applications. They worked with attorneys when it came to the applications. There was a real spirit of facilitation then. (US-A3)

The above remarks allude to the geographic variability and randomness that one would assume would not be a factor in a rather lengthy and seemingly well-thought-out trade document such as NAFTA. In fact, the above comments touch on what one attorney (US-A5) referred to as the 'climate' at the border. Another attorney (C-A2) noted that a good attorney should keep up with the 'culture' in operation at the different POEs and be in constant contact with other attorneys to find out what the overall current 'spirit of facilitation and/or restrictiveness' might be at each POE even down to the individual immigration officials. This information was crucial for attorneys when they instructed their clients as to what borders to travel through, what time of day, and which border official to be looking for.

6.8.2 The Geography of Port Shopping along the US Border

Two US immigration attorneys (US-A5 and 8) stressed that general training and education did not play as heavy a role in the interpretation of NAFTA applications as the actual 'culture' of each POE, and the levels of professionalism displayed by each port director. In fact, one US immigration attorney summed it up well with the idea of the 'climate' of immigration at each POE, meaning that the interpretation of NAFTA regulations was heavily dependent not only on how the regional economy was faring, but also the personalities and attitudes towards NAFTA of key personnel at the POE. She stated:

> The gate-keeping mechanism at the POEs is based on economics and politics. The US economy does influence how the applications are interpreted at the border. For example, they [the immigration officers] get their ideas from the newspaper. There is the idea of a 'climate' at the border. DHS has its political objectives. When it changes its officers [and port directors], the opinions of the border changes. This shapes the climate at the border. It is implicit. It is hard to nail down with concrete pinpoints, but can be described as a 'climate.' (US-A5)

Three attorneys (US-A4, 7, and 8) argued that rather than having to think through a complex NAFTA application it was much easier for the border official to just deny it. They discussed that this leads to a culture of 'No', or refusal of a complex application; but it was a local 'culture' that varied greatly from port to port. This, in turn, led to the phenomenon of port shopping. In fact, the following quotes (by US-A4 and 7) touch on some of these complex topic areas:

> ... There is much work for graphic designers within the high-tech arena. However, immigration officers have not made this connection yet. The high-tech field grows so rapidly, that it is hard to have a system that keeps up with it. Immigration officers like things to be simple and consistent. When it gets complicated for them, it leads to confusion and frustration. [This could lead to the application being denied] ... (US-A7)

> Obviously it [NAFTA] has enhanced labor mobility ... Now one can just go straight to the POE. However, NAFTA's biggest benefit, being POE adjudication is also its biggest drawback. It exposes these kinds of applications to inexperienced officers and their own agenda when it comes to admitting Canadians. We have experienced too many denials not warranted under the law. There is too much discretion to the actual officers at the border. They do not have enough training in adjudicating. They are extremely rigid, and they have very little guidance. It makes it too easy to find defects on which a denial can be based. There are still too many defects within NAFTA. (US-A4)

These circumstances have led many immigration attorneys to track the times of work shifts of experienced officers, and recommend to their clients to go through the various POEs at these times of day. For example:

> [You] do not want to file a TN or an L over the weekend because the Free Trade Officer is not there. On the weekend, an applicant will not get an officer who is experienced. The attitude [at the POE] is that it is easier to deny an application rather than do anything else. (US-A4)

The above quotes begin to touch on the almost 'default' mechanism that US POE officers resort to when reviewing NAFTA applications. Although there is some formal education and training around NAFTA, which was discussed in detail in Chapter 5, it appears to US immigration attorneys that it is much easier to refer to the reviewing officers' own judgments and the general climate of 'restrictiveness' or 'facilitativeness' within each POE. This is true to such an extent that former legacy US INS Commissioner, James Ziglar, issued a memorandum of understanding in late March of 2002 to all Regional and District INS Directors regarding a 'Zero Tolerance Policy'. Essentially, the memo read as follows:

> Effective immediately [March 22, 2002], I am implementing a zero tolerance policy with regards to INS employees who fail to abide by Headquarters-issued policy and field instructions. I would like to make it clear that disregarding field guidance or other INS policy will not be tolerated. The days of looking the other way are over.
>
> Regional Directors and District Directors are expected to read and understand all field guidance and then it is their responsibility to ensure that the substance of all field guidance is properly and effectively communicated to all personnel, in a timely manner.
>
> It is also imperative that each employee review and understand issued field guidance. Each supervisor is to ensure that each employee has not only read the field guidance, but that they are also implementing the guidance. Individuals who fail to abide by issued field guidance or other INS policy will be disciplined appropriately. (Ziglar, 2002)

This memo was eventually rescinded, apparently due to its strong tone, but the awareness of the problem of disregarding policy and formal training manuals in the field is rather apparent. Since the writing of this memo, there have been deliberate efforts to better educate US immigration field personnel, but with overall mixed results. In fact, a year and a half later, in October 2003, one attorney (US-A4) reported that there was still tremendous variability between each POE, even under the guise of the new US DHS.

6.9 PERCEIVED PROBLEMS/OPPORTUNITIES WITH US/CANADIAN BORDER OFFICIALS

This section examines the role of training programs in the professional development of border officials in the Cascadia region. After 9/11, there was a concern with three US immigration attorneys (US-A4, 6, and 7) that US immigration officers would receive even less training on immigration matters than before 9/11 since these officers would also be responsible for agriculture and customs in addition to immigration. One US attorney summed it up well:

> With the DHS, the officers have very little training in these matters, and now that they are also responsible for customs and agriculture, there will probably be even less training than they had previously [on immigration matters]. (US-A7)

6.9.1　US Attorneys

Based on their discontent with the training and educational aptitude of US immigration officers, three US attorneys (US-A1, 3, and 7) stressed that they would like to see the US's system be based more on the Canadian immigration training system. There was a general impression that the Canadian system was more comprehensive and current. All attorneys stressed that the way NAFTA applications were understood rested heavily on the 'culture' of interpretation and local procedures used at each POE. A more uniform nationwide ongoing training and education for all immigration officers (as used in Canada) would help to broaden the reviewing immigration officers' perspectives and create a more predictable and consistent means of understanding NAFTA applications for all US POEs. One immigration attorney (US-A3) noted that the Canadian approach, which emphasized frequent and ongoing education for their immigration officers, would also be advantageous to the US immigration officers. This attorney suggested that it would be a positive step if Canadian and US immigration officers were given the same training, especially since NAFTA rules applied, in theory, equally to both Canada and the US (and, of course, Mexico also). The attorney noted that Canada seemed to be much more progressive and professional in keeping its reviewing officers updated and educated about immigration policies and procedures as compared to the situation in the US.

6.10　THE ROLE OF THE PORT DIRECTOR

It should be mentioned that three US immigration attorneys (US-A2, 3, and 4) stressed that the single most important factor regarding the spirit of NAFTA rests with the attitude of each port director. Thus, much of the culture or climate of each POE may be traced back to the attitude of the particular port director. One attorney (US-A4) provided a lengthy statement about the variability of each POE and the important role that the port director played in his/her attitudes towards NAFTA.

In terms of specific POEs, Blaine is consistent, but there are some old school people. Regarding the Pacific Highway Crossing, Jones is OK, but Swansea can be difficult.[3] Remember this can change. [For example], Sweetgrass, Montana used to be the place to take it to if you was denied everywhere else. This has changed now. Now it [Sweetgrass] is more difficult. It [Sweetgrass, Montana POE] knows now that it is seen as a 'soft touch,' and has to reverse this image. Calgary is good with Management Consultants. Edmonton and Winnipeg are to be avoided. Not because they are harsh, it is just that they do not understand the process. They commit rookie type errors like not giving them an I-94 Card (showing that you have been admitted).

Vancouver – you can get a fair adjudication.

The Peace Bridge in Buffalo is the only place to go in the more eastern regions along the Canada–US border. For example, John Cardiff [at the Port Huron POE] is seen as the worst immigration officer along the Canada–US border when it comes to adjudicating TN statuses. He has mentioned that he does not like foreigners. My experience with him is that he was only willing to approve TN applications for companies that he had heard of. Thus, Canadians [working for smaller lesser-known firms] will not get a fair review.

Right now, Pearson Airport in Toronto is seen as the best. The Port Director understands NAFTA and its process. He is accessible, answers his phone, and responds to faxes. He also will not outright deny an application. He will call the attorney, and ask for more information to be faxed. At the moment, this is THE BEST POE along the Canada–US border. In my experience, Ottawa is also one of the better ports. The consulate in Ottawa is also very good. The visa consular, Catherine Bremen, expects professionalism from her staff. (US-A4)

The above quote stresses that the professionalism and attitudes surrounding NAFTA appeared to be highly dependent on how the port director perceived NAFTA, and what he/she expected from his/her staff. Once again, this commentary also demonstrates the lack of uniformity along the Canada–US border for US POEs as discussed in Chapter 5. This was in direct contrast to the Canadian POEs. Additionally, the above quote alludes to the broader regional nature or culture at specific POEs. The specific 'culture' of decision making at any port, strongly dependent on the personality of each particular port director, appeared to contribute to the success (or failure) of a NAFTA application. It was emphasized by US attorneys that, in addition to the attitudes of the port director, the POE's 'level of experience' with applications and the movement of business people also contributed to how NAFTA applications were received and interpreted. Thus, airport ports of entries, such as Vancouver and Toronto, saw many more Canadians moving through for purposes of work compared to the so-called land borders. Therefore, these POEs had a higher likelihood of understanding and approving a NAFTA application. Additionally, the central North American POEs, located between Detroit–Windsor and Buffalo–Niagara Falls may be considered better than the west, Calgary/ Edmonton, Alberta (preflight), and the four most western land crossings and the Vancouver International Airport. One attorney (US-A4) stressed that the culture of POEs was always subject to change, and so had to be monitored. This is one reason why attorneys, acting as intermediaries in the NAFTA process, were so important. This particular concept, the role of attorneys in the NAFTA process, was discussed earlier in the chapter. However, the following subsection explores one possible alternative to POE adjudications of NAFTA applications in an effort to overcome this rather complicated and ever changing practice of port shopping.

6.11 ALTERNATIVES TO PORT OF ENTRY ADJUDICATIONS?

6.11.1 US Attorneys

When posed with the question about what were the possible alternatives to POE adjudications in order to address the issue of port shopping, the only response that came to mind for many of the US attorneys was the use of a more centralized processing center, such as the facility in Vermont, which now processed NAFTA applications. However, based on past experiences with legacy US INS/US DHS central processing centers, two attorneys (US-A4 and 8) did not see this as providing a solution for more predictable adjudications of NAFTA applications. In fact, despite the seemingly complicated port shopping strategies, in addition to the general frustrations with local POE adjudications discussed earlier, US attorneys for the most part stressed that they preferred the POE adjudications when compared to sending in the NAFTA status applications to a US DHS Citizenship and Immigration Services case processing center. Attorneys noted that there was a high degree of variability with the time that it took to issue a NAFTA status when dealing with a case processing center, such as the ones located in Nebraska or Vermont, for example. One attorney summed it up well with his reaction to the question about doing away with port of entry adjudications and moving all NAFTA applications to the case processing centers.

> . . . The other option is to adopt the strategy of not going through the border. Have the person change his/her status once they are in the US. We have something called premium processing. So, for a $1250 fee the person's application will be processed within two weeks. Before premium processing, the time delays were prohibitive. The problem with this is that the petition is no longer preferential, which is one of the mandates under NAFTA. This would be inconsistent with the NAFTA. NAFTA applicants would have to get in line with everyone else. I would fight that strongly if it occurred. Even though I'm moaning about

port of entry [adjudications] being very inconsistent, I think it would be a tremendous step backwards if we moved NAFTA applicants to the Vermont Processing Center. (US-A4)

In fact, three attorneys (US-A2, 3, and 4) stated they preferred the more local or regional nature of NAFTA status adjudications at the actual POEs. Despite the fact that there were specific officers that the attorneys wanted to avoid, it was also a strength to know the particular immigration officers on duty who might be conducting the adjudication and issuing of the NAFTA status. One attorney (US-A8) stated that when one sent materials off to Nebraska or Vermont, it was like sending materials off to a 'black hole'. Historically, there was no way to follow an application, let alone getting through on the telephone when an application was being processed at one of the case processing centers. Thus, the relatively quick turn-around time for the majority of NAFTA status applications directly at POEs in addition to the fact that attorneys could call the POEs to follow up their applications, and until recently, attorneys could even accompany their client to the border POE. These were all seen as real advantages over the way things were once done when the servicing center in Nebraska was the only option. In fact, one US attorney (US-A2) stressed,

> I want to deal locally with people that I know. I do not want to send it into the [Service] Center to people I do not know, and where I have to wait. (US-A2)

The above quote was made in July 2002, approximately ten months after 9/11. At this time there was still a feeling of familiarity and comfort with the local POEs. However, another interview with an attorney in April of 2004 revealed that the cultures at the local POEs had changed considerably, and there was a growing attitude of 'distance' between the (now) US DHS officers and immigration attorneys. Additionally, there were many new people working at the local ports who came directly from Washington DC, or POEs located along the US–Mexico border. One attorney (US-A6) stated:

> There are still inconsistencies [regarding NAFTA]. There is now even more work than ever for attorneys after 9/11. I used to phone the border regarding my clients' applications. However, since August, no one can have an attorney present with them at the border. DHS is using this as a wedge to push us away. I do not know the new people with the DHS at the border now. (US-A6)

These quotes help to demonstrate the ever-changing nature of the POEs, and how critical it was that attorneys knew who worked at each POE. Perhaps more importantly, that they had physical access to these officers.

One attorney (US-A2) stressed that this was essential for him to being able to do his job. Additionally, there was a stronger and stronger legal effort on the part of the US DHS to not allow attorneys' access to the POE, unless his/her client was being charged criminally. These topics will be discussed in detail in an upcoming section.

In summary, the above section revealed why port shopping with US POEs had become such a prevalent factor in issuing NAFTA statuses. Although there were deliberate efforts to curtail this activity, which was discussed in Chapter 5, port shopping still continues for US POEs.

6.11.2 Canadian Attorneys

Interestingly, Canadian attorneys, for the most part, tended not to stress that port shopping was an issue. Two Canadian attorneys noted that they found that most of the Canadian POEs, especially the larger ones found in the three busiest corridors, namely Vancouver–Seattle, Windsor–Detroit, and Niagara Falls–Buffalo, have rather consistent adjudications along the Canada–US border. In fact, one Canadian attorney (C-A4) stressed,

> We do not have the TN horror stories that you hear about with Canadians trying to enter the U.S. . . ..Basically, the INS [now DHS] plays a human resource role under NAFTA [i.e. making adjudications according to the strength of the US economy]. They should not be doing this. They [as an organization] really are not designed for this. We have pretty consistent adjudications at the borders. Where we get our variability is with ESDC. The spirit of the ESDC varies considerably from region to region. This is where we as [Canadian] attorneys are helpful in addition to other reasons. (C-A4)

The above quote helps to demonstrate the varying nature not only of the experience of NAFTA applicants from one side of the Canada–US border to the other, but also the different roles that immigration attorneys see themselves playing, based on which country they practice law in. The next section continues to explore the comments of immigration attorneys and the changing roles that they have played in the NAFTA process after the events of 9/11.

6.12 CHANGES SINCE 9/11 AND LABOR MOBILITY UNDER NAFTA

Although the chapter has alluded to the impact of 9/11 on labor mobility and the work of immigration attorneys in many ways, this particular section shall briefly cover some of the major impacts that 9/11 has had on labor mobility and adjudication of NAFTA visas at US POEs, through the experiences of immigration attorneys.

6.12.1 US Attorneys

Three US attorneys (US-A1, 2, and 3) stressed that 9/11 was absolutely devastating to labor mobility across the border and to their practices. However, about two months after 9/11, business began to rebound for various reasons not associated with offering professional help in attaining a NAFTA status. For example, many clients post 9/11 now needed a waiver of excludability for former drug convictions due to the fact that the legacy US INS was reaching deeper and deeper into its databases, in order to search for possible terrorists, which was not the case prior to 9/11. Attorney (US-A3) explained,

> Initially, immediately after 9/11, it was devastating to my practice. However, after a couple of months, it started to pick up. Interestingly, we started getting a high volume of calls from Canadians who needed something called a 'waiver of excludability.' This is needed if a person has been convicted of possession of drugs or other criminal charges, and would then normally not be allowed into the US. What was happening was that the [legacy] INS was digging deeper into their databases and going farther back into people's histories, which was usually not the case before 9/11. Also, they [US immigration officials] were reading NAFTA applications much more narrowly after 9/11, and people were being rejected who did not have problems in the past. Thus, foreigners were subject to a much higher level of scrutiny, and needed the help of a lawyer now more than ever. (US-A3)

Another attorney commented on the culture and seemingly unchecked power of US immigration officials at the border, which grew after 9/11,

> Their people [immigration officials] are law enforcement. They really do not want to review paperwork [like NAFTA applications]. They have a lot of power. For example, they can do the following: 1. Search without a warrant 2. Interrogate 3. A person stopped at the border does not have a right to counsel 4. A person can be barred from entering the United States for up to five years at the border through the expedited removal process. Did you know that the INS can search without a warrant within 25 miles of the border? . . . Now, after 9/11, they have even looser restrictions in regards to what they can do. Larger companies, such as Microsoft or Sierra, have vast legal resources and human resource departments that can help their foreign employees negotiate around the growing obstacles at the border. However, smaller firms do not have these resources, and stumble around trying to find help. Once a person is denied entry at the border, it is very hard for them to get reentry. This is when we are usually contacted [as attorneys]. However, now the smaller firm usually pays more since we have to

undo what they are tangled up with at the border, and get them admitted into the US. (US-A10)

As discussed in the previous section, all immigration attorneys noted that there was a spirit of heavy enforcement at the US border; and they had noticed that more of their clients' applications were being rejected, than before 9/11, due to a seemingly more narrow reading of NAFTA. Finally, due to this spirit of greater enforcement at the borders, firms on both sides of the border, especially smaller ones, were more likely to seek the professional advice of attorneys, which had not been done in the past due to the costs involved.

6.12.2 Canadian Attorneys

Two Canadian immigration attorneys (C-A1 and 2) noted that the CIC has also stepped up security for applicants entering into Canada. In fact, they were concerned that Canadian immigration officials were becoming more like those in the US in their spirit of 'restrictiveness'. Thus, Canadian immigration officers were also heavily scrutinizing everyone entering Canada. This is where an applicant would also need the help of a Canadian immigration attorney if she/he was convicted of possession of drugs or drunk driving, for example, and wanted to work in Canada. Essentially, the person would need a temporary residential entry, which is difficult to attain without the professional help of an attorney. Attorneys equated this to the experiences that Canadians, who had old drug convictions, were having with trying to enter into the US on NAFTA TNs after 9/11.

6.12.3 The Growing Distance between US Attorneys and US Immigration Officers, post 9/11

Overall, one major outcome of 9/11 on the US side of the border appeared to be a growing 'distance' between US immigration officers at POEs and US immigration attorneys. As discussed previously, immigration attorneys said that knowing the US immigration officials at the various POEs was seen as a real (informal) strength in the NAFTA process. However, since 9/11, there were many new officers at the US ports. In addition, US attorneys reported that they felt more of a feeling of 'distance' between the officers and attorneys. One attorney (US-A6) stressed,

I have to spend some time getting to know the new DHS people at the border. Essentially, one has to make all new friends now. (US-A6)

Based on interviews and visits to the actual POEs since 9/11, it was the author's observations that there was, indeed, an increased amount of turn-over at the POEs between Seattle and Vancouver, especially at the director level. It appears that this will continue to be the case in the future, and that much of the day-to-day activities dealing with border management and adjudicating NAFTA statuses is being executed by the seemingly more permanent, lower level staff. Other attorneys also noted the many new faces at the POEs, and discussed how they were responding in developing relationships with a new array of immigration officials. One immigration lawyer (US-A8) stated:

> It takes a while to create positive relationships with these people. I try and give them applications that are easy and straightforward, initially. This builds up trust. So, if I submit more complex applications later on, there is an established record of credibility. (US-A8)

6.12.4   Expedited Removal in the US

Probably the most direct blow to the US immigration attorney–US immigration officer relationship since 9/11 was a memo written by Michael P. D'Ambrosio, Customs and Border Protection Director of Field Operations, Buffalo, New York, to New York American Immigration Lawyers Association (AILA) Chair, Mark Kenmore, in August of 2003. Essentially the memo advised Mr. Kenmore and the AILA membership that attorneys were no longer allowed to assist their clients in primary or secondary inspections at US POEs unless the client became the focus of a criminal investigation and had been taken into custody, or the inspect-ing officer requested the services of the client's attorney, on behalf of the client. D'Ambrosio argues that the reason for this action was to '. . . increase security at our POEs'. However, Boos and Pauw (2004) in a general statement rebuffing this new approach argue that it is unclear within the memo exactly how barring immigration lawyers from POEs would increase port security.

Although the legacy US INS had not officially allowed immigration attorneys to be present while their foreign clients go through primary and secondary inspection at the US POEs for the past 20 years, attor-neys used to accompany their clients to POEs for a variety of immigra-tion related issues, ranging from applications for humanitarian parole to processing of NAFTA related immigration matters (Boos and Pauw, 2004). However, as of August 2003, the US DHS took a rather hard and direct approach to this matter, by reminding attorneys that they were not allowed to represent their clients in primary and secondary inspections. Boos and Pauw (ibid.) argue in their opening paragraphs that, in the stage of secondary processing at POEs, a foreigner may be subjected to something called 'expedited removal', and especially in these situations an attorney could possibly defuse such a rather draconian outcome for the foreigner. Essentially, expedited removal bars a foreigner from entering the US (from anywhere from five years to a lifetime) who has made a material misrepresentation in the entry process or who lacks required document- ation for entry.[4] US immigration attorneys consider this new procedure 'draconian' since the order is drawn up by the reviewing officer at the POE and is subject to only a review by his/her supervisor before the foreigner is effectively removed from the US.

Since early 1997, when expedited removal was first implemented under the US's Illegal Immigration Reform and Immigrant Responsibility Act (IIRIRA), signed in 1996, this measure continued to expand in use. For example, expedited removal was usually applied to asylum seekers who allegedly failed to articulate a fear of persecution if removed from the US. As of 25 May 2001, inspecting US DHS officers can now put Canadian NAFTA applicants into expedited removal proceedings if the US POE officers make the determination that the applicant was not eligible for the NAFTA status, and the applicant declined to withdraw the applic- ation. Prior to 25 May 2001, the government's denial of a TN status for a Canadian citizen was subject to the review of an immigration judge. Boos and Pauw (2004: 389) argued that the 'hard-line' approach of expedited removal became a tactic used by the US federal government to remove adjudication in NAFTA TN matters from any formal review process.

6.12.5 US Expedited Removal Expanding to Canada?

Up to the mid-2000s, there were less than 30 expedited removals for Canadian citizens seeking TN statuses at the POEs between Seattle and Vancouver (interview with C-A1). However, the US attorneys interviewed considered that the growing lack of checks and balances between the US government and the judiciary process, and its officers, namely attorneys, was a possible cause for alarm. Currently, the new hard-line approach only applies to POEs in the US. However, the Canadian government passed the Preclearance Act in 1999, a law that grants extraterritorial powers, such as the right to detail and arrest, to US DHS officers stationed at Canadian preflight inspections, which includes the Vancouver International Airport. Boos and Pauw (2004) stressed that the US government might eventu- ally allow expedited removal proceedings to be practiced at US preflight inspections within Canada under this new Canadian law.

The above complexity and added security provisions at US POEs since 9/11 suggest a growing role for the US attorneys of Canadian clients when attaining a NAFTA status. Additionally, there appears to be a growing distance between immigration attorneys and US DHS field officers, especially at US POEs. This was demonstrated by the reported barring of US attorneys from POEs when they attempted to represent their clients. This was causing considerable concern within the community of immigration lawyers, especially in light of the use of expedited removal proceedings and the seemingly growing unchecked powers of US immigration officers at POEs.

The above subsection has highlighted increasing complexity in administering NAFTA statuses in the US following 9/11. But what about the Canadian situation? The following section now turns to the Canadian immigration attorney's experience in the NAFTA process in the post 9/11 era and their relationship with Canadian immigration officers.

6.13   THE CANADIAN EXPERIENCE: A STRAINED RELATIONSHIP?

The NAFTA process for Americans seeking entry into Canada can be considered a relative 'nonevent' compared to the 'roll of the dice' (as one US attorney (US-A6) put it) for Canadians seeking entry into the US. However, the Canadian attorneys reported a more subtle set of interactions between Canadian immigration attorneys and POE officers and in their interviews alluded to a much more strained and complicated relationship than appeared on the surface. This subsection examines this complex and rather tense relationship.

To begin with, two Canadian attorneys (C-A4 and 6) stated that for the most part, entering Canada under NAFTA was extremely straightforward, compared to seeking entry into the US under NAFTA. As stated previously one Canadian attorney (C-A4) stressed that the Canadian side does not have the NAFTA 'horror stories' that one could hear from the US immigration attorneys. However, he did note that smaller companies, ranging from special effects firms in the Vancouver film industry to small manufacturing firms, did need the help of attorneys in navigating through the NAFTA status provisions. He also noted that Canadian attorneys were also hired for auxiliary purposes if a person was seeking a NAFTA status to work in Canada. For example, he stated:

> An attorney is usually needed if the applicant had a previous drug or drunk driving conviction, visa expiration, or wanted to bring his/her spouse into Canada while he/she was on a NAFTA status. (C-A4)

Another Canadian attorney (C-A1) also stressed that it was advisable that NAFTA applicants sought professional help since the NAFTA status process could be confusing. So, despite an overall approval of NAFTA status provisions, Canadian attorneys also reported that a professional could help a prospective applicant avoid possible problems before they arose. One attorney stressed that this ran counter to the viewpoint of the CIC, which stated that a person only needed an attorney if and when problems were to arise. (CIC's perspective regarding its own ideas about its role in the NAFTA process were explored in Chapter 5.) This attorney stressed:

> How is the person to know if there are problems until they are discovered by the CIC? Once this happens, the person has to prove his or her innocence, and an attorney is definitely needed. Now, [in such a case] the application process is usually twice as long and twice as expensive as compared to if an attorney was hired in the first place. (C-A1)

The attorney also noted that there was much confusion and spectacular misunderstandings as to business people seeking entry into Canada and the appropriate work statuses/visas they required. This attorney went on to provide the example of a recently hired US executive who was coming into Canada for a preliminary meeting with his new company under the NAFTA classification as a 'business visitor', meaning he could 'visit' a business office, but not to work.

> Yes, the CIC POE immigration officer tried to be magnanimous and granted him a TN status as a management consultant for one year. Basically, they gave him an incorrect job classification. It was quite clear from the letter, which the executive was carrying, that he was the new chief executive officer of a Canadian company and coming into Canada for two days just for a meeting, not for work. He was clearly a senior manager and not a professional, which is what the job states TN classification was drawn up to cover. My client asked the immigration officials to call me, *I am his attorney*, since I could better explain to CIC exactly what my client needed. However, the immigration officer said that they would call the company in Canada, but not the CEO's attorney, namely me . . . There is a bad attitude towards attorneys at the Canadian POEs. (C-A1)

The above attorney argued that CIC did not want attorneys to review their decisions, especially at the POEs, and this particular example clearly demonstrated this. In fact, at the time of the interview, the attorney was going through the process of changing this particular client's work status from the incorrect 'management consultant' category which was incorrectly issued at the POE to the more suitable 'executive' category. He stated,

> All of this is taking additional time and money which could have been avoided had they [the CIC] called me. (C-A1)

Other Canadian attorneys interviewed noted the seemingly deliberate distance between immigration officers and attorneys in addition to the immigration officers' lack of professional competence towards NAFTA and Canadian immigration matters in general. Two Canadian immigration attorneys (C-A6 and C-A3) explained:

> ... Look at the Globe and Mail article this coming Thursday. There is an internal audit of the CIC. If we (as a law firm) had this many errors, we would be shut down. (C-A6)

> Politically, any immigration official is terrified of immigration attorneys. They are political appointees, but we know immigration and the law. It's our profession. Many immigration officials are afraid to speak out on immigration matters since they know we will crush them ... NAFTA is safe. If immigration officials don't understand and facilitate NAFTA, then what does this say about the rest of the immigration system? (C-A3)

The above short, but direct, comments on the role of Canadian immigration in the NAFTA process puts considerable emphasis on a greater tension between immigration attorneys and Canadian immigration officials, which goes beyond NAFTA. The control of power and authority over the process of immigration appears to be a growing one for Canada. The above commentary suggests the tension and frustration of certain attorneys over what they perceive as an increasing lack of accountability of the Canadian government, and the seeming disrespect that government officials have for attorneys and their legitimate role in the process of immigration and labor mobility into Canada.

6.14 HAS NAFTA FACILITATED CROSS-BORDER LABOR MOBILITY IN CASCADIA?

All immigration attorneys interviewed were asked to reflect on whether the NAFTA status provisions had indeed been favorable in facilitating the growth of the Cascadia corridor to cross-border labor mobility. This section reviewed the responses given to this question and the following section deals with the broader implications of NAFTA in the region.

Although attorneys spent considerable time in the interviews discussing how NAFTA was imperfect, in many ways, all attorneys interviewed emphasized that NAFTA was a positive force in allowing greater cross-border mobility in the Cascadia corridor. Since its inception, NAFTA had improved flows of North American professionals across the Canada–US border by providing a wider range of mechanisms to move legitimately across North American borders. The attorneys also commented that it had influenced positively their own practices by adding a new component of client services, which was not so much in demand before NAFTA and the Canada–US Free Trade Agreement (NAFTA's predecessor).

Many attorneys stressed that NAFTA has been a tremendous boon for the Canadian professional worker since many now had considerable access to firms in the US as well as Canada. One attorney (US-A10) explained:

> In terms of Canadians, NAFTA is a tremendous benefit! They do not have to go through the H-1B process, and the TN application is much faster. Additionally, over 60 percent of all Canadians live within 90 minutes of the border, so NAFTA has opened up employment prospects in the US, which were not accessible before NAFTA. (US-A10)

NAFTA has also been good for smaller firms who need to move people quickly and efficiently across the border without the time and cost that an H-1B requires. Overall, this has helped the growing number of small but expanding high-tech firms in the Cascadia region. For example, one attorney (US-A10) was emphatic about how helpful NAFTA has been for high-technology in the region,

> The software industry has been liberalized! It is a fact of life [in this region] that people must travel back and forth over the border for work. (US-A10)

However, usually in the same breath, many attorneys (US-3, 4, 5, 6, 9, and 10) stressed that NAFTA does have its drawbacks, especially with POE adjudications. One attorney articulated,

> Obviously it [NAFTA] has enhanced labor mobility. [NAFTA] has made mobility much more rapid than if the person was not a Canadian national. You do not need a petition. Now, one can just go straight to the POE. However, NAFTA's biggest benefit, being POE adjudication is also its biggest drawback. It exposes these kinds of applications to inexperienced officers and their own agenda when it comes to admitting Canadians. We have experienced too many denials not warranted under the law. (US-A4)

6.15 NAFTA'S BROADER INFLUENCES

From a structural perspective, NAFTA was designed to primarily allow only degreed professionals mobility across North American borders. Thus, many attorneys argued that NAFTA did not allow key people within industries who do not have degrees. Two attorneys (C-A5 and C-A4) stressed:

NAFTA does not apply to people who did not get smart through an education. For example, Bill Gates would not pass on a NAFTA TN. (C-A5)

> Much of NAFTA is based on experience and education . . . for example, there was a Korean national that had never attained an educational certification, but he was a recognized leader in his field. In fact, he had authored key books on the subject matter and was constantly being requested to speak at key events. He was clearly ahead of the industrial curve. Essentially, he was merited, but not accredited. This type of person would not be eligible for TN status [if he were Canadian] or other related professional Canadian work statuses. (C-A4)

NAFTA's extensive list of 65 professions for a TN status mandates that all should have a bachelor's degree except for two (management consultant and scientific technician). This has put a stop to professionals without degrees who moved freely across the border prior to NAFTA. For example, one immigration attorney (US-A3) discussed the predicament that journalists found themselves in after the Canada–US Free Trade Agreement was signed in 1989. She explained:

> . . . An interesting example of this is journalists. They were originally listed on the Canada–US Free Trade Agreement. However, with this Free Trade Agreement, one almost always needs a 4-year degree and many journalists do not have 4-year degrees. So, after the FTA was implemented, many journalists could not move back and forth across the border. Thus, they petitioned to remove themselves from the list. (US-A3)

Finally, the above attorney (US-A3) went on to stress that NAFTA had much potential when it was first created in the early 1990s. However, over the past 20 years of NAFTA's existence, she noticed that NAFTA, which was designed as an agreement to facilitate cross-border labor mobility, had become somewhat stagnant. Part of the idea behind Chapter 16 of NAFTA was to include a wide range of contemporary professional jobs to move freely within North America's borders, and to reflect and respond to the professional human resource needs of a robust new IT economy. Unfortunately, much of NAFTA was written in the mid- to late-1980s as part of the original Canada–US FTA, and so the economy and its human resource needs then were rather different than in the early twenty-first century. Additionally, the wording of the NAFTA agreement was now difficult to change, even with the NAFTA labor mobility working group that had reviewed NAFTA annually since 1994. She explained,

> The TN status has made movements of certain professionals more difficult. It does not fit certain categories listed. For example, the 'code jockey' and the 'programmer' do not fall under the TN. The TN category is used to try and fit

these people into various related professions, which they really don't fit. They are not systems analysts nor are they software engineers because they do not have an engineering degree, and they are not management consultants. *They do not fit into these three categories.*

Right now, firms try and fit high-tech professionals who do not fall under NAFTA or into the H-1B category. Some of these jobs are 'doing' things. They do not fit into the three categories of NAFTA that I listed earlier. One of the problems is that NAFTA is so rigid in terms of updates. Programmers are not listed. They [programmers] must get on a broader computer list. Now we are bringing them in under H-1Bs. The primary reason [for lack of a broader listing of computer professions] is that the three countries could not agree on which high-tech professions should be included. Also, the high-tech industry evolves so rapidly. However, NAFTA is not designed to respond to the rapid changes in the new economy. It is very inelastic. In fact, NAFTA's rigidity is showing with age . . . in order for Chapter 16 of NAFTA to continue to be a success, it needs to be a living growing treaty rather than something set in stone. (US-A3)

The above quote summarizes much of the wider frustration that all attorneys felt towards NAFTA beyond the day-to-day adjudications at different POEs. Although NAFTA has provided many options that were not available prior to the early 1990s, NAFTA as a structural document appeared to be rather rigid and had considerable difficulty responding to the ever changing needs of the high-tech industry, which is now found in all sectors of the economy. (See Richardson 2011 for an in-depth discussion on the industries and professions that NAFTA does not include.[5]) Chapters 3 and 5 examined more closely the policy development side of Chapter 16 of NAFTA and why, from a regulator's perspective, NAFTA was so difficult to change (see also Richardson, 2006a; 2010.)

6.16 CONCLUSION

This chapter has reported on a wide range of issues, such as port shopping, the relationship between attorneys and POE officials, and the role taken by attorneys in the NAFTA status approval process. The material underscores that there is a clear geography of border administration in Cascadia, with the attorneys having quite different remarks whether they were on the American or Canadian side of the border, and different experiences at POEs along the international border. One key point regarding the inception of Chapter 16 of NAFTA was that attorneys were not supposed to be needed for NAFTA's short-term and seemingly easily accessible foreign work statuses. However, over the course of the past 15 years, and especially in light of 9/11, attorneys were needed more and more for both Canadian

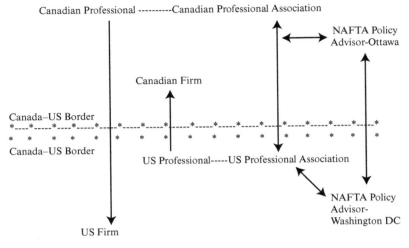

Canadian Side

Canadian Professional ----------Canadian Professional Association

NAFTA Policy
Advisor-Ottawa

Canadian Firm

Canada–US Border

Canada–US Border

US Professional-----US Professional Association

NAFTA Policy
Advisor-
Washington DC

US Firm

US Side

Note: *=Port of Entry

Source: Richardson, 2010 (pub. UBC Press).

*Figure 6.1   Envisioned system of communication and influence under
Chapter 16 of NAFTA*

and American professionals seeking entry into their NAFTA counterparts. Over time, the structural problems of NAFTA are becoming increasingly apparent, in addition to the varied cultures at each US POE, and the deliberate distance and the seemingly growing unaccountability of immigration officers at POEs, especially since 9/11.

Overall, all the 23 attorneys interviewed felt that immigration officials were using 9/11 as a reason to put distance between themselves and attorneys, but they felt they had a legitimate and rightful place in the process of immigration and foreign labor mobility. Many Canadian attorneys were concerned that Canadian officials were becoming more like the US in their 'restrictive' spirit when it came to interpreting NAFTA provisions. Conversely, it appeared that US immigration officers were actually becoming more like Canadian officers in their deliberate efforts to deny US attorneys access to POEs on behalf of the attorney's client. Figures 6.1 and 6.2 depict the envisioned relational geography of Chapter 16 of NAFTA and the realistic relational geography between immigration attorneys, their

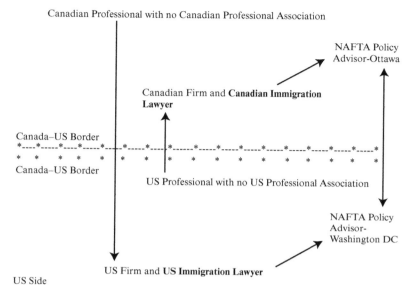

Canadian Side

Canadian Professional with no Canadian Professional Association

NAFTA Policy
Advisor-Ottawa

Canadian Firm and **Canadian Immigration Lawyer**

Canada–US Border

Canada–US Border

US Professional with no US Professional Association

NAFTA Policy
Advisor-
Washington DC

US Firm and **US Immigration Lawyer**

US Side

Note: *=Port of Entry

Source: Richardson, 2010 (pub. UBC Press).

Figure 6.2 Chapter 16 of NAFTA's realistic system of communication and influence

clients, the POEs, and key decision makers in Ottawa and Washington DC. Overall, the final effects of 9/11 on professional labor mobility throughout North America remain to be seen.

NOTES

1. Only two new professions, plant pathologist and actuary, have been added to the original list of 63 professions since NAFTA's inception in 1994.
2. Since 2008, NAFTA statuses can now be issued for up to three years.
3. All names used have been changed to protect the confidentiality of these people.
4. INA 212(a)(6)(c) in Boos and Pauw (2004).
5. Chapter 16 of NAFTA does not include many of the ever evolving professions found in high-technology and biotechnology, and the newly emerging professions found in the creative design industries. Richardson (2011) also found that Chapter 16 of NAFTA did not recognize human resource professionals and executives as allowed professions under the NAFTA.

PART III

The conclusion

7. Conclusion

7.1 INTRODUCTION

This chapter provides a conclusion to the study. The chapter begins with a summary of the empirical findings, which explore if the international border really is an impediment to the development of a high-tech region between Vancouver and Seattle. It then moves to determining what type of border bisects the transnational region of Cascadia and comments on the geography and border administration with regard to knowledge worker mobility. It closes with examining what are the implications of this study for theory, policy, and further research.

7.2 SUMMARY OF FINDINGS

Against a background of long-term international trends in the location of economic activity, North American integration following NAFTA is having a significant and lasting impact on the organization of economic activity with regions, cross-border region or otherwise, becoming central economic players and key engines of growth. Many suggest a new approach for regional development and industrial policies, including harmonization of government policies (Ohmae, 1995). Cascadia in particular has been seen as a new cross-border that has potential for growth based on knowledge intensive production and services. In this way it is qualitatively different from other cross-border regions in North America, and throughout the world, that focus on the movements of goods across international borders rather than people – examples of the former type include Toronto/Detroit; Atlantic (Atlantic Canada, southern Quebec, northeastern United States); the Singapore Growth Triangle; and the Tijuana–San Diego border region (see Chapters 2 and 3).

Much previous literature on Cascadia has focused upon the need for transportation connections and other improvements in infrastructure (see Chapter 3). But with the understanding that the people (including tourists) in this cross-border region are more important than manufactured products, the purpose of this study has been to examine whether or not the international border that divides Cascadia has been a significant impediment to the cross-border movement of knowledge based and skills based employees; and in turn, whether the border had constrained the formation of a cross-border cluster of synergistic economic activity based on high-technology industries, such as software, advanced bioengineering, and so on, stretching from Seattle to Vancouver. Indeed, very little previous literature has focused on the administration of border regimes per se as either facilitating or constraining cross-border interaction of knowledge workers necessary for high-technology regional development. To pursue this issue in the Cascadian context the study examines not only provisions of the NAFTA, which in great measure was a trigger to the Cascadia concept in the early 1990s, but also the study conducted interviews with firms that send employees across the border and the border officials themselves, as well as the attorneys who were hired by firms to facilitate the transfer of employees across the international border within the Cascadia region.

This section provides a brief review of the key points from Chapters 4–6 of the study, which explored the research findings for over 80 interviews conducted with firms, immigration officials, and immigration attorneys primarily in the Cascadia region, but also elsewhere in North America.

7.2.1   The Firms

7.2.1.1   The Vancouver firms
Overall, all firms needed to cross the Canada–US border for a variety of reasons, including sales, finance, follow-up services, and the recruitment of labor. For the Vancouver firms, all were outward looking in their growth strategy, by focusing on the US as either their prime market, or the rest of the world. Neither regional nor national markets in Canada were seen as a priority for these firms. Perhaps most interesting is that these firms' sales connections within the Cascadia region was less than 10 percent of the time for all but one firm (Firm-V6). Thus, the study found that these firms had far-reaching connections across international borders (beyond Cascadia per se) in order for their business operations to be successful. A critical factor in each one of the firms' successes was the ability to hire from outside their immediate area and to move people back and forth across the Canada–US border. Firms had certain frustrations moving their knowledge intensive workers across the border but did not perceive it as an overriding barrier or shield to professional worker mobility. Although 9/11 has not stopped the movement of their employees, this event did make the firms even more aware of just how much they depended on an open and predictable border, and how seemingly powerless each firm was in actually influencing Canada–US border management.

7.2.1.2 The Seattle firms

The Seattle firms had different yet similar needs as the smaller Vancouver firms. For one Seattle firm, it had the resources to hire people locally to do jobs rather than move one person around North America for many jobs, stressing that it would be a lot easier if one firm could move their people freely throughout North America without any labor certifications or statuses. For the second Seattle firm, the preservation of the Canada–US border ensured the viability of a unique Vancouver spirit and culture (as also identified by Firms-V5 and 9), which inspired innovation and creativity, and helped each of these firms to grow.

7.2.2 The Canadian and US Immigration Officials

7.2.2.1 The Canadian immigration officials

Overall, both firms and immigration attorneys saw the Canadian officials as being much more facilitative towards NAFTA status applicants than US officials. In part, this reflects the different norms and values in the two immigration organizations (as predicted by Finnemore and Sikkink, 1998) and points to an intriguing geography of how NAFTA is implemented; a geography of difference not only between Canada and the US, but also along the Canada–US border in Cascadia. Reasons for this include a greater understanding of the importance of foreign professionals working in Canada's domestic economy and a general acceptance of foreigners seeking entry into Canada's labor markets. Canadian immigration officials at ports of entry (POEs) also had mandatory and extensive training programs regarding their jobs and interpretations of Chapter 16 of NAFTA. Thus, there was a spirit of education and willingness to learn and understand new rules and regulations as they developed. There was also a deliberate iterative system of communication between POEs and CIC headquarters in Ottawa and vice versa regarding interesting or contested cases, and questions on how NAFTA was interpreted and implemented. This led to a more standard and predictable approach to implementing NAFTA rules. By comparison, the US side exhibited more ad hoc instruction, which led to a phenomenon of port shopping along the US side of the border by US attorneys and their clients.

The relationship between Canadian immigration officials and Canadian immigration attorneys was seen as a strained one, with Canadian immigration officials not recognizing the legitimate role of immigration attorneys in the NAFTA process. This was demonstrated by Canadian immigration officers' refusal to contact a NAFTA applicant's attorney from the POE to not allowing immigration attorneys on the premises of the POEs. Finally, Canadian immigration officials were perceived as becoming more enforcement driven (i.e. using a stricter interpretation of NAFTA rules) as opposed to facilitative. This trend began to occur before the repercussions of 9/11, and was in some ways due to the growing numbers of foreigners wanting entry into Canada.

7.2.2.2   The US immigration officials

When compared with Canadian officials, the US has had seemingly erratic interpretations regarding Chapter 16 of NAFTA, which led to the phenomenon of port shopping. Port shopping occurred when NAFTA applicants (firms and attorneys) took their applications to US POEs that were seen as more liberal in interpreting NAFTA applications. Chapter 5 explored this problem in detail; but to summarize, much of this variability was attributed to the US POE officers' limited professional training regarding NAFTA, the varying attitude of the port director at each POE, and the subsequent culture at each POE between all officers (see Table 5.1).

On a more positive note, there was a general level of professional respect by US officers towards US immigration lawyers, and an understanding as to where lawyers fit within the process of Chapter 16 of NAFTA. However, as of August 2003, US immigration attorneys were no longer allowed to accompany their clients to US POEs, which was seen as an acceptable norm prior to this date. Additionally, since 9/11, there were many new US DHS personnel at the US POEs between Seattle and Vancouver, which made developing relations of trust difficult for the US attorneys. Thus, there was a growing distance within the relationship between immigration officials and lawyers, which was once seen as a rather symbiotic one. The events of 9/11 also brought about changes in the way that US immigration officials were trained, and how they behaved at POEs. Mandatory constant training is now the norm for all US DHS personnel. Additionally, professionalism training was one of the first modes of education mandated by Tom Ridge, former Secretary of the US DHS. Thus, the US model has become more closely aligned to the Canadian model in regards to education and codes of conduct.

7.2.3   The Immigration Attorneys

As noted in Chapter 3 of the study, Chapter 16 of NAFTA was originally envisioned as a very simple process, which would not require much paperwork and the subsequent professional advice of lawyers (see Richardson, 2006a). However, as explored in Chapter 6, lawyers were needed by firms and their employees (and potential employees) more frequently due to the local variability between US ports (POEs), as well as the repercussions following 9/11 with border security. Thus, lawyers had become crucial mediators between the firms and immigration officials. In their role as mediators they had developed sharp insights into the actual workings of NAFTA adjudications at POEs as well as reflections on the broader implications of Chapter 16 of NAFTA.

In light of the empirical findings, the study can now reflect on the key research question: Has the Canada–US border impeded the creation of a high-tech region in Cascadia? The following section explores some of the answers to this question and additional themes that have developed as a result of the empirical research.

7.3 IS THE CANADA–US BORDER AN IMPEDIMENT TO THE DEVELOPMENT OF A HIGH-TECH CLUSTER BETWEEN SEATTLE AND VANCOUVER?

The various frustrations with the Canada–US border reported by firms and their attorneys might lead one to think that the Canada–US border was a serious impediment to firms moving their people around North America as a part of NAFTA. So, when asked the question: Is the Canada–US border an impediment to a high-tech cluster between Seattle and Vancouver?, surprisingly, many of the firm respondents, after a few moments of reflection, said that overall, it was not. Despite all of the negatives that the border brings to moving employees across the border post 9/11, it is still relatively open, and, NAFTA Chapter 16, overall, provides many more options for companies than before it existed.

So despite of all of the misgivings at the border, there is still ample opportunity for mobility within North America. Overall, it appears that the present administration of the border acts more like a sieve (perhaps keeping out some IT workers who do not clearly fall within the 65 professional classifications of Chapter 16) than a shield that bars entry except for those few brave enough or patient enough to petition governments and use high priced attorneys. However, it should also be stressed that seeking entry into Canada is not without its problems, and more attention needs to be given to the changing categories of IT workers (Richardson, 2011). Some interviewees have heralded Canadian rules and norms as an example for the US to follow; but some firms stressed that Canada could be just as difficult as the US, and was becoming more enforcement driven, as opposed to facilitative, especially after 9/11.

7.4   WHAT TYPE OF CLUSTER IS CASCADIA?

Apart from the key question: Is the Canada–US border an impediment to the development of a high-tech cluster between Seattle and Vancouver?, the research also had implications for Cascadia and more broadly for theories of regional development. Accordingly, this section provides a succinct analysis as to what type of high-tech cluster may be developing in both Vancouver and Seattle, and whether or not what are currently two separate clusters may one day be considered one large symbiotic cluster.

7.4.1   Vancouver

The above reflections on the role of the border in acting as a sieve or shield to mobility in Cascadia begs the question: What type of regional cluster is Cascadia, anyway? As explored in Chapter 3, Rees (1999) did extensive work on this topic regarding the greater Vancouver area. He found that Vancouver was all 'ring and no core'. This concept refers to Storper's idea (1999) that a region such as Vancouver is characterized by a lack of a core lead firm (similar to Boeing and Microsoft Corporation in Seattle) and a horizontal production system of products, as opposed to a hierarchical system. Its system of governance may be similar to the Marshallian industrial districts of Italy, where there are many highly creative local firms (Piore and Sabel, 1984). However, Rees (1999) stresses that these firms are different from their Marshallian counterparts in the sense that there is an absence of intraregional collaboration between firms within the greater Vancouver area, which mitigates against the development of a true regional innovative network. This is true even despite the fact that both Microsoft Corporation and Amazon.com have established key R&D facilities in the greater Vancouver area over the past ten years, and now a smaller Seattle based software firm, Tableau Software, Inc., has set up a temporary development office in downtown Vancouver in late 2015. This may be due to the nature of R&D facilities, and nascent firms in general, since there is usually little synergy between firms due to concerns of intellectual property, and perhaps equally important, the poaching of hard-won highly skilled employees. Thus, the mix of innovation in high-technology coupled with fragmentation may be deemed as being 'territorial innovative, but without milieux' (Camagni, 1995 cited in Rees, 1999). This all ring, no core structure characterized by predominantly external collaborative linkages describes many Vancouver based firms as they continue to seek complementary access to basic research, testing, and marketing-oriented activities.

Historically, this has been especially true for the biotechnology sector.

The broader high-technology industry has significant external linkages derived from increasingly foreign ownership/major investments and information flows extending beyond the local Vancouver area and Canada, generally. A majority of these external linkages for both high-technology and biotechnology lead to California. The eastern United States and Western Europe also have strong linkages with biotechnology. However, as both the high-tech and biotechnology clusters grow, they are increasing the local availability of human capital, whether foreign or domestic. In fact, the Vancouver biotechnology sector through their human resource professionals has formed a group dedicated to retaining foreign and domestic talent within the region (Richardson, 2016). This strategy has worked well over the past ten years, with more and more biotechnology professionals being able to move from one employer to another within the local region, and junior executives are increasingly seeing growth opportunities with fledgling firms within the immediate region. Thus, it appears that perhaps the Vancouver biotechnology cluster may be on the brink of not only having a strong capacity towards territorial innovation, but also the ability to create systems of intraregional collaboration. This may lead Vancouver to creating a cluster that is 'territorial innovative *with* milieux' (Camagni, 1995; Richardson, 2016).

7.4.2 Seattle

Seattle, on the other hand, may be considered a classic American hub and spoke city that hosts one or more industries, each with one or a few dominant hub firms surrounded by smaller firms which are tied, through origin and/or ongoing exchange relationships, to the larger firm (Gray et al. 1999a). However, the hubs are also usually engaged in relationships, such as branch plants, suppliers, customers, and competitors, outside of the region, which can range anywhere from national to international in nature. Microsoft Corporation is also seen as a strong 'hub' within the hub and spokes model of the local software industry, and has strong national and international connections. In fact, Microsoft Corporation's greatest contribution to the Seattle region is a growing pool of highly skilled professionals, both domestic and foreign. Seattle's software cluster is not seen as collaborative in the sense of Silicon Valley as described by Saxenian (1994). In fact, it may be seen as a more parasitic relationship with the smaller high growth firms luring away top Microsoft executives to run these other local firms with much potential (Gray et al. 1999a). Microsoft Corporation's recent efforts to establish a key development and innovation center in Vancouver, with Amazon.com and Tableau Software, Inc. now following suit, may begin to change the cross-border regional dynamics between Vancouver and Seattle's high-tech economy. This possibility of an eventual cross-border high-tech cluster emerging over the next ten years is somewhat fragile at best, since there was some speculation that Seattle and Vancouver could develop a cross-border biotechnology cluster in the late 1980s. This assertion was based on Michael Smith, a UBC professor and Nobel Laureate, helping to create Zymogenetics in Seattle in the early 1980s. However, Amgen pulled the emerging local biotechnology sector towards California with the purchase of Immunex (Seattle's largest biotechnology firm) in 2002 (Richardson, 2006a). By the 2010s, two of Seattle's larger biotechnology firms, namely Turbion Pharmaceuticals and Zymogenetics, were acquired by large pharmaceutical companies based in Maryland and New York. Thus, Seattle's biotechnology cluster continues to lose a critical mass of its local autonomy to the regional forces of California and the east coast.

7.4.3   Summary of Cluster Types

The above commentary helps to depict a pattern that Vancouver and Seattle high-tech clusters, although similar in their development, have grown and changed *in different ways* with different connections and networks that reach far beyond the region of Cascadia to the US and the rest of the world. Vancouver, on the one hand, is more dependent on foreign investment, expertise, and sales and marketing that originate internationally, but primarily from the state of California. However, Vancouver is growing rapidly and it is developing its own local cluster of expertise, which may contribute to a factor of milieux to accompany the idea of territorial innovation, especially when it comes to biotechnology. However, when reaching beyond the boundaries of the local it was the biotechnology cluster's preference to draw from California for professional expertise and finances as opposed to Seattle (Richardson, 2016). Possible reasons for this include just the sheer numbers of available experts in the state of California in addition to the fact that the largest concentration of biotechnology firms in the world are located in California (Biocom, 2006), which substantiate the regional gravity model of Helliwell (1999). Seattle, however, is highly dependent on a 'hub and spokes' model initiated by the Boeing Company and Microsoft Corporation has followed with the software industry. This includes strong local interactions, but also being dependent on connections and networks throughout the US and the rest of the world. This is similar to Vancouver, but historically, each city has had its own long established networks and connections with other regions in the US and the rest of the world. Microsoft Corporation, Amazon.com, and Tableau Software, Inc.'s new connections to Vancouver are nascent and somewhat fragile at best.

Thus, it will take considerable time to determine the extent and robustness of ties, if not clustering effects, between the two cities when it comes to high-technology and related industries.

Overall, the above comments underscore that although Vancouver and Seattle are physically close cities with very similar histories, and comparable new industries, such as high-technology and biotechnology, their clustering strategies and networks with other regions have historically been separate and different for a variety of reasons, which is similar to the findings of Trippl (2012). Both cities' key new industries originated and operate well within the local cluster. However, the new industries in both cities have had to recruit highly skilled professionals at critical stages of firm development, who were not accessible within the local clusters. Both cities' industries have had to turn to sources of financing outside of the local region at critical stages of an individual firm's growth, and both cities' new industries reach to the rest of the US and the world for markets and sales. Despite all of these similarities, both Vancouver's and Seattle's high-technology and biotechnology clusters have historically operated independently of one another. Now, with both Microsoft Corporation and Amazon.com's new and significant R&D facilities being established in Vancouver, there is anticipation that a more robust high-technology cross-border cluster might emerge between Seattle and Vancouver over the next ten years. In fact, Brad Smith, President and Chief Legal Officer of Microsoft Corporation, when speaking at the grand opening of the Microsoft Canada Excellence Centre in downtown Vancouver in June of 2016 stressed the beginnings of a 'Cascadia high tech corridor' that would start a regional high-tech movement, which would span between Vancouver, Seattle, and beyond. He elaborated,

> We want to also start talking about and really investing in this region not just as a single city or one important country but as a corridor that actually connects two big important cities and two countries. Brad Smith, President, Microsoft Corporation (Levy, 2016)

Smith's long-term vision for an all-encompassing Cascadia innovation corridor, or cluster, is a long-awaited advancement for the future of both high-tech and biotechnology connectivity within the region of Cascadia. In fact, many may find it reassuring to see this generation of high-tech leadership demonstrating a maturity to the point that firms are not only taking responsibility for their own growth and success, but also the cluster, or region, as a whole. Nevertheless, there is cautious optimism with this approach since, historically, the larger Seattle based software firms have not been known for their spirit of collaboration when it comes to advancing the needs of Seattle's high-tech cluster as a whole, especially when it comes to regional firm mobility regarding labor (Gray et al., 1999a), unlike Vancouver's biotechnology sector (Richardson, 2016) and firms found within Silicon Valley (Saxenian, 1994).

7.5   WHAT TYPE OF BORDER BISECTS THE CASCADIA CORRIDOR?

The above discussion leads to the question: What type of border bisects the Cascadia corridor? Wu (1998; 2001) and Bertram (1998) did excellent foundational work in categorizing and discussing the many facets of border regions. As discussed in Chapter 2, Wu (2001) has worked to develop three different types of border regions; namely border regions, cross-border regions, and transborder regions, with the latter being the most open and fluid. Key contributing factors towards these assessments include economic and institutional relationships, infrastructure networks, labor costs, and migration factors. Wu (2001) stressed that actual cross-border regions usually do not fit neatly into these categories set out in the typology. However, the typology does encourage a continuum of development, which moves from a frontier as a barrier, to the border as a filter, then to a border region as a zone of contact (Ratti, 1993 in Wu, 2001). This recognized fluidity of the constant transitioning of borders helps to explain Cascadia's typology. *Cascadia waivers between a cross-border region and a transborder region*, due to its partial allowance of free mobility of people, especially under NAFTA, but not absolute free mobility of people as is the case in the EU, which constitutes a transborder region according to Wu (2001).

Prior to 9/11 Cascadia was moving towards a transborder region with its deliberate policy developments around Chapter 16 of NAFTA, which should ensure fluid movements of professionals in addition to the general movements of residents within the Cascadia transborder area. However, following 9/11, there was a strong retrenching of firms and people back into the confines of one's nation state, despite the more open labor mobility policies still in place. This culture of retrenchment was also manifested at the actual POEs with both Canadian and US immigration officials becoming more enforcement driven in the way they approached their work. Despite the nascent movements of some high-tech professionals and executives between Seattle and Vancouver as a result of Microsoft Corporation and Amazon.com's establishment of key R&D facilities in greater Vancouver over the past ten years, there is still nowhere near a critical mass of networking, or symbiosis of flows, occurring between the two city-regions, especially when one considers labor mobility flows found in other economically advanced cross-border regions. For example, as a result of the EU's common labor market and the Schengen Border Accord, the Saar–Lor–Lux border region (a geographical area that transcends the borders of Germany, France, Luxembourg, and the Walloon region of Belgium) facilitated over 70,000 cross-border commuters on a daily basis by the late 1990s (Dörrenbächer and Schulz, 1999).This indicates that Cascadia continues to waiver between a cross-border region and a trans-border region in its economic relations and private enterprises according to Wu (1998; 2001). Eventually, this cross-border region may begin to elicit signs of a Stage II semi-integrated cross-border innovation system as described by Lundquist and Trippl (2013) with increasing levels of professionals affiliated with powerful Fortune 500 companies crossing the Vancouver–Seattle border region on a regular basis. Thus, this anticipated increased movement of professionals may lead to greater change along the Canada–US border when it comes to better facilitating flows of professionals and, eventually, a more integrated cross-border regional innovation system. Nevertheless, many of the Vancouver firms continued to use the land POEs to collect their NAFTA statuses (stating that they are going to a Seattle firm for a meeting) then fly out of the Vancouver International airport for US destinations beyond the Seattle area a few days later. Thus, the actual border region between Seattle and Vancouver continues to be used as a staging area for not only international goods, but also the internationally highly skilled as they prepare for their foreign professional journeys, which, for many, include California as well as extending beyond the region of Cascadia.

7.6 INTERNATIONAL LABOR MOBILITY OF THE HIGHLY SKILLED

As discussed in Chapter 2, the regional international movements of the professional highly skilled have taken place for over 300 years. Currently, the need for the internationally highly skilled is perhaps even greater than any other time in the history of the global capitalist system, due to fierce competition between industries at a global level. In fact, one key feature to creating and maintaining an innovative and competitive economy is access to the highly skilled, both foreign and domestic (Florida, 2002; 2005). This need has given rise to many different types of industries depending on the professional abilities, cultural fluidity, and international mobility of the highly skilled. Over the past 50 years, multinational corporations (MNCs) have dominated the movements of the professionally highly skilled as these corporations expanded beyond the boundaries of the firm's original nation state in an insatiable appetite for overseas markets as has been demonstrated by Beaverstock and Smith (1996); Beaverstock and Hall (2012); and Findlay et al. (1996).

Now, a rising trend is the movement of the professionally highly skilled and executives that work for younger, smaller, yet aggressive, firms in the areas of high-tech and biotechnology. This trend has been demonstrated initially by Saxenian (2000; 2002) and Boyle and Motherwell (2005).

Thus, the growing trend of smaller, yet aggressive, high-tech firms needing to become global has put an added layer of responsibility and professional obligation for all executives and professionals that these types of firm hire. This includes the ability to be internationally mobile and culturally fluid for either short- or long-term assignments for a vast majority of professionals and executives. This growing trend is especially apparent with the finding for this particular study with all participating firms having anywhere from 10 to 35 percent of all professional staff conducting a variety of firm operations in foreign countries at the time of the research interviews. In fact, firms interviewed stressed that a majority of their sales, markets, and finances were directly tied to the US, especially California, and it was essential to maintain a constant flow of firm professionals and executives between Vancouver and California, in addition to the larger US and the world. All firms also stressed that they hired a number of professionals and executives from the US and relocated these people to Vancouver. Thus, there was considerable need to have a predictable and efficiently operating border, especially between Canada and the US. This predictability was needed not only for these firms to move their people, but also to ensure a seamless operation of business between their firm in Vancouver and the rest of the world, with particular emphasis on the US.

All of these operational requirements were a tall order for a firm just beginning to make its way. In fact, these vast global operational requirements added complicated work time and expensive costs to the existing obligations of these nascent firms. Additionally, these smaller mobile firms were not similar in size or structure to the vast MNCs. Thus, these smaller firms and their personnel were seen as having somewhat of a hindrance when trying to cross the boundaries of international borders, especially between Canada and the US since they usually do not fit the profile of the MNC's ideal type. Overall, these firms' smaller size and their highly skilled professionals and executives were somewhat disadvantaged compared to the larger MNCs when it came to gaining access to a foreign nation state at the actual local POEs between Canada and the US.

7.7 POLICY IMPLICATIONS: INSTITUTIONS THAT AFFECT LABOR MOBILITY

The research has certain policy implications, especially regarding the management of the border in Cascadia. As has been discussed in Chapters 2 and 3, there are a variety of institutions that range from the global to the local which affect the movements of the internationally highly skilled. The primary focus of the study was to examine how NAFTA has affected labor mobility for high-tech professionals moving across the international border between Vancouver and Seattle. Overall, NAFTA was seen as one of many different institutional options that the participating firms could use when needing to move existing or potential employees within North America or beyond. NAFTA TN statuses, overall, were seen as the most accessible and least costly of all the foreign work status options. However, the NAFTA status was not without its drawbacks. As discussed in Chapter 6, and substantiated by Richardson (2011) and Cryne (2013), the NAFTA professions are increasingly out of date with professions found in industries such as high-technology, biotechnology, and creative design. Overall, there is a greater need to rethink the underpinnings of the original Chapter 16 of NAFTA – for instance, what are its objectives, why was it crafted, and does it serve the modern information and knowledge economy era? As well, will the Trans-Pacific Partnership better address the shortcomings of Chapter 16 of NAFTA? There also needs to be a greater awareness of the importance of the knowledge worker, and how this type of professional's growth and circular cross-border flows contribute to the overall development of Vancouver's, Seattle's, and the greater San Francisco/Silicon Valley's future economic prosperity within the region of Cascadia.

The following subsection shall summarize NAFTA's overall effect on labor mobility and its broader influences.

7.8 POLICY IMPLICATIONS: BORDERS AND LABOR MOBILITY MANAGEMENT

Perhaps what the preceding section leads to is more consistent and predictable management within each POE along the Canada–US border that facilitates labor mobility under NAFTA. At present, the border appears to act as an unpredictable sieve, with some POEs more tightly controlled than others, both when the Canadian side is compared to that of the US, and also along the border at various POEs. Portions of Chapters 2 and 3 have explored some of the norms and rules that influence how decisions surrounding international trade policies are actually implemented

as well as developed. Chapter 5 of the study, which explored the role
of both Canadian and US immigration officials, demonstrated that the
actual border management and policies towards NAFTA varied considerably between Canada and the US, and especially between US POEs.
Interestingly, Yale-Loehr et al. (2005), Meyers (2005), and Richardson
(2006a) separately argued that the ongoing, mandatory, and extensive
training that the US DHS POE officers began to receive in the early 2000s
was viewed as an advancement towards better Canada–US border management. However, more recent studies, such as Richardson (2011) and
Cryne (2013), demonstrated that there remains a growing unpredictability
in crossing the Canada–US border despite the rise of ongoing training and
professionalism within the US DHS.

Thus, there is still a tension between US federal concerns, namely
shield effects, of heightened security coupled with cross-border economic
regional needs for more flexible and predictable border management,
namely sieve effects. This dual mandate of Canada–US border management highlights the bipolar nature that the Canada–US border, as it relates
to Chapter 16 of NAFTA, continues to be embroiled within – continued
mandates towards greater North American regional integration (sieve
effects) but still dictated by strong federal policy directives in a post 9/11
climate (shield effects). The former Canadian Policy Research Initiative in
its November 2005 *Interim Report* captured this tension well in the following quote regarding Single-Door Diplomacy:

> Pressure on Single-Door Diplomacy
> The growing emergence of cross-border regions that display a high level of
> involvement of sub national governments in Canada–US issues would have
> an important impact in the context of how foreign diplomacy is conducted.
> Traditionally, state-to-state relations were largely the domain of the president or
> prime minister, ambassadors, and foreign ministers. Cross-border cooperation
> and the multiplicity of sub-national actors and linkages raise new challenges
> of co-ordination for the Government of Canada. Similarly, the cross-border
> regions and their institutions become a channel of communication between
> sub-national and national governments that cannot be ignored.
> (Policy Research Initiative, 2005)

On a positive note, as has been demonstrated throughout this study, the
Canadian model of local POE adjudications has received less criticism
from the firms interviewed. In fact, many of the study's participating attorneys have lauded the Canadian system of constant ongoing training with
a strong culture of iterative communication from front-line POE officers
to headquarters based in Ottawa as an example the US should continue
to follow. These are learning and management strategies that the recently

created US DHS is just beginning to embrace and use. Nevertheless, the variability of each US POE's culture can still be attributed to the attitude of each port director and other strong personalities within each particular port, despite the rise of ongoing training and professionalism over the past ten years. This continues to lead to considerably varying interpretations of NAFTA applications, and had significant impacts as to whether or not a NAFTA applicant would be allowed an uneventful entry into the US. As a response to claims of inconsistent interpretations of NAFTA applications, as of late 2014, the US DHS has created something called Optimized Processing at 14 designated US POEs. These particular POEs have specially trained US DHS POE officers who are available during certain times of day to specifically adjudicate NAFTA TN and L-1 applications. The intent of the program is to provide a more predictable experience for the NAFTA applicant. However, a trial program that was similar in nature that ran from December 2010–11 at the US Pacific Highway POE was shut down by the US DHS for lack of use, and perhaps misuse, by certain immigration attorneys and their clients (Richardson, 2011).

Thus, it remains yet to be seen as to whether or not these broader mandated training policies and a NAFTA Optimized Processing program stemming from US DHS headquarters in Washington DC will create more consistent and predictable interpretations of NAFTA TN applications between US POEs. Overall, it is a step in the right direction for all professionals seeking labor mobility throughout North America under NAFTA.

7.9 FURTHER RESEARCH

This study has implications for further research of the Cascadia region, and especially whether or not the construct of Cascadia is a useful one for high-tech and biotechnology firms located in both Vancouver and Seattle. Historically, there was very little connectivity within Cascadia per se for the majority of the firms interviewed. Their links were much wider to other parts of North America, especially California, and beyond. Historically, Vancouver and Seattle developed both their high-technology and biotechnology sectors in different ways. Now, key Seattle based firms have begun to establish significant R&D facilities within the greater Vancouver region over the past ten years. Thus, the notion of a high-tech cross-border cluster, and eventual cross-border innovation system, between Seattle and Vancouver may begin to emerge within the next 10 to 20 years. So, the notion of a 'Cascadia innovation corridor' might become a reality in time. Overall, it would appear that more research needs to be conducted regarding the continental and global networks of the firms in Seattle and

Vancouver. Additionally, comparative work also needs to be conducted on border management involving knowledge workers along the US–Mexico border, in the Singapore Growth Triangle, between Australia and New Zealand, and within the dynamic zone between Eastern and Western Europe and beyond. In an era of increasing use of information technology in growth oriented business and regions there is a need for further research generally regarding the international regional movements of the highly skilled.

Bibliography

Abella, M. and C. Kuptsch (2006), *Competing for Global Talent*, Geneva: International Labor Office, International Institute for Labor Studies.

American Civil Liberties Union (2009), press release on the US–Mexico Border Crossing Deaths Are a Humanitarian Crisis, According to Report from the ACLU and CNDH, 30 September 2009, accessed 10 March 2016 at https://www.aclu.org/news/us-mexico-border-crossing-deaths-are-humanitarian-crisis-according-report-aclu-and-cndh.

Anderson, J. and L. O'Dowd (1999), 'Borders, border regions and territoriality: contradictory meanings, changing significance', *Regional Studies*, **33** (7), 593–604.

Anderson, M. (2000), 'The transformation of border controls: a European precedent?', in P. Andreas and T. Snyder (eds), *The Wall Around the West: State Borders and Immigration Controls in North America and Europe*, New York: Rowman and Littlefield Publishers, pp. 15–30.

Andreas, P. (2000), *Border Games: Policing the US–Mexico Divide* (1st ed.), Ithaca and London: Cornell University Press.

Andreas, P. (2003), 'A tale of two borders: the US–Canada and US–Mexico lines after 9–11', in P. Andreas and T. Biersteker (eds), *The Rebordering of North America: Integration and Exclusion in a New Security Context*, New York: Routledge, pp. 1–23.

Andreas, P. (2009), *Border Games: Policing the US–Mexico Divide* (2nd ed.), Ithaca and London: Cornell University Press.

APEC (Asia Pacific Economic Cooperation) (2006), official web site, accessed 10 December 2015 at http://www.apecsec.org.sg/.

Artibise, A. (1996), 'Cascadian adventures: shared visions, strategic alliances, and ingrained barriers in a transborder region', paper presentation at On Brotherly Terms: Canadian–American Relations West of the Rockies Symposium, University of Washington, Seattle, 12–14 September.

Artibise, A. (2005), 'Cascadian adventures: shared visions, strategic alliances, and ingrained barriers in a transborder region', in H. Nicol and I. Townsend-Gault (eds), *Holding the Line: Borders in a Global World*, Vancouver: UBC Press, pp. 239–67.

Aydalot, P.A. (ed.) (1986), *Milieux Innovatuers en Europe*, Paris: CEE.

Aydalot, P. and D. Keeble (eds) (1988), *High-technology Industries and Innovative Environments: The European Experience*, London: Routledge.

Badie, B. and M.C. Smouts (1999), *Le retournment du monde: Sociologie de la scene internationale*, Paris: Presses de la Fondation Nationale des Sciences Politique.

Barnes, T. (1996), 'External shocks: regional implications of an open space economy', in J.H. Britton (ed.), *Canada and the Global Economy: The Geography of Structural and Technological Change*, Montreal: McGill-Queen's University Press, pp. 48–68.

BC TIA (Technology Industries Association) (2003), *Technology Industries in BC: A 2002 Report Card*, Vancouver, British Columbia: BC TIA.

BC TIA (Technology Industries Association) (2015), general information home page, accessed 10 December 2015 at http://www.bctia.org.

Beaverstock, J. (1996), 'Sub-contracting the accountant! Professional labor markets, migration and organizational networks in the global accountancy industry', *Environment and Planning A*, **28** (2), 303–26.

Beaverstock, J. and S. Hall (2012), 'Competing for talent: global mobility, immigration, and the City of London's labor market', *Cambridge Journal of Regions, Economy, and Society*, **5** (2), 271–88.

Beaverstock, J. and J. Smith (1996), 'Lending jobs to global cities: skilled international labor migration, investment banking and the City of London', *Urban Studies*, **33** (8), 1377–94.

Bertelsmann, W. (1914), *Das passwesen: eine völkerrechtliche studie*, Strassburg: Heitz and Mündel.

Bertram, H. (1998), 'Double transformation on the eastern border of the EU: the case of the Euroregion pro Europa Viadrina', *Geojournal*, **44** (3), 215–24.

Beyers, W. (1993), 'Producers services development processes: some preliminary evidence', paper presented at the North American Regional Science Association Meeting, Houston, 11–14 November.

Biersteker, T. (2003), 'The rebordering of North America? Implications for conceptualizing borders after September 11', in P. Andreas and T. Biersteker (eds), *The Rebordering of North America: Integration and Exclusion in a New Security Context*, New York: Routledge, pp. 153–68.

Biocom (2006), *Biotechnology Industry Facts*, San Diego, California: Biocom.

Bloemraad, I. (2012), 'Understanding "Canadian exceptionalism" in immigration and pluralism policy', report for the Migration Policy Institute, Washington DC: Migration Policy Institute, July.

Boos, G. (2002), 'Interpreting NAFTA narrowly: recent INS positions regarding Treaty-NAFTA (TN) matters', submission to the Canadian House of Commons, Standing Committee on Foreign Affairs and International Trade (SCFAIT), 6 May.

Boos, G. and R. Pauw (2004), 'Reasserting the right to representation in immigration matters arising at POEs', *Bender's Immigration Bulletin*, 9, 385–93.

Boyle, M. and S. Motherwell (2005), 'Attracting and retaining talent: lessons for Scottish policy makers from the experiences of Scottish expatriates in Dublin', research paper for the *Fresh Talent Scotland Initiative*, Glasgow: Skills Development Scotland, accessed 10 March 2015 at http://www.researchonline.org.uk/sds/search/taxonomy.do?action=document&pager.offset=0&ref=Y6130&taxonomy=EMI Http://www.scotecon.net/publications/Boyle.

Bresnahan, B. and A. Gambardella (eds) (2004), *Building High-tech Clusters: Silicon Valley and Beyond*, Cambridge: Cambridge University Press.

Briner, H. (1986), 'Regional planning and transfrontier cooperation: the Regio Basiliensis', in O. Martinez (ed.), *Across Boundaries: Transborder Interaction in Comparative Perspective*, El Paso, Texas: Texas Western Press, pp. 45–56.

Bristow, J. (2010), 'A western Canadian contribution to Canada–US border policy development', draft working paper, Policy Horizons Canada, Ottawa: Government of Canada.

Brunet-Jailly, E. (2004), 'NAFTA, economic integration, and the Canada-American security regime in the post-September 11, 2001 era: multi-level governance and transparent border?', *Journal of Borderlands Studies*, 19 (1), 123–42.

Brunet-Jailly, E. (2006), 'NAFTA and cross-border relations in Niagara, Detroit, and Vancouver', *Journal of Borderlands Studies*, 21 (2), 1–19.

Brunet-Jailly, E. (ed.) (2007), *Borderlands: Comparing Border Security in North America and Europe*, Ottawa: University of Ottawa Press.

Brunet-Jailly, E. (2008), 'Cascadia in comparative perspectives: Canada–US relations and the emergence of cross-border regions', *Canadian Political Science Review*, 2 (2), 104–24.

Business in Vancouver (2015), 'Biggest BC based tech companies in 2015', *BC Tech*, Business in Vancouver: Vancouver, June, accessed 15 March 2016 at https://www.biv.com/datatables/biggest-bc-based-tech-companies-in-2015/.

Callenbach, E. (1981), *Ecotopia Emerging*, Berkeley: Banyan Tree Books.

Camagni, R.P. (1995), 'The concept of innovative milieu and its relevance for public policies in European lagging regions', *Papers in Regional Science*, 74 (4), 317–40.

Camagni, R.P. (ed.) (1991), *Innovation Networks: Spatial Perspectives*, London: Belhaven Press.

Cappellin, R. (1993), 'Interregional cooperation in Europe: an introduction', in R. Capellin and P.W.J. Bately (eds), *Regional Networks, Border Regions and European Integration*, London: Pion, pp. 1–23.

Carlos, A. and S. Nicolas (1988), 'Giants of an early capitalism: the chartered trading companies as modern multinationals', *Business History Review*, **62** (3), 398–420.

Cascadia Cross-Border Law (2015), 'Improving the process of adjudicating TN status', *Border Policy Brief*, **10** (4), 1–4, accessed 12 January 2017 at http://www.wwu.edu/bpri/files/2015_Fall_Border_Brief.pdf.

Castells, M. and P. Hall (1994), *Technopoles of the World: The Making of Twenty-first-century Industrial Complexes*, London: Routledge.

Castles, S., H. de Hass, and M. Miller (2009), *The Age of Migration: International Population Movements in the Modern World* (5th ed.), London: The Guilford Press.

CBC (2013), 'Amazon.com set for major expansion in Vancouver', Canadian Broadcast Company, 23 October, accessed 10 April 2016 at http://www.cbc.ca/news/canada/british-columbia/amazon-com-set-for-major-expansion-in-vancouver.

Chanda, R. (2001), 'Movement of natural persons and the GATS', *The World Economy*, **24** (5), 631–54.

Chase, R. (1991), *A Review and Outlook of the Washington State Software Industry, 1990*, Seattle: Washington State Department of Trade and Economic Development.

Cheetham, J. (ed.) (2001), *Immigration Practice and Procedure under the North American Free Trade Agreement* (2nd ed.), Washington, DC: American Immigration Lawyers Association.

Cheetham, J., W. Reich, J. Apa, R. Han, and S. Wang (eds) (2006), *Immigration Practice under NAFTA and Other Free Trade Agreements* (3rd ed.), Washington, DC: American Immigration Lawyers Association.

Citizenship and Immigration Canada (2016), official web site, accessed 23 May 2016 at www.cic.gc.ca/english.

Citizenship and Immigration Canada (2017a), International Mobility Program: North American Free Trade Agreement, official web site, accessed 7 January 2017 at http://www.cic.gc.ca/english/resources/tools/temp/work/international/nafta.asp.

Citizenship and Immigration Canada (2017b), Operational Bulletins and Training Manuals, official web site, accessed 7 January 2017 at http://www.cic.gc.ca/English/resources/manuals/index.asp.

City of Richmond, British Columbia (2016), official web site, accessed 23 May 2016 at http://www.richmond.ca/home.htm.

Clarke, S.E. (2000), 'Regional and transnational discourse: the politics of ideas and economic development in Cascadia', *International Journal of Economic Development*, **2** (3), 360–78.

Clarke, S.E. (2002), 'Spatial concepts and cross-border governance strategies: comparing North American and Northern European experiences', paper presented at the EURA Conference on Urban and Spatial European Policies, Turin, Italy, 18–20 April.

Clarke, S.E. (2004), 'Cross-border regionalism: from the bottom up – challenges to government and governance', Policy Research Initiative/ SSHRC Round Table, Government of Canada, Ottawa, 16 June.

Coenen, L., J. Moodysson, and B. Asheim (2004), 'Proximities in a crossborder regional innovation system: on the knowledge dynamics of Medicon Valley (DK/SE)', paper presented at the 4th Congress on Proximity Economics: Proximity, Networks and Co-ordination, Marseille, 17–18 June.

Cohn, T. (1999), 'Cross-border travel in North America: the challenge of US section 110 legislation', *Canadian–American Public Policy*, **40** (1).

Collett, E. (2013), 'Faltering Schengen cooperation? The challenges to maintaining a stable system', in R. Hansen and D. Papademetriou (eds), *Managing Borders in an Increasingly Borderless World*, Washington, DC: Migration Policy Institute.

Cooke, P. (2002), 'Regional innovation systems and regional competitiveness', in M. Gertler and D. Wolfe (eds), *Innovation and Social Learning: Institutional Adaptation in an Era of Technological Change*, New York: Palgrave Macmillan, pp. 177–203.

Cooke, P., M. Parrilli, and J. Curbelo (2012), *Innovation, Global Change and Territorial Resilience*, Cheltenham, UK and Northampton, Massachusetts: Edward Elgar Publishing.

Cortright, J. and H. Mayer (2002), *Signs of Life: The Growth of Biotechnology Centers in the U.S.*, Washington, DC: Brookings Institution.

Cox, K. (ed.) (1997), *Spaces of Globalization: Reasserting the Power of the Local*, New York: Guilford Press.

Cronin, M. (2000), 'Guidance for processing applicants under the North American Free Trade Agreement', US Department of Justice, Immigration and Naturalization Service, Washington, DC, 24 July.

Cryne, S. (2013), 'Canada–US mobility: a competitive advantage in the global economy', Barriers to Cross-Border Labor Mobility for Professionals Doing Business in Canada and the United States Symposium, Wilson Center, Woodrow Wilson International Center for Scholars, Washington, DC, *One Issue: Two Voices*, 16, 11–17, accessed 12 January 2017 at https://www.wilsoncenter.org/sites/default/files/FINAL%20publication% 20proof.pdf.

Darby, M., Q. Li, and L. Zucker, (1999), 'Stakes and stars: the effects of intellectual human capital on the level of variability of high-tech firms', Market Values, NBER Working Paper, No. 7201.

Darwent, D.F. (1969), 'Growth poles and regional centres in regional planning: a review', *Environment and Planning*, **1** (1), 5–31.

Dawson, L. (2012), 'The Canada–US border action plan: this time it's for real, Charles Brown', A Safe Smart Border: The Ongoing Quest in US Canada Relations Symposium, Wilson Center, Woodrow Wilson International Center for Scholars, Washington, DC, *One Issue: Two Voices*, 15, 9–14, accessed 12 January 2017 at https://www.wilsoncenter.org/sites/default/files/CI_120828_One%20Issue%20Two%20Voices%2015_FINAL.pdf

Demay, D. (2015), 'Has Amazon killed Seattle? One writer thinks so', *Seattle Post Intelligencer*, 18 August.

Desiderio, M.V. and K. Hooper (2016), *The Canadian Expression of Interest System: A Model to Manage Skilled Migration to the European Union?*, Brussels: Migration Policy Institute Europe.

DeVol, R. and A. Bedroussian (2006), *Mind to Market: A Global Analysis of University Biotechnology Transfer and Commercialization*, research report, Santa Monica, California: Milken Institute.

DeVoretz, D.J. and C. Iturralde (2001), 'Why do highly-skilled Canadians stay in Canada?', *Policy Options: Montreal*, **22** (2), 59–63.

Donald, B., M. Gertler, and P. Tyler (2013), 'Regional resilience: theoretical and empirical perspectives', *Cambridge Journal of Regions, Economy, and Society*, **6** (1), 3–21.

Dörrenbächer, P. and C. Schulz (1999), 'Cultural and regional integration: the case of the Saar-Lor-Lux cross-border labor market', in M. Koter and K. Heffner (eds), *Multicultural Regions and Cities: Regions and Regionalism*, **4**, Lódż/Opole: University of Lódż/Silesian Institute, pp. 125–39.

Dunford, M. and G. Kafkalas (1992), *Cities and Regions in the New Europe: The Global–Local Interplay and Spatial Development Strategies*, London: Belhaven Press.

The Economist (2008), 'Crisis? What crisis?', *The Economist*, 17 July.

Edgington, D. (1995), 'Trade, investment, and the new regionalism: Cascadia and its economic links with Japan', *Canadian Journal of Regional Science*, **18** (3), 333–56.

Edgington, D. and M. Goldberg (1992), 'Vancouver: Canada's gateway to the Rim', in E. Blakely and R. Stimson (eds), *New Cities of the Pacific Rim*, Berkeley: University of Berkeley Press, pp. 7.1–7.13.

Edgington, D., M. Goldberg, and T. Hutton (2003), 'The Hong Kong Chinese in Vancouver', RIIM Working Paper Series, The Metropolis Project: Government of Canada.

Elliott, L. (2014), 'Foreign workers: Microsoft gets green light from Ottawa for foreign trainees', Canadian Broadcast Company (CBC), accessed on 13 December 2015 at http://www.cbc.ca/news/politics/

foreign-workers-microsoft-gets-green-light-from-ottawa-for-foreign-tra
inees-1.2870289http://www.cbc.ca/news/politics/foreign-workers-microso
ft-gets-green-light-from-ottawa-for-foreign-trainees-1.2870289.

Eyre, J.D. (1968), 'Japanese–Soviet territorial issues in the Southern Kurile Islands', *Professional Geographer*, **20** (1), 11–15.

European Free Trade Association (2017), official web site, accessed on 3 January 2017 at http://www.efta.int/eea/eea-agreement/eea-basic-features#3.

Faulconbridge, J., J. Beaverstock, and S. Hall (2009), 'The "war for talent": the gatekeeper role of executive search firms in elite labour markets', *Geoforum*, **40** (5), 800–808.

Findlay, A. (1995), 'Skilled transients: the invisible phenomenon?', in R. Cohen (ed.), *The Cambridge Survey of World Migration*, Cambridge: Cambridge University Press.

Findlay, A.M., F.L. Li, A.J. Jowett, and R. Skeldon (1996), 'Skilled international migration and the global city: a study of expatriates in Hong Kong', *Transactions of the Institute of British Geographers*, **21** (1), 49–61.

Finnemore, M. and K. Sikkink (1998), 'International norm dynamics and political change', *International Organization*, **52** (4), 887–917.

Fischer, P., E. Holm, G. Malmberg, and T. Straubhaar (2000), 'Why do people stay? Insider advantages and immobility', HWWA Discussion Paper 112, Hamburg: HWWA.

Florida, R. (1995), 'Towards the learning region', *Futures*, **27** (5), 527–36.

Florida, R. (2002), *The Rise of the Creative Class*, New York: Basic Books.

Florida, R. (2005), *The Flight of the Creative Class: The New Global Competition for Talent*, New York: HarperCollins Books.

Florida, R. and M. Kenney (1994), 'The globalization of Japanese R&D: the economic geography of Japanese R&D investment in the US', *Economic Geography*, **70** (40), 344–69.

Folsom, R. (1999), *NAFTA in a Nutshell*, St. Paul: West Group.

Fontana, A. and J. Frey (2000), 'The interview: from structured questions to negotiated text,' in N. Denzin and Y. Lincoln (eds), *Handbook of Qualitative Research*, London: Sage Publications, pp. 645–72.

Forshee, S. (2015), 'Exclusive: Amazon reveals Washington state head-count for first time', *Puget Sound Business Journal*, 23 July.

Fraser, G.M. (1989), *The Steel Bonnets: The Story of the Anglo-Scottish Border Reivers*, reprinted in O. Martinez (1994), *Border People: Life and Society in the US–Mexico Borderlands*, Tucson: The University of Arizona Press.

Friedmann, J. (1965), *Regional Development Policy: A Case Study of Venezuela*, Cambridge, Massachusetts: MIT Press.

Frobel, O., J. Heinrichs, and O. Kreye (1980), *The New International Division of Labor: Structural Unemployment in Industrialized Countries*, Cambridge: Cambridge University Press.

Garreau, J. (1981), *The Nine Nations of North America*, New York: Avon Books.

Gates, D. (2016), 'Record deliveries keep Boeing ahead of Airbus', *The Seattle Times*, 7 January, accessed on 7 January 2016 at http://www.seat tletimes.com/business/boeing-aerospace/boeing-2016.

Gertler, M. (2002), 'Technology, culture, and social learning: regional and national institutions of governance', in M. Gertler and D. Wolfe (eds), *Innovation and Social Learning: Institutional Adaptation in an Era of Technological Change*, New York: Palgrave Macmillan, pp. 111–34.

Gertler, M. (2004), *Manufacturing Culture: The Institutional Geography of Industrial Practice*, Oxford: Oxford University Press.

Gertler, M. and D. Wolfe (eds) (2002), *Innovation and Social Learning: Institutional Adaptation in an Era of Technological Change*, New York: Palgrave Macmillan.

Granovetter, M. (1985), 'Economic action and social structure: the problem of embeddedness', *American Journal of Sociology*, **91** (3), 481–510.

Gray, M., E. Golob, and A. Markusen (1999a), 'Seattle: a classic hub-and-spoke region', in A. Markusen, Y.S. Lee, and S. DiGiovanna (eds), *Second Tier Cities: Rapid Growth Beyond the Metropolis*, Minneapolis: University of Minnesota Press, pp. 267–90.

Gray, M., E. Golob, A. Markusen, and S. Park (1999b), 'The four faces of Silicon Valley', in A. Markusen, Y.S. Lee, and S. DiGiovanna (eds), *Second Tier Cities: Rapid Growth Beyond the Metropolis*, Minneapolis: University of Minnesota Press, pp. 291–310.

Gwinn, M. (2003), 'The gloom in the boom', *Seattle Times*, 29 September, E 1.

Gwyn, R. (1985), *The 49th Paradox: Canada in North America*, Toronto: McClelland & Stewart.

Hacker (Thomas) and Associates, Architects (1997), *Western Washington/ Lower British Columbia Border Comprehensive Plan*, prepared for US General Services Administration, Public Services, Region 10, Auburn, Washington.

Hampson, F. and M. Molat (2000), 'Does the 49th parallel matter any more', in M. Molat and F. Hampson (eds), *Vanishing Borders: Canada among Nations 2000*, Don Mills, Ontario: Oxford University Press Canada, pp. 1–23.

Harvey, F. (2004), *Smoke and Mirrors: Globalized Terrorism and the Illusion of Multilateral Security*, Toronto: University of Toronto Press.

Harvey, F. (2007), 'The homeland security dilemma: imagination, failure, and the escalating cost of perfect security', *Canadian Journal of Political Science*, **40** (2), 283–316.

Held, D. and A. McGrew (2000), *The Global Transformation Reader: An Introduction to the Globalization Debate*, Malden, Massachusetts: Polity Press.

Held, D., A. McGrew, D. Goldblatt, and J. Perraton (1999), *Global Transformations: Politics, Economics, and Culture*, Oxford: Blackwell Publishers.

Helliwell, J. (1998), *How Much Do National Borders Matter?*, Washington, DC: The Brookings Institution.

Helliwell, J. (1999), 'Checking the brain drain: evidence and implications', *Policy Options: Montreal*, **20** (7), 6–17.

Henry, P. (2003), 'The two way influence of national policy measures and international trade agreements', paper presented for Migration and International Trade Investment: North American Experience and Policy Development, International Metropolis Conference, Vienna, Austria, 15–19 September.

Hodder, B.W. (1968), 'The ewe problem', in C.A. Fisher (ed.), *Essays in Political Geography*, London: Methuen.

Holbrook, J., M. Salazar, N. Crowden, S. Reiblling, K. Warfield, and N. Weiner (2004), 'The biotechnology cluster in Vancouver', in D. Wolfe and M. Lucas (eds), *Cluster in a Cold Climate*, Montreal and Kingston: McGill-Queen's University Press, pp. 95–112.

Holmes, J. (2000), 'Regional economic integration in North America', in G.L. Clark, M.P. Feldman, and M.S. Gertler (eds), *The Oxford Handbook of Economic Geography*, Oxford: Oxford University Press.

Holmes, J. (2003), 'Spatial distribution of economic activities in North America', in J. Holmes and J.J. Stevens (eds), *Handbook of Regional and Urban Economics*, Minneapolis: University of Minnesota Press, pp. 2797–843.

Holsti, K. (2004), *Taming the Sovereigns: Institutional Change in International Politics*, Cambridge: Cambridge University Press.

Houston, D., A.M. Findlay, R. Harrison, and C. Mason (2008), 'Will attracting the "creative class" boost economic growth in old industrial regions: a case study of Scotland', *Geografisha Annaler: Series B, Human Geography*, **90** (2), 133–49.

Hudson, D., Vancouver (IFC) (2000), Introductory Remarks for First Cross-border Venture Capital Seminar, International Financial Centre, The Waterfront Centre Hotel, Vancouver, 26 April.

Hutton, T. (1998), *The Transformation of Canada's Pacific Metropolis: A Study of Vancouver*, Montreal: IRPP.

Hutton, T. (2015), *Cities and the Cultural Economy*, New York: Routledge.

Innis, H. (1962), *The Fur Trade in Canada: An Introduction to Canadian History*, Toronto: University of Toronto Press.

Innis, H. with A. Ray (1999), *The Fur Trade in Canada: An Introduction to Canadian Economic History*, Toronto: University of Toronto Press.

Jimenez, M. (2009), *Humanitarian Crisis: Migrant Deaths at the U.S.–Mexico Border*, a report, San Diego and Imperial Counties and Mexico City: American Civil Liberties Union and National Commission on Human Rights (Mexico).

Jones, J.L. (2004), 'Seattle trudges towards recovery', *National Real Estate Investor*, 1 March.

Kenney, M. (ed.) (2000), *Understanding Silicon Valley: The Anatomy of an Entrepreneurial Region*, Stanford: Stanford University Press.

Kerwin, D. (2005), 'Special ABA Committee report: the Canada–US border – balancing trade, security and migrant rights in the post 9/11 era', *Georgetown Immigration Law Journal*, **19** (2), 199–219.

Klein, N. (2003), 'Fortress continents: the US and Europe are both creating multi-tiered regional strongholds', *The Guardian* (United Kingdom), 16 January.

Konrad, V. and H. Nicol (2008), *Beyond Walls: Reinventing the Canada–US Borderlands*, Farnham: Ashgate Press.

KPMG (2014), 'Bordering on the big play: taking our tech sector to the next level', *British Columbia Technology Report Card*, Vancouver: KPMG Canada.

Kresel, P. (1992), *The Urban Economy and Regional Trade Liberalization*, New York: Praeger.

Lawrence, D. (2013), 'Two Canadian companies leading the way in BC's biotech revival', *Canadian Business*, 27 November, accessed on 27 November 2015 at http://www.canadianbusiness.com/companies-and-industries/two-companies-are-leading-the-way-in-b-c-s-biotech-revival/.

Lee, C.M., W. Miller, M. Hancock, and H. Rowen (eds) (2000), *The Silicon Valley Edge: A Habit for Innovation and Entrepreneurship*, Stanford: Stanford University Press.

Lee, K.S. (1998), 'The role of the border city Hunchun on Tumen River, China', *Geojournal*, **44** (3), 249–57.

Levy, N. (2016), 'Microsoft opens new Vancouver BC development center with visit from Prime Minister', Geekwire, 17 June, accessed at http://www.geekwire.com/2016/trudeau-speak-opening-microsoft-vancouver-facility/.

Ley, D. (1996), 'Urban geography and cultural studies', *Urban Geography*, **17** (6), 475–77.

Ley, D. (2005), *Indicators of Entrepreneurial Success among Business Immigrants in Canada*, RIIM Working Paper Series, The Metropolis Project: Government of Canada.

Ley, D. (2011), *Millionaire Migrants: Trans Pacific Life Lines*, New Jersey: Wiley-Blackwell.

Ley, D, D. Hiebert, and G. Pratt (1992), 'Time to grow up? From urban village to world city, 1966–91', in G. Wynn and T. Oke (eds), *Vancouver and its Region*, Vancouver: UBC Press, pp. 234–66.

Lifesciences BC (2015), official web site accessed on 10 December 2015 at http://www.lifesciencesbc.ca/.

Linn, A. (2006), 'Boeing sets record for commercial plane sales', *The Globe and Mail*, Toronto, 6 January, B4.

Littlemore, R. (2015), 'Vancouver's high-tech makeover', *The Globe and Mail*, Toronto, 2 March.

Losch, A. (1954), *The Economics of Location*, New Haven: Yale University Press.

Lucassen, J. (1987), *Migrant Labor in Europe, 1600–1900*, London: Croom Helm.

Luger, M. and H. Goldstein (1990), *Technology in the Garden*, Chapel Hill: University of North Carolina Press.

Luke, T. (1991), 'The discipline of security studies and the codes of containment: learning from Kuwait', *Alternatives: Global, Local, Political*, **16** (3), 315–44.

Lundquist, K.J. and M. Trippl (2013), 'Distance, proximity and types of cross-border innovation systems: a conceptual analysis', *Regional Studies*, **47** (3), 450–60.

MacDonald, N. (1987), *Distant Neighbors: A Comparative History of Seattle and Vancouver*, Lincoln: University of Nebraska Press.

Mackie, J. (2000), 'Who needs Seattle?', *The Vancouver Sun*, 25 May, A1.

Macleod, S. and T.G. McGee (1996), 'The Singapore–Johore–Riau Growth Triangle: an emerging extended metropolitan region', in F. Lo and Y. Yeung (eds), *Emerging World Cities in Pacific Asia*, New York: United Nations University Press, pp. 417–64.

Mahapatra, R. (2005), 'Microsoft lays bet on India with expansion', *The Globe and Mail*, Toronto, 8 December.

Maillat, D. and J.C. Perrin (1992), 'La relation des entreprises innovatrices avec leur milieu', in D. Maillat and J.-C. Perrin (eds), *Entreprises innovatrices et développement territorial*, Neuchâtel: GREMI/EDES.

Maillat, D., O. Crevoisier, and B. Lecoq (1990), 'Innovation and territorial dynamism', Paper for the Flexible Specialisation in Europe Workshop, Zurich, 25–6 October.

Maillat, D., M. Quévit, and L. Senn (1993), *Réseaux d'innovation et milieux innovateurs*, *Réseaux d'innovation et milieu innovateurs: un pari pour le développement regional*, Paris: GREMI/EDES.

Markusen, A., P. Hall, and A. Glasmeier (1986), *High-tech America: The*

What, How, Where, and Why of the Sunrise Industries, Boston: Allen and Unwin.

Martin, P. (2001), 'Policies for admitting highly skilled workers into the United States', in Organisation for Economic Co-operation and Development (ed.), *International Mobility of the Highly Skilled*, Paris: Organisation for Economic Co-operation and Development.

Martinez, O. (1986), *Across Boundaries: Transborder Interaction in Comparative Perspective*, El Paso, Texas: Texas Western Press.

Martinez, O. (1994), *Border People: Life and Society in the US–Mexico Borderlands*, Tucson: The University of Arizona Press.

McCloskey, D. (1989), 'On ecoregional boundaries', *Trumpter*, **6** (4), 127–31.

McCloskey, D. (1994), 'Cascadia', in D. Aberley (ed.), *Futures by Design: The Practice of Ecological Planning*, Gabriola Island, British Columbia: New Society Publishers, pp. 98–105.

McCloskey, D. (2014), 'Cascadia' (map), Seattle: CascadiaInstitute.org, accessed on 12 January 2017 at http://cascadia-institute.org/.

McHale, J. (2003), 'Canadian immigration policy in comparative perspective', in C. Beach, A. Green, and J. Reitz (eds), *Canadian Immigration Policy for the 21st Century*, Kingston, Ontario: John Deutsch Institute, Queen's University, pp. 217–54.

Meinig, D.W. (1986), *The Shaping of America: A Geographical Perspective on 500 Years of History, Volume 3 Transcontinental America 1850–1915*, New Haven: Yale University Press.

Merritt, C.D. (1996), *Free Trade: Neither Free Nor About Trade*, Montreal: Black Rose Books.

Meyers, D. (2005), *One Face at the Border: Behind the Slogan*, Washington, DC: Migration Policy Institute.

Michaels, E., H. Handfield-Jones, B. Axelrod (2001), *The War for Talent*, Boston: Harvard Business School.

Mitchell, K. (1996), 'Visions of Vancouver: ideology, democracy, and the future of urban development', *Urban Geography*, **17** (6), 476–501.

Monger, R. and M. Mathews (2011), 'Nonimmigrant admissions to the US: 2010', Annual Flow Report 2011, Office of Immigration Statistics, Policy Directorate, US Department of Homeland Security, Washington, DC.

Moodysson, J., M. Nilsson, and H. Svennsson (2005), 'Contextualizing clusters in time and space: long-term dynamics, systems of regions, and extra-regional interdependencies', paper presented at the DRUID Tenth Anniversary Summer Conference on Dynamics of Industry and Innovation: Organizations, Networks and Systems, Copenhagen, 27–29 June.

Morgan, O. (2002), 'Embattled Seattle flies on one wing: Boeing is suffering, but what is the real reason for west coast job cuts?', *The Observer*, 8 September.

Muir, R. (1983), *Modern Political Geography* (2nd ed.), London: The Macmillan Press.

Nevins, J. (2002), *Operation Gatekeeper: The Rise of the 'Illegal Alien' and the Making of the US–Mexico Boundary* (1st ed.), New York: Routledge.

Nevins, J. (2010), *Operation Gatekeeper and Beyond: The War on 'Illegals' and the Remaking of the US Mexico Boundary* (2nd ed.), New York: Routledge.

Niosi, J. (2003), 'Alliances are not enough: explaining rapid growth in Canadian biotechnology', *Research Policy*, **32** (5),737–50.

Niosi, J. and T. Bas (2004), 'Canadian biotech policy: designing incentives for a new technology', *Environment and Planning C: Government and Policy*, **22** (2), 233–48.

OECD (Organisation for Economic Co-operation and Development) (2013), *Regions and Innovation: Collaborating across Borders*, OECD Reviews of Regional Innovation, Paris: OECD Publishing.

Ohmae, K. (1990), *The Borderless World: Power and Strategy in an International Economy*, New York: Harper Business.

Ohmae, K. (1995), *The End of the Nation State: The Rise of Regional Economies*, New York: Free Press.

Ong, A. (1999), *Flexible Citizenship: The Cultural Logics of a Transnationality*, Durham, North Carolina: Duke University Press.

Park, D. and P. McCaffrey (2013), *The Economic Importance of the Life Sciences Sector in British Columbia: Revised Report*, Vancouver, British Columbia: D.E. Park and Associates.

Parkhurst, E. (2015), 'Dreams delayed: Canada profits as US immigration maze costs the Puget Sound prized tech talent', *Puget Sound Business Journal*, 15 May.

Peck, J. (2005), 'Struggle with the creative class', *International Journal of Urban and Regional Research*, **29** (4), 740–70.

Perkmann, M. (2003), 'Cross-border regions in Europe significance and drivers of regional cross-border co-operation', *European Urban and Regional Studies*, **10** (2), 153–71.

Perkmann, M. (2007), 'Construction of new territorial scales: a framework and case study of the EUREGIO cross-border region', *Regional Studies*, **41** (2), 253–66.

Perloff, H.S. and V.W. Dodd (1963), *How a Region Grows: Area Development in the United States*, New York: Committee for Economic Development.

Piore, M. and C. Sabel (1984), *The Second Industrial Divide*, New York: Basic Books.

Piro, G. (1995), *Toward Sustainable Development on Cascadia's Main Street*, Vancouver, British Columbia: International Centre for Sustainable Cities, p. 3.

Policy Research Initiative (2004), *North American Linkages*, Ottawa: Government of Canada, June.

Policy Research Initiative (2005), *Interim Report on Cross-border Regions*, Ottawa: Government of Canada, November.

Policy Research Initiative (2006), *The Emergence of Cross-border Regions*, Ottawa: Government of Canada, February.

Prescott, J.R. (1965), *The Geography of Frontiers and Boundaries*, London: Hutchinson's University Library.

PricewaterhouseCooper (2002), *Managing Mobility Matters: A European Perspective*, London: PricewaterhouseCooper.

Public Service Alliance of Canada (2004), official web site, accessed on 7 January 2016 at http://psacunion.ca/.

Puget Sound Business Journal (2015), *Puget Sound Business Journal Complete Book of Lists*, Seattle: Puget Sound Business Journal.

Ratti, R. (1993), 'How can existing barriers and burden effects be overcome? A theoretical approach', in R. Cappellin and P.J. Batey (eds), *Regional Networks, Border Regions and European Integration*, London: Pion.

Rees, K. (1999), *Innovation in the Periphery: Networks or Fragments in High-technology Industries of Greater Vancouver?*, unpublished dissertation, Department of Geography, Simon Fraser University.

Rees, K. (2004), 'Collaboration, innovation and regional networks: evidence from the medical biotechnology industry of Greater Vancouver', in A. Lagendijk and P. Oinas (eds), *Proximity, Distance and Diversity: Issues on Economic Interaction and Local Development*, London: Ashgate.

Richardson, K. (1998), 'Whatcom county, Washington and the Greater Vancouver region: what is so enticing over the border', *Canadian Journal of Regional Sciences*, Spring.

Richardson, K. (2006a), *Sieve or Shield: High-tech Labor Mobility in the Cascadia Corridor under NAFTA and Post 9/11*, unpublished dissertation, Department of Geography, The University of British Columbia.

Richardson, K. (2006b), 'International mobility of the highly skilled: a case study of the biotechnology sector in Vancouver, BC', working paper for Industry Canada, Human Resources and Skills Development Canada and Social Science and Humanities Research Council Partnership on the International Mobility of Highly Skilled Workers, June.

Richardson, K. (2010), 'NAFTA, labor mobility, and dispute resolution within a North American context', in P. Potter and L. Biukovic (eds), *Globalization and Local Adaptations in International Trade Law*, Vancouver: University of British Columbia Press, pp. 76–105.

Richardson, K. (2011), 'Understanding the Canada–US border's impact on the movement of people to support the movement of goods and ideas under and beyond the North American Free Trade Agreement (NAFTA)', published working paper, Policy Horizons Canada, Government of Canada, Ottawa, June.

Richardson, K. (2016), 'The retaining of the foreign highly skilled in times of global crisis: a case study of Vancouver, British Columbia's biotechnology sector', *Population, Space, and Place*, **22** (5), 428–40.

Richardson, K. (2017), 'Highly skilled professional labor and the Trans-Pacific Partnership: is the deal the best next step beyond the NAFTA for Canada and the U.S.?', as part of the Canada–U.S. Fulbright, State University of New York, Plattsburgh and University of Hawaii at Manoa invitation only colloquium on the Trans-Pacific Partnership and its implications for the Canada–U.S. relationship, Honolulu, Hawaii, 21–4 February.

Richardson, K., R. Florida, and K. Stolarick (2012), 'The potential of place: using location to attract global talent', in J. Johansson, D. Karlsson, and D. Stough (eds), *Innovation, Technology and Knowledge: Their Role in Economic Development*, New York: Routledge, pp. 328–51.

Rosenau, J. (1997), *Along the Domestic–Foreign Frontier: Exploring Governance in a Turbulent World*, Cambridge: Cambridge University Press.

Rudd, D. and N. Furneaux (eds) (2002), *Fortress North America? What 'Continental Security' Means for Canada*, Toronto: The Canadian Institute of Strategic Studies.

Rushworth, W.D. (1968), 'Defining a frontier in the Andes', *Geographical Magazine*, **40** (11), 972–81.

Rutten, R. and F. Boekema (2007), *The Learning Region: Foundations, State of Art, Future*, Cheltenham, UK and Northampton, Massachusetts: Edward Elgar Publishing.

Sahlins, P. (1989), *Boundaries: The Making of France and Spain in the Pyrenees*, Berkeley: University of California Press.

Sassen, S. (1996), *Losing Control: Sovereignty in an Age of Globalization*, New York: Columbia University Press.

Sassen, S. (2000), 'Excavating power: in search of frontier zones and new actors', *Theory, Culture, and Society*, **17** (1), 165–70.

Sassen, S. (2012), *Cities in a World Economy* (4th ed.), Los Angeles: Sage.

Saxenian, A. (1994), *Regional Advantage*, Cambridge, Massachusetts: Harvard University Press.

Saxenian, A. (2000), 'Silicon Valley's new immigrant entrepreneurs', Working Paper No. 15, University of California San Diego: The Centre for Comparative Immigration Studies.

Saxenian, A. (2002), 'Brain circulation: how high-skilled immigration makes everyone better off', *The Brookings Review*, **20** (1), 28–31.

Saxenian, A. (2006), *The New Argonauts: Regional Advantage in a Global Economy*, Cambridge, Massachusetts: Harvard University Press.

Saxenian, A. (2012), 'The new Argonauts, global search and local institution building', in P. Cooke, M. Parrilli, and J. Curbelo (eds), *Innovation, Global Change and Territorial Resilience*, Cheltenham, UK and Northampton, Massachusetts: Edward Elgar Publishing, pp. 25–42.

Scott, A. (1993), *Technopolis*, Los Angeles: University of California Press.

Scott, A. (1998), *Regions and the World Economy*, Oxford: Oxford University Press.

Scott, J. (1998), *Seeing Like a State: How Certain Schemes to Improve the Human Condition Have Failed*, New Haven: Yale University Press.

Scott, J.W. (1999), 'European and North American contexts for cross-border regionalism', *Regional Studies*, **33** (7), 605–17.

Seattle Times (2016), 'King County home prices hit new highs, inventory new lows', *The Seattle Times*, 6 January, accessed on 6 January 2016 at http://www.seattletimes.com/business/real-estate/king-county-home-prices-hit-a-new-record-in-december/.

Shotwell, L. and A. Yewdell (2013), 'Crossing the northern border: the challenges of labor mobility from the United States to Canada and a risk-based solution', Barriers to Cross-Border Labor Mobility for Professionals Doing Business in Canada and the United States Symposium, Wilson Center, Woodrow Wilson International Center for Scholars, Washington, DC, *One Issue: Two Voices*, 16, 3–10, accessed on 12 January 2017 at https://www.wilsoncenter.org/sites/default/files/FINAL%20publication%20proof.pdf

Solimano, A. (2008), 'The international mobility of talent and economic development: an overview of selected issues', in A. Solimano (ed.), *The International Mobility of Talent: Types, Causes, and Development Impacts*, Oxford: Oxford University Press.

Sparke, M. (2000), 'Excavating the future in Cascadia: geoeconomics and the imagined geographies of a cross-border region', *BC Studies: The British Columbian Quarterly*, 127, 5–44.

Sparke, M. (2003), 'Passports into credit cards: borders and spaces of neo-liberal citizenship', in J.S. Migdal (ed.), *Boundaries and Belonging: States and Societies in the Struggle to Shape Identities and Local Practices*, Cambridge: Cambridge University Press, pp. 251–83.

Sparke, M. (2005), *In the Space of Theory: Postfoundational Geographies of the Nation-State*, Minneapolis: University of Minnesota Press.

Stewart, A. (2016), 'Microsoft doubles Vancouver presence with new engineering center,' *Puget Sound Business Journal*, 17 June.

Storper, M. (1982), *The Spatial Division of Labor: Technology, the Labor Process, and the Location of Industries*, unpublished PhD dissertation, Department of Geography, University of California Berkeley.

Storper, M. (1999), 'The resurgence of regional economies', in T. Barnes and M. Gertler (eds), *The New Industrial Geography: Regions, Regulation, and Institutions*, London: Routledge.

Storper, M. and B. Harrison (1991), 'Flexibility specialization and regional industrial agglomeration: the case of the US motion picture industry', *Annals of the Association of American Geographers*, 77, 104–17.

Sunley, P. (1992), 'An uncertain future', *Progress in Human Geography*, 16, 58–70.

Tam, P.W. (2006), 'Help wanted in Silicon Valley, but only the skilled need apply', *The Wall Street Journal* in *The Globe and Mail*, 8 January.

Taylor, J. (2010), 'Trade in goods and tasks: an analysis of border impacts and costs', draft working paper, Policy Horizons Canada, Ottawa: Government of Canada.

Tichenor, D. (2002), *Dividing Lines: The Politics of Immigration Control in America*, Princeton: Princeton University Press.

Todd, D. (2008), *Cascadia the Elusive Utopia: Exploring the Spirit of the Pacific Northwest*, Vancouver British Columbia: Ronsdale Press.

Tödtling, F., P. Lehner, and M. Trippl (2006), 'Innovation in knowledge intensive industries: the nature and geography of knowledge links', *European Planning Studies*, **14** (8), 1035–58.

Tolley, E. (2002), 'Introduction', *Journal of International Migration and Integration*, **3** (1), 1–16.

Torpey, J. (2000), *The Invention of the Passport: Surveillance, Citizenship, and the State*, Cambridge: Cambridge University Press.

Torpey, J. (2001), 'The great war and the birth of the modern passport system', in J. Caplan and J. Torpey (eds), *Documenting Individual Identity: The Development of State Practices in the Modern World*, Princeton: Princeton University Press.

Trippl, M. (2010), 'Developing cross-border regional innovation systems: key factors and challenges', *Tijdschrift voor economische en sociale geografie*, **101** (2), 150–60.

Trippl, M. (2012), 'Innovation networks in a cross-border context: the case of Vienna', in M. van Geenhuizen and P. Nijkamp (eds), *Creative*

Knowledge Cities: Myths, Visions and Realities, Cheltenham, UK and Northampton, Massachusetts: Edward Elgar Publishing, pp. 273–302.

US Department of Homeland Security (Various years), *DHS Statistical Yearbook*, Washington, DC: US Department of Homeland Security.

US Immigration and Naturalization Service (1994–2014), *INS Statistical Yearbook*, Washington, DC: US Immigration and Naturalization Service.

Van Houtum, H. and M. van der Velde (2004), 'The power of cross-border labor market immobility', *Tijdschrift voor Economische en Sociale Geografie*, **95** (1), 100–107.

Vance, A. (2011), 'Strategic business responses to the border', published working paper, Policy Horizons Canada, Ottawa: Government of Canada.

Vanneph, Alain (2001), 'Frontera norte: De las redes a la región transfronteriza', in P. Wong-Gonzalez (2001), 'New strategies of transborder regional development', in D. Edgington, A. Fernandez, and C. Hoshino (eds), *New Regional Development Paradigms: New Regions, Concepts, Issues, and Practices*, Vol. 2, London: Greenwood Press, pp. 57–74.

Vazquez-Azpiri, A.J. (2000), 'Through the eye of a needle: Canadian information technology professional and the TN category of the NAFTA', *Interpreter Releases*, **77** (24), 805–22.

Waters, J. (2000), *Flexible Families: The Experiences of Astronaut and Satellite Households amongst Recent Chinese Immigrants to Vancouver, British Columbia*, unpublished MA thesis, Department of Geography, University of British Columbia.

Waters, J. (2004), *Geographies of Cultural Capital: International Education, Circular Migration and Family Strategies between Canada and Hong Kong*, unpublished dissertation, Department of Geography, the University of British Columbia.

Welch, M. (2002), *Detained: Immigration Laws and the Expanding I.N.S. Jail Complex*, Philadelphia: Temple University Press.

Winters, A. (2002), *Liberalizing Labor Mobility under the GATS*, London: Commonwealth Secretariat.

Wolfe, D. and M. Gertler (2004), 'Clusters from the inside and out: local dynamics and global linkages', *Urban Studies*, **41** (5–6), 1071–93.

Wong-Gonzalez, P. (2001), 'New strategies of transborder regional development', in D. Edgington, A. Fernandez, and C. Hoshino (eds), *New Regional Development Paradigms: New Regions, Concepts, Issues, and Practices*, Vol. 2, London: Greenwood Press, pp. 57–74.

Wu, C.T. (1998), 'Cross-border development in Europe and Asia', *Geojournal*, **44** (3), 189–201.

Wu, C.T. (2001), 'Cross-border development in a changing world: re-defining regional development policies', in D. Edgington, A. Fernandez, and C. Hoshino (eds), *New Regional Development Paradigms: New Regions, Concepts, Issues and Practices*, Vol. 2, Westport: Greenwood Press, pp. 21–38.

Yale-Loehr, S., D. Papademetriou, and B. Cooper (2005), *Secure Borders, Open Doors: Visa Procedures in the Post-September 11 Era*, Washington, DC: Migration Policy Institute.

Yuan, L. (1997), 'Growth triangles in Singapore, Malaysia, and ASEAN: lessons for subregional cooperation', in E. Chen and C.H. Kwan (eds), *Asia's Borderless Economy: The Emergence of Sub-regional Zones*, New South Wales: Allen and Unwin, pp. 89–135.

Ziglar, J. (2002), 'Zero tolerance memo', US Department of Justice, Immigration and Naturalization Service, Washington, DC, 22 March.

Zisman, R. (2004), 'The US admission and inspection process in a nutshell', presentation and informational packet presented to Pacific Corridor Enterprise Council in conjunction with The British Columbia Institute for Studies in International Trade, SFU Harbour Centre, Vancouver, 13 May.

Zucker, L. and M. Darby (1999), 'Star scientist linkages to firms in APEC and European countries: indicators of regional institutional differences affecting competitive advantage', *International Journal of Biotechnology*, **1** (1), 119–31.

Zucker, L. and M. Darby (2007), 'Star scientists, innovation and regional and national immigration', (No. w13547), US National Bureau of Economic Research.

Index